Acceptance and Change in Couple Therapy

A Therapist's Guide to Transforming Relationships

Acceptance and Change in Couple Therapy

A Therapist's Guide to Transforming Relationships

Neil S. Jacobson
University of Washington

Andrew Christensen
University of California at Los Angeles

W.W. NORTON & COMPANY
New York • London

Originally published under the title INTEGRATIVE COUPLE THERAPY:
Promoting Acceptance and Change
For information about permission to reproduce selections from this book,
write to Permissions, W. W. Norton & Company, Inc., 500 Fifth Avenue,
New York, NY 10110.

Composition by Eastern Composition
Manufacturing by Haddon Craftsmen

Library of Congress Cataloging-in-Publication Data

Jacobson, Neil S., 1949–
   [Integrative couple therapy]
   Acceptance and change in couple therapy : a therapist's guide to
transforming relationships / Neil S. Jacobson, Andrew Christensen.
     p.   cm.
   "Norton professional book."
   Previously published: Integrative couple therapy. New York :
Norton, 1996.
   Includes bibliographical references and index.
   ISBN-10: 0-393-70290-1

   ISBN-13: 978-0-393-70290-3
   1. Marital psychotherapy. I. Christensen, Andrew. II. Title.
RC488.5.J349   1998
616.89'156—dc21   98-19060 CIP

W. W. Norton & Company, Inc., 500 Fifth Avenue,
New York, N.Y. 10110
http://www.wwnorton.com
W. W. Norton & Company Ltd., 10 Coptic Street, London WC1A 1PU

Contents

Preface and Acknowledgments

I remember getting a computer print-out that depressed me, sometime in 1985. It told me that this treatment I had been developing since graduate school, this treatment I had written a book about in 1979, was not all it was cracked up to be. Traditional behavioral couple therapy (TBCT) was yielding results that were, at least to me, disappointing. At about the same time, my colleagues Bill Follette, Dick Revenstorf, and I were developing statistics to measure the "clinical significance" of treatment effects and applying those statistics to behavioral marital therapy. I discovered, along with colleagues Kurt Hahlweg, Don Baucom, and Gayla Margolin, that other labs were producing similar findings. Then, perhaps a year later, I completed a study with Karen Schmaling, Victoria Follette, Lisa Wood, and Janice Katt, showing that novice graduate students, with no previous clinical experience, could produce outcomes with behavioral marital therapy that were as good as or better than those produced by trained professionals.

Thus, I began a decade of experimentation, soul-searching, reading, and listening, which culminated in the writing of this book. I am not sure of the exact chronological order. But I know that I took a year off from reading "the literature" and instead read novels. I wanted to see relationships through the eyes and ears of creative writers. Sue Johnson, who was then a graduate student at the University of British Columbia, would travel down to Seattle for training and the exchange of ideas. She brought with her a very different way of looking at couples, which she had developed along with her mentor Les Greenberg, whom I was to meet soon thereafter. Sue and Les told us about their "emotion-focused marital therapy." Not only did these two creative clinicians influence my thinking, but they actually sent me back to reading B. F. Skinner because, despite the fact that their approach seemed about as anti-behavioral as one could imagine, there was something about it that led me to explore Skinner's distinction between contingency-shaped and rule-governed behavior. This distinction was to prove central in the development of the approach described in this book.

My friend and colleague Bob Kohlenberg was also extremely influential in this process. Bob is a radical behaviorist who knows and understands the philosophical roots of behaviorism in a way that went far beyond my training. He showed me how far behavior therapists had strayed from contextualism, the true philosophical root of behaviorism. He helped me to understand what it really meant to take a functional approach to studying marital interaction. Even though we had together taught a graduate course on "behavior change" for a number of years, I didn't "get it" until sometime after 1985.

There was also something funny going on in my private practice. I was not following a set of rules; rather, I was opening myself up to natural contingencies and letting myself respond as those contingencies dictated. I was having more success with my clients, but without a theory to explain why. I had always known that my private practice was two or more years ahead of whatever treatment I was testing in a clinical trial. But this time the discrepancy seemed particularly striking.

And finally, there was Dan Wile, a therapist in Oakland who had written a provocative book in 1981 that both critiqued currently existing approaches and proposed an alternative. At first, Wile's approach seemed to me much too simple to have much applicability, but the more I looked, the more wisdom I saw in Wile's work. Strategies that are currently at the core of acceptance work, such as "unified detachment," were directly shaped by Wile's concept of the "platform." Wile also taught me that conflict can be good for a relationship, that it can be used to make couples closer. Perhaps most importantly, Wile taught me that the common belief that humans are inclined to wallow in self-pity is erroneous; quite the opposite is true. In their heart of hearts, people berate themselves for their imperfections, condemn themselves for their natural foibles, and walk around feeling incompetent a good part of the time. Human beings do not need more confrontation; they are already confronting themselves—too much—and need validation, compassion, and sympathy.

It was sometime between 1989 and 1991 that I started to use the term "acceptance" to describe what I was aiming for with couples. Within behavior therapy, my colleague Marsha Linehan had been a pioneer in introducing Eastern notions of acceptance into her treatment of parasuicidal behavior. I listened to her talk about her approach, which seemed to be mainly about self-acceptance rather than acceptance of the other, and thus did not seem directly relevant to couples work. But as we started to formalize our work, the importance of Marsha's work became more apparent. So did the work of Steve Hayes, who had begun to integrate acceptance with radical behaviorism: the result was an approach that is now called "acceptance commitment therapy." I was first introduced to it when Steve wrote a chapter for a book that I was editing in 1987, and the "acceptance work" embedded within it was compelling.

In 1989, I received a Research Career Development Award from the National Institute of Mental Health. This award paid 75% of my university salary so that I was able to focus almost exclusively on clinical research. I also received "recapture" money from the Psychology Department at the University of Washington to bring visiting scholars into the laboratory. In February 1991, I brought in Andy Christensen, a professor from UCLA. Andy was already a friend and colleague. I met him through Gayla Margolin, who was a close friend and collaborator of Andy's and his former graduate school classmate at the University of Oregon. I had always admired Andy's work and liked him personally. What I admired most about his work was its integrity: he never overinterpreted his results, he replicated all of his findings, he was extremely cautious (as a scientist should be), and, as a result, his findings consistently stood the test of time. I brought him to the laboratory primarily to talk about his research on marital conflict, but I also asked him to give a clinical presentation. Since he was trained in the same behavioral mold in which I had been trained, I was astonished to hear that Andy and I were thinking along very similar lines clinically. In fact, we were both using the term "acceptance" to describe our work.

During that visit, I began to complicate Andy's life. I am not sure that he will ever forgive me. I suggested that we start collaborating. First, we got a grant to fund a pilot study of a treatment we developed together. As we explain in Chapter 1, that pilot study had validated our conviction that any complete approach to couple therapy must integrate acceptance and change, and now we have completed this book, which is, to date, the most comprehensive account of this approach.

In the process of writing books, grant proposals, and chapters, and giving workshops over the past five years, Andy and I have become close friends as well as collaborators. In fact, Andy performed the wedding ceremony when Virginia Rutter and I were married on July 2, 1995. It has been an easy, delightful, and highly productive collaboration from day one, one that will continue—I suspect—for the remainder of our careers.

Many others have contributed to this book in various ways. Although Andy and I did all of the writing, we received helpful feedback at points along the way, most notably from our editor, Susan Munro. Susan deserves an award for patience, since the original book contract called for a completed manuscript by December 31, 1989—before Andy and I had even begun collaborating. Virginia Rutter has provided valuable feedback on several chapters. Julie Cisz helped tremendously with Chapter 10 on diversity. My graduate student Stacey Prince was a major intellectual force during our pilot study, and Kelly Koerner helped me to understand aspects of my clinical work that I could not see from watching my own tapes. James Cordova, Jaslean La Taillade, Julia Babcock, and Michael Addis were graduate students who also provided valuable feedback on integrative couple therapy, as were the first group of professionals whom we trained in our approach: Deborah Wilk, Peter Fehrenbach, Susan Price, Steve Clancy and Joan Fiore. Sara Berns, a current student, supplied a slogan that perhaps best sums up our approach: "Dig it, change it, suck it up, or split!" Somehow, our final version of the text did not include this brilliant aphorism, perhaps because it is an admonition to couples and this whole book is about freeing partners from admonitions. Joan Giacommi, who has been my assistant for sixteen years, worked hard to whip this book into publication readiness.

And finally, I would like to acknowledge John Gottman, another collaborator, friend, and colleague at the University of Washington. John and I have been studying domestic violence together for almost a decade, but our friendship extends well beyond that collaboration. We have spent many hours over the years discussing marriage, close relationships, and couple therapy. John has been an important force in my development and I am sure that this book reflects his influence in numerous places.

Neil S. Jacobson
Seattle, April 1996

When I went to graduate school at the University of Oregon in the early 1970s, it was a hotbed of applied behaviorism. Jerry Patterson and Steve Johnson were experimenting with behavior modification in families. Robert Weiss and Patterson were developing behavioral approaches for couples. Joe LoPiccolo was trying out behavior therapy with sexual dysfunctions. I was trained in state-of-the-art behavior therapy.

I remember my first marital case in graduate school with the clarity that is only provided by trauma. The spouses' contempt for each other was matched by their steadfast attachment. Angry conflict, destruction of each other's property, and accusations of affairs led to threats of separation and divorce, but, unfortunately for them at the time, the threats were empty. They stuck together in their mutual misery. They desperately wanted and needed help, but seemed relatively immune to whatever counsel my cotherapist and I provided.

Fortunately, I had Gayla Margolin as my cotherapist and Robert Weiss as my supervisor. They made this trial by fire a learning experience for me, despite the fact that it violated an important principle: start with a success! Nonetheless, I joined Weiss's legendary marital therapy team at Oregon. His humor, astute clinical observations of couples, and his accumulated wisdom about them made this experience a highlight of my clinical training. As the culmination of my marital therapy work in graduate school, Gayla and I matched up again, with Weiss as our supervisor, to conduct a therapy group for couples. Here we were successful. So even if I didn't start with a success, I did end with one. More importantly for these acknowledgments, my imprinting experience in couple therapy was with Robert Weiss as supervisor and Gayla Margolin as cotherapist.

After graduate training and an internship at Rutgers, I ended up at UCLA. Fortunately, my colleague and cotherapist from graduate school, Gayla Margolin, also ended up in southern California, first at UC, Santa Barbara, and then at the University of Southern California. Both of us were intrigued by family systems theory. We were products of our training at Oregon; we believed in a functional analysis of behavior that sought the causal determinants of behavior in the environmental antecedent and consequent stimuli for that behavior. Yet, influenced by the family systems theory, we conceptualized antecedents in terms that emphasized family dynamics, and we looked for antecedent and consequent influences that were not so immediately proximal to behavior. A child might misbehave not just because of the immediate, specific antecedent of a sibling's teasing remark, but because of a marital conflict the night before.

We decided to collaborate on a grant proposal to examine some of the ideas from family systems theory. As part of our grant proposal, we conducted both behavioral marital therapy and behavioral family therapy with multiproblem families who had a distressed marriage and a child with behavior problems. Gayla and I worked together on this project for several years as co-investigators, as co-supervisors, and most importantly, as friends. We were fellow explorers moving beyond the narrow behavioral dyad to the larger family constellation. Gayla's influence and support during this period and throughout my career are greatly appreciated.

During my early years at UCLA, Harold Kelley formed a group of nine social and clinical psychologists throughout the country to examine the literature on close relationships and give direction to it. He asked me to join this group. Supported by a grant from the National Science Foundation, we met for five weeks over about three years and developed a framework for viewing close relationships. In our book, entitled *Close Relationships* (Kelley et al., 1983), we presented this framework and applied it to various content areas of close relationships. My major goal was to apply the framework to intervention in close relationships. In writing this chapter of the book (Christensen, 1983), I explored the commonalties and differences in the major approaches to couple and family treatment. This experience provided the intellectual background for my own growth and development as a scholar and practitioner of couples therapy. I am grateful to the whole group, but especially to Harold Kelley, our leader.

Philosophers of science often make a distinction between the context of discovery and the context of verification. The former concerns the generation of ideas; the latter, the logic for testing those ideas. Scientific principles and methodology belong in the context of verification. Here logic rules. In the context of discovery, experience, intuition, and creativity rule. Although I was aware of the data that others collected on the outcome of behavioral therapy and acutely aware of the data that Gayla and I collected, these data were only a small reason for my movement away from the behavioral techniques I had learned in graduate school. My context of discovery has centered around my clinical work with couples, my supervision of students learning traditional behavioral couple therapy (TBCT), and, to a lesser extent, my own experiences in relationships.

As I tried to implement TBCT, I experienced its common difficulties. Sometimes couples wouldn't do the assignments. Even when they did them, sometimes the assignments would not have their intended effects. At times my efforts and theirs to create change seemed counterproductive. In my own relationship with my wife, I experimented with TBCT techniques and found them limited at best. Contingency contracting just didn't usually serve us well. During conflict, I found it difficult to use "I statements" or paraphrase and reflect my partner's positions (and she found it similarly difficult). She taught me that it was more important to be honest than to be nice. I discovered that a focus on change was often counterproductive for my clients and myself. Sometimes people want a voice more than they want a resolution. Sometimes people can experience intimacy not when they have achieved change from the other, but when they have given up the battle to change the other.

In my own work with couples, I then moved away from the change-oriented techniques I was taught. I still operated under the flag of behaviorism and conceptualized problems in that perspective. However, my strategies in therapy seemed less like the bag of tricks I had learned at Oregon. It is hard to specify all that influenced me during this period. My earlier interest in religion and philosophy clearly played a role. That influential undergraduate course on world religion that I took from Huston Smith, a scholar who was recently featured in a PBS special with Bill Moyers, exposed me to Eastern ideas. For years I had been an avid practitioner of transcendental meditation. These influences had shown me that the Western idea of direct attack, of changing the things that upset you, was not the only way to resolution. Acceptance of the world as is was an alternative.

Along this journey. I came across the work of Dan Wile. I attended two of his workshops in Southern California and read some of his writings. Many of his ideas about working with couples fit with and shaped my emerging views. I wasn't sure what kind of a therapist I was becoming.

I had known Neil Jacobson casually for years. I had even served as consultant on the early book on couple therapy that he wrote with Gayla Margolin. In February 1991 he invited me to come to Seattle and give a research colloquium on my work on the demand/withdraw interaction pattern. I was happy to do that, but he also asked me to give a clinical talk. This was more challenging. To be honest, I would have to describe what I was currently doing in couple therapy in front of someone who was the leading researcher on TBCT and who probably assumed, given my background, that I was another chip off the old behavioral block. It would probably lead to some interesting, challenging, perhaps even controversial discussions.

I was surprised by Neil's reactions. Not only did he not disagree with or challenge my approach to couple therapy, but he revealed that he had independently been going in a similar direction. In our discussions, we found that we had both moved to similar therapeutic ground. During this visit he proposed that we collaborate on a grant proposal where we would test this new approach that we had independently pursued. Later that year, Neil drafted the grant proposal and I drafted the treatment manual for this new approach. Thus was born integrative couple therapy.

In the five years since that visit to Seattle, Neil and I have worked closely on clinical work and research. I have come to admire his abilities in both areas; he is clearly a model clinical scientist. He has kept me anchored in the behavioral theoretical framework. Our collaboration has been successful and fun—clearly the best of both worlds. Perhaps one of us could have done this work alone, but it would not have been as good or as enjoyable. And as an added bonus, in the process I gained a true friend.

During our pilot study of integrative couple therapy, Neil and I trained five professionals in this approach: Deborah Wilk, Peter Fehrenbach, Susan Price, Steve Clancy, and Joan Fiore. I spent hours watching and listening to the tapes of those therapists and hours discussing those tapes. These interactions assisted in the evolution and definition of our approach. The many graduate students that I have trained over the years in couple therapy have similarly helped stimulate my thinking and refine my approach to couples. They are too numerous to mention but their assistance is nonetheless appreciated.

For the actual work of getting this manuscript completed, two people deserve special credit. Susan Munro, our editor, provided excellent editing and feedback. Joan Giacomini worked patiently and energetically to get this manuscript together. They both deserve a special thanks.

Although I have gotten wonderful assistance from all those mentioned above and many others as well, my continuing learning laboratory of love remains my family—my wife Louise, my daughter Lisa, and my son Sean. My experiences with these three delight and challenge me and my ideas and feelings about what can and should be changed, what can be accepted, and what intimacy with another human being means.

Andrew Christensen
Los Angeles, April 1996

1

FROM CHANGE TO
ACCEPTANCE

When we were being trained in the early 1970s, behavior therapy was not yet part of mainstream clinical psychology. However, the application of behavioral principles to clinical problems was generating a great deal of enthusiasm from an increasingly vocal minority. By the end of the decade, behavior therapy had entered mainstream clinical psychology, and it revolutionized the discipline as much as family therapy revolutionized the overall practice of psychotherapy. However, this chapter, and in some sense the entire book, says as much about the excesses of behavior therapy as it does about its achievements.

The first applications of behavioral principles to the treatment of couples were by Richard B. Stuart (1969), who was then at the University of Michigan, and a group of psychologists lead by Gerald R. Patterson and Robert L. Weiss at the University of Oregon and the Oregon Research Institute (Weiss, Hops, & Patterson,1973). These creative clinical researchers began by applying techniques and methodologies that had worked well with other populations to the vagaries of marital distress. For example, token economy programs had shown promise in the treatment of institutionalized schizophrenia, so Stuart, as described in his pioneering article on behavioral marital therapy, had couples form token economy programs in the home. The Oregon group put a greater emphasis on skills training, extrapolating from a growing body of literature which conceptualized interpersonal problems as deficiencies in social skills. Others were also experimenting with behavioral techniques (e.g., Liberman, 1970); Knox (1971) even wrote a book based on the use of behavioral principles with couples.

Most of this early work was put forth very tentatively, with an explicitly acknowledged need for the collection of experimental evidence to support the efficacy of these clinical innovations. Jacobson became interested in conducting an experimental test of these and

1

similar techniques as a masters thesis project (1977). This study became the very first randomized clinical trial on the efficacy of couple therapy. With Jacobson as the sole therapist and a small sample size (five couples in the treatment group and five in the control group), the study found significant effects for the behavioral treatment condition. Encouraged by these findings, Jacobson continued this line of research into his doctoral dissertation, establishing not only that this behavioral approach was effective, but also that its effects were specific to the approach and not attributable to those aspects common to all couple therapies (Jacobson, 1978a). In fact, while on internship at Brown University Medical School, Jacobson (1979) conducted a third study suggesting that this approach was promising even with inpatient psychiatric patients and their spouses.

Jacobson continued this line of research after taking a faculty position in the psychology department at the University of Iowa. In the major study conducted there, Jacobson and Anderson (1980) found that communication and conflict resolution skills are most likely to be effectively learned when a standard behavioral skills training package is applied in its entirety: instructions, behavior rehearsal, and videotaped feedback followed by tasks designed to foster generalization from the clinic to the home were all necessary to ensure skill acquisition.

Christensen studied marital therapy under Robert Weiss at the University of Oregon in the early 1970s. With Weiss and fellow graduate student Gayla Margolin, he published an early paper on marital therapy illustrated with a case study. Entitled "Contracts, cognition, and change: A behavioral approach to marriage therapy," this paper anticipated some of the cognitive emphases that were to emerge in behavioral marital therapy (Margolin, Christensen, & Weiss, 1975). In 1976, Christensen took a faculty position at UCLA. Soon after, in 1978, he began a lengthy collaboration with eight other social and clinical psychologists across the country to develop a framework for analyzing close relationships. The influential book based on this work (Kelley et al., 1983) emphasized the affective, cognitive, and observable events that the make up the stream of behavior of interacting partners, put these events on equal footing, and outlined the broad causal conditions that might influence those events. Christensen (1983) used this conceptual framework for analyzing existing marital and family intervention approaches, including the existing behavioral approaches.

During Jacobson's internship year at Brown and his first year at the University of Iowa, he and his colleague Gayla Margolin turned their version of behavioral couple therapy, which by now had been applied in four controlled studies, into a treatment manual. At this point in time, Christensen began his first collaboration with Jacobson, because

Jacobson and Margolin hired him as their consultant on the writing of the manual, which became *Marital Therapy: Strategies Based on Social Learning and Behavior Exchange Principles* (1979).

Principal Components of Traditional Behavioral Couple Therapy

Thus, by 1979, an approach had evolved that set the stage for, and coincided with, a great deal of research activity all over the world in the decade to come. Stuart published his own version of behavioral couple therapy in 1980. This book described an approach that went well beyond the token economies depicted in the original 1969 article. Robert Liberman and colleagues (1981) published yet another book on the subject that same year. John Gottman and his students at Indiana University had written a manual for couples on behavioral communication skills (Gottman et al., 1976). This manual was converted by Howard Markman and his associates into a prevention program called PREP, which has continued to evolve and is now used all over the world (see Floyd et al., 1995). In Germany, Kurt Hahlweg, Dirk Revenstorf and colleagues applied this treatment approach to German couples with similar outcomes (1984). Paul Emmelkamp and collaborators (1984) did the same thing in the Netherlands. Donald H. Baucom and colleagues developed a major program of research in the early 1980s, which culminated in the incorporation of cognitive therapy (Baucom & Epstein, 1990; Baucom, Epstein, & Rankin, 1995). Attempts were successfully made to use this basic behavioral approach as a treatment for depression (Jacobson et al., 1991; O'Leary & Beach, 1990), alcoholism (McCrady & Epstein, 1995; O'Farrell, 1986), and agoraphobia (Craske & Zoellner, 1995). The approach was somewhat different at each site, but it seemed to have at least two major components in common: *behavior exchange* and *communication/problem-solving training*.

Behavior Exchange

Behavior exchange procedures began with techniques derived from social psychological exchange theories (Thibaut & Kelley, 1959), as well as behavioral principles. They included the early token economy techniques of Stuart, "caring days" (Stuart, 1980), and "love days" (Weiss et al., 1973), as well as a number of strategies described by Jacobson and Margolin (1979). Behavior exchange strategies all involve attempts to increase the ratio of positive to negative behaviors exchanged by couples at home. Research by Gottman (1993) has suggested that an optimal balance of positive to negative behaviors seems necessary in order for marriages to remain satisfying and stable. Behavior exchange strategies use tasks presented by therapists to couples for completion at home as the primary vehicle to increase this ratio of positive to negative behaviors. For this reason, we think of behavior exchange techniques as "instigative," in that they are designed to increase positive, or decrease negative, behaviors at home. The emphasis in behavior exchange interventions is on behavior at home rather than behavior in the session. In this sense, behavior exchange in its extreme form is less concerned with the communication process between partners in the session, than with solving presenting problems as directly and expeditiously as possible. The role of the therapist is that of a conductor, actively suggesting tasks and debriefing the couple during the subsequent treatment session.

In the early 1980s, Jacobson's model of therapy stipulated that behavior exchange (BE) should bring about rapid change, but that the changes should not be expected to last forever. Why? Because couples who receive nothing but BE are not taking anything out of therapy to help them become their own therapists in the future. There is no training in communication skills when the therapist is conducting BE. In short, the theory of change predicts that BE in and of itself generates rapid but transient changes. It solves presenting problems rapidly but only temporarily.

Communication/Problem-solving Training

Communication/problem-solving training (CPT) is the antithesis of BE. Presenting problems are de-emphasized. Short-term changes in the ratio of positive to negative behaviors are ignored. Instead, couples are taught to be their own therapists through the training in communication and conflict resolution skills. The theory of change is that if couples can be taught to solve their own problems, then they can function on their own in the future, after therapy is over, when problems recur, as they inevitably do. If one were to treat couples using nothing but CPT, the theory of change predicts less rapid and profound changes than in BE. However, the changes that do occur would be expected to last longer. More importantly, the theory predicts continued change after therapy is over, since the couples can continue to have their own "therapy" sessions at home to solve problems as they arise. These therapy sessions at home have been called "state of the relationship" sessions (Jacobson & Holtzworth-Munroe, 1986).

BE and CPT were expected to work together synergistically. Couples were to get short-term benefits from BE, and these short-term benefits were expected to sustain them long enough for the skills taught in CPT to become strengthened, at which point the skills would take over and promote long-term benefits. BE generated immediate change; CPT extended the change process and prevented relapse.

Traditional Behavior Therapy Is Not Enough

The theory of change described in the previous section was tested in a study first reported in 1984 (Jacobson, 1984; Jacobson & Follette, 1985; Jacobson, Follette, & Pagel, 1986; Jacobson, Schmaling, & Holtzworth-Munroe, 1987). In a randomized clinical trial, Jacobson and colleagues assigned couples to a complete treatment involving both BE and CPT (CO); treatment which was limited to BE only; one that was limited to CPT only; or a waiting-list control group (WL). First, they found that in the short run couples in the BE group were more likely to improve than those in any of the other conditions, although all treatments were significantly better than no treatment at all. Second, BE was more successful than the other treatment conditions in changing the ratio of positive to negative behaviors at home. Third, CPT was more successful than BE at changing communication and conflict resolution skills for the better; in fact, it was the only treatment condition that exceeded the control group on direct measures of communication. Fourth, BE couples relapsed at a very high rate, and within six months. In contrast, couples receiving CPT were slower to relapse, but, interestingly enough, two years later there was more divorce in the CPT group than there was in the BE group. It appeared that when a couple received CPT without BE, and the relationship was particularly fragile, their communication skills simply led them expeditiously to the conclusion that divorce was the best course of action. In other words, without BE to generate increases in positive behavior, CPT was somewhat risky. Nevertheless, for couples who stayed together, CPT as well as CO produced significantly lower decreases in marital satisfaction than BE, and a substantial proportion of couples in both CPT and CO continued to improve even after therapy ended.

Overall, CO outperformed its components—BE and CPT—when they were presented in isolation. Improvements in marital satisfaction were maintained to a greater degree over the course of the two-year follow-up, and not a single couple in the CO condition had split up by the end of the follow-up period. Although staying together is not necessarily a favorable outcome in the absence of increased marital satisfaction, the combination of marital stability and satisfaction clearly justified the CO treatment, with both of its components contributing to a whole that was more than the sum of either of its parts.

Unfortunately, the presentation of research findings thus far has simply told one side of the story, the side where the glass is half full. This often happens when statistically significant differences between groups are used as the sole criterion for evaluating treatment efficacy. Since Jacobson's laboratory was committed to a careful examination of the clinical significance of treatment effects, rather than simply relying on statistical significance (Jacobson, Follette, & Revenstorf, 1984, 1986; Jacobson & Revenstorf, 1988; Jacobson & Truax, 1991), they found that the glass was quite literally half empty as well as half full. Even in the CO treatment condition, about one-third of the couples failed to improve during the course of therapy, and of those who did improve about one-third relapsed during the course of the two-year follow-up, most between the first and second year. In essence they were helping about half of the couples who were presenting for therapy: the ones who significantly improved and sustained their improvements during the follow-up period. The rest either failed to respond during the acute treatment phase or to maintain their improvements during the follow-up period. When they applied their clinical significance analysis to other published clinical trials, they found that other investigators had even a lower percentage of couples manifesting sustained improvement (Jacobson et al., 1984). As we were later to discover, this 50% success rate is characteristic of marital therapy outcome research in general; it is not unique to this traditional behavioral approach (Jacobson & Addis, 1993). Clearly, our approach was helping a substantial proportion of those who were receiving it: the glass was half full. Just as clearly, there were substantial numbers of couples who were not benefiting: the glass was half empty.

What was missing from the traditional behavioral approach to treating couples? For that matter, what was missing from these other couple therapies, which were also yielding comparable but certainly not substantially better success rates?

Factors Affecting the Success of Traditional Behavior Therapy

Jacobson and his colleaagues decided to begin their quest to improve the efficacy of their approach by first identifying the couples who responded positively and negatively to it (Jacobson, Follette, & Pagel, 1986; Jacobson et al., 1987). They identified five couple factors that discriminated between success and failure within the traditional behavioral approach.

Commitment

Couples who were more committed to staying together, independent of the outcome of therapy, were more likely to improve than those who saw couple therapy as a last-ditch effort to prevent divorce. This is not to say that couples on the brink of divorce were never helped by our approach. Nor does it mean that couples committed to staying together were always successful in therapy. However, all other things being equal, the stronger the commitment, the more successful their response.

Age

Younger couples responded more positively to our approach than did older couples. Just as with "commitment" or with any of the other predictor variables, there were no magical cutoff points, and there were many exceptions. We cannot say that below a certain age a positive outcome is guaranteed. Nor would we refuse to treat an older couple because this approach was often successful with older couples. Nevertheless, on the average, younger couples were more likely to benefit.

They investigated the possibility that the "age" effect was an artifact of marriage duration: perhaps chronological age was inversely related to outcome simply because couples who were older tended to have been married longer. In other words, perhaps the relevant hypothesis was: the longer a couple has been together, the harder they are to change. Despite the intuitive appeal of this interpretation, they tested it empirically and found it wanting. The effect was attributable to chronological age. Couples in their fifties together only a short time were harder to treat than couples in their forties who had been together for many years.

Emotional Engagement

Couples who were emotionally engaged were more likely to benefit from behavior therapy than disengaged couples. By emotional engagement, we mean the continued "chemistry" between the two people, despite their areas of conflict. For example, when couples continue to show sexual interest, their prognosis improves considerably with the

Jacobson and Margolin (1979) approach. However, it is a bad prognostic sign when sex has ceased or is extremely infrequent. Discrepan-
cies between the partners in desired frequency is also a bad prognostic
sign.

Emotional engagement also refers to whether or not the couple engages in or avoids conflict. Christensen and Heavey's (Christensen,
1987; Christensen & Heavey, 1993) work on demand/withdraw interaction has shown that male withdrawal is a predictor of decline in
marital satisfaction (Heavey, Christensen, & Malamuth, 1995). Gottman's (1994) research shows that withdrawal is a reliable predictor of
marital instability, more so than criticism, and even more predictive
of divorce than contempt. When the couple is still arguing, there is
more hope than when they have stopped arguing and live together in
seething silence.

Traditionality

Our approach was more successful with egalitarian marriages or what
Pepper Schwartz has referred to as "peer" marriages (Schwartz, 1994),
than it was with couples who had relatively traditional marriages. For
our purposes traditionality can be divided into three components. The
first has to do with who takes responsibility for and controls finances.
In single breadwinner couples, our approach did not work as well as it
did with dual-career couples, especially those in which the spouses'
incomes were equally important in determining the lifestyle of the
family, and particularly those where spouses shared decision-making
about how money was to be spent.

Traditionality also refers to "who does what." In traditional marriages, tasks are assigned based on gender-role stereotypes. In peer or
egalitarian marriages, tasks are assigned or shared according to a system that is less dependent on cultural norms. When couples entered
therapy believing, for example, that housework was women's work,
we were less likely to help them than we were when housework was
shared.

The third dimension of traditionality pertained to whose job it was
to maintain the emotional well-being of other family members. Traditionally, it is the wife or mother's responsibility to make sure that
everyone else in the family is healthy and happy. When husbands attended to the affective well-being of their partners and were willing to
discuss difficult, emotion-laden topics without waiting for their wives
to bring them up, the behavioral approach was more successful.

Convergent Goals for the Marriage

Some couples share similar goals for the marriage despite major areas of conflict. To put it another way, most partners have a point of view on what an ideal relationship with their spouse would look like. To the extent that these points of view converged within a particular relationship, couples were more likely to benefit from a behavioral approach. For example, in one instance Henry and Louise believed in remaining childless and "living for today." They wanted to spend most of their free time together and liked to travel. They shared an "existential" view of life: they both pointed out that the world could end any day for them and so they wanted to enjoy life while it lasted, together. Unfortunately, they also argued a lot, for a variety of reasons: they were both formidable debaters and when they disagreed about, for example, who should contribute how much to their new car, the disagreements were loud and vitriolic. However, since their goals converged, at least they were working toward the same ends.

Couples like Henry and Louise are easier to treat with behavior therapy than those who don't even want the same type of marriage. Since these couples have very different goals for their relationship, it is harder to generate successful behavioral couple therapy. For example, Dan wanted a wife but didn't want to spend a lot of time with her. He preferred the company of his drinking buddies. He also believed that the man should be the head of the household and that the instrumental tasks of marriage should be compartmentalized along the lines of traditional gender roles. He didn't talk much, but he defended his role on the basis of his being a good breadwinner and a reliable, dependable partner who didn't drink too much, batter, or engage in infidelity. Linda agreed with many of these ideas in principle, but she found herself changing during the course of their years together. By the time they entered therapy she wanted a different kind of partner, a different kind of marriage. She wanted to share raising the kids, making financial decisions, and doing the housework. She wanted her husband to be a friend in whom she could confide. Dan thought that she needed her own therapist to help her overcome these unrealistic expectations. As far as he was concerned, their marriage was just fine the way it was and her requests for change amounted to a "bait and switch." When they had taken their vows, they had agreed implicitly on a marriage contract, and he had no intentions of renegotiating it. He entered therapy determined to maintain his vision of their marriage. She entered therapy hoping that his vision would change, that they would leave therapy with a shared vision. Dan and

Linda represented a prototype of a couple with divergent goals, not to mention contradictory views of marriage. Such couples are not good candidates for traditional behavior therapy.

Acceptance: The Missing Link in Traditional Behavior Therapy

The key to discovering what was missing from traditional behavior therapy was ascertaining the common thread among the factors predicting responsiveness to it. All five of the above factors—commitment, age, emotional engagement, traditionality, and convergent goals—relate to partners' capacity for accommodation, compromise, and collaboration. In other words, the more committed, younger, emotionally engaged, egalitarian couples with relatively convergent goals for the relationship were more likely to be able and willing to accommodate one another, to make compromises with one another, and to collaborate with one another in a relationship-enhancing treatment. In contrast, when couples are on the brink of divorce, older, disengaged, traditional, and unable to agree on what a good marriage looks like, they are unlikely to be able or willing to compromise, accommodate, and collaborate.

Here's the rub. Traditional behavior therapy places great emphasis on accommodation, compromise, and collaboration. When couples enter therapy with the ability and willingness to adopt these stances, therapy proceeds quite smoothly—or at least works eventually. However, when couples cannot or will not compromise, accommodate, or collaborate, for one or more of the reasons identified earlier, traditional behavior therapy has little to offer them. Jacobson and Margolin (1979), recognizing the intractability that characterizes many couples seeking therapy, proposed strategies for inducing a *collaborative set* so that accommodation, compromise, and collaboration would be possible anyway. For example, couples would be asked to make a commitment to engaging in collaborative behavior despite their feelings, with the presumption that once the change process got started the desire to collaborate would follow along with increased marital satisfaction, thereby strengthening and maintaining subsequent collaborative behavior. Unfortunately, we now know that all too often these *collaboration induction* techniques had the effect of *force-feeding* change. Even when they were successful, the changes that couples made during the course of therapy were unlikely to persist for long after termination. The changes they were making were rule-governed; they were not maintained by natural contingencies. We will say more about this distinction between rule-governed and contingency shaped behavior later, because it is a crucial distinction in understanding our integrative approach to treating couples. For now, it is important to know that behavior therapy in its traditional form had a significant limitation: it only worked for couples who were able and willing to change.

The fact is that some couples enter therapy with truly irreconcilable differences. As Daniel B. Wile (1981) has noted, some marital problems are unsolvable. And yet, couples with irreconcilable differences and unsolvable problems are not uncommon among therapy consumers, and they often want to try to work things out despite these differences and problems. When direct efforts to change are blocked by incompatibilities, irreconcilable differences, and unsolvable problems, the only way to generate relationship improvement is by promoting acceptance of what seems at first glance unacceptable. Yet, there is nothing in behavioral technology that suggests strategies for promoting acceptance of incompatibilities, differences, or marital problems. *Acceptance* is the missing link in traditional behavior therapy.

The notion that "acceptance is essential to a successful marriage" is probably as old as the institution itself. It undoubtedly appears on a Hallmark card somewhere. Our culture considers it a sign of growth if one accepts things that one can't change. It is even embedded in the vernacular of pop psychology. The serenity prayer used by Alcoholics Anonymous states, "God, give us grace to accept with serenity the things that cannot be changed, courage to change the things that should be changed, and the wisdom to distinguish the one from the other." However, it is one thing to advocate for the acceptance of things that cannot be changed; it is quite another to make it happen. Generating acceptance of one's partner is nice work if you can get it, but it is far easier said than accomplished in therapy.

Nevertheless, beginning in 1986, we independently decided that any complete approach to couple therapy needed to integrate strategies for fostering both acceptance and change. In the development of this integrative approach, we were influenced by a number of clinician writers, most notably Dan Wile (1981, 1995), experiential therapists such as Leslie Greenberg and Susan Johnson (e.g., Johnson & Greenberg, 1995), and strategic therapists, especially those from the Mental Research Institute (e.g., Shoham et al., 1995). Finally, in 1991, our readings as well as our experimental clinical work led us to discover one another, and we have been collaborating ever since. In 1991, we began collaborating on a research project to examine our new treatment against traditional behavioral couple therapy (TBCT). Jacobson drafted the grant proposal to the National Institute of Mental Health for this project; Christensen drafted the treatment manual for integrative couple therapy (ICT) (Christensen & Jacobson, 1991). Later that year, when Jacobson was President of the Association for the Advancement of Behavior Therapy, he first spoke of this collaborative effort in his presidential address (Jacobson, 1992). Finally, in 1995, we published the first clinical description of our approach (Christensen, Jacobson, & Babcock, 1995). This book represents the next step: both a detailed treatment manual and a discussion of special issues related to theory, assessment, and research. A companion book for couples will be published soon (Christensen & Jacobson, 1997). Despite the varying order of authorship on the various books and papers, we view ourselves as joint, equal, co-developers of ICT.

What Is Acceptance in the Context of Intimate Relationships?

The College Dictionary defines acceptance as "the act of taking or receiving something offered" or "favorable reception; approval." These definitions actually come quite close to what we mean by acceptance, even though they differ somewhat dramatically from the connotations of the word as it is commonly used in our culture. *Acceptance* is often used to mean *resignation* or "the act of submission or yielding."

In other words, acceptance could be taken to mean grudgingly giving in to the inevitable status quo. Luckily, this is not what we mean by acceptance. If it were, we would be advocating a sexist form of therapy. Accepting the status quo usually means that men continue to get what they want from marriage, while women don't get the change that they want from therapy. Women typically seek marital therapy because they want their husbands to change; husbands are often reluctant to come to therapy at all because they are quite happy with the current marriage, if only the wife would stop complaining about it (Baucom et al., 1990; Jacobson, 1989; Margolin, Talovic, & Weinstein, 1983). An acceptance-based therapy runs the risk of colluding with the husband and denying the wife precisely what she typically seeks from couple therapy. This risk would exist, that is, if we meant by acceptance *resignation* or preservation of the status quo.

However, acceptance has two components to it in our integrative approach. The first is an attempt to convert problems into vehicles for intimacy. Most approaches to couple therapy define problems as things that have to be eradicated in order for therapy to be successful. However, as Wile (1981) has pointed out, it is actually possible to improve a relationship through the conflict itself: problems can be ways of generating closeness. Our integrative approach is based in part on the premise that if the proper conditions are created in therapy, partners can build a closer, more intimate relationship *because of* their problems and conflict areas, rather than in spite of them. Thus, we offer a radically new way of conceptualizing a conflict or a marital problem. When the problem or conflict successfully brings partners closer together, good things happen. These good things will be detailed later in the chapter; however, it should be noted that none of the positive outcomes requires that either spouse leave therapy frustrated because of not having received what she or he wanted. When our approach works, both get changes *and* acceptance.

The second dimension of acceptance is derived from helping partners "let go" of the struggle to change each other. First, they let go of the premise that differences between them are intolerable, especially when these differences result in one or both of them not getting what they want from the relationship. Second, they let go of the struggle to remold their partner in terms consistent with their idealized image of a husband or wife. As Paul Watzlawick, John Weakland, Richard Fisch, and others (cf. Shoham, Rohrbaugh, & Patterson, 1995) have been telling us since 1967, there are times when efforts to change one's partner actually have the opposite effect. Direct attempts to change an intimate partner are often self-defeating, both because the particular efforts are misguided and because such attempts are likely to have the opposite effect. If one can let go of the struggle to make these changes, a contextual shift can occur where the changes one couldn't get through direct efforts come about because the social context supports the changes.

We describe our approach as integrative, and for heuristic purposes we create a dichotomy between *change* and *acceptance*. In actuality, however, it is a false dichotomy, since both types of interventions foster change: it is simply a matter of who is doing the changing and the nature of the change. With traditional change techniques, the change typically takes the form of one person (the complainee) accommodating the requests for change coming from another person (the complainant); during the course of therapy, partners often switch back and forth between these two roles. With acceptance work, it is the complainant who is changing. The complaint disappears or is transformed into something else. Change involves increases or decreases in the frequency or intensity of behavior; acceptance involves a change in emotional reactions to behavior.

The *change vs. acceptance* dichotomy is also false because, as we mentioned above, acceptance techniques can often be one of the most effective methods available for generating change. Why? First, because partners' strategies for changing each other have often become the primary problem by the time they seek therapy. And second, because *acceptance* means, in part, letting go of the struggle to generate change in one's partner. Therefore, truly letting go of that struggle is often the best way to generate change.

In short, acceptance work is undertaken in order to deal with incompatibilities, irreconcilable differences, and unsolvable problems. The goal of this work is to promote greater intimacy in the relationship by using these incompatibilities, irreconcilable differences, and unsolvable problems as methods of generating closeness, rather than attempting to eradicate them. Short of this goal, partners can often learn to better tolerate things that they don't like about each other, even if they would prefer that these behaviors disappeared. Ideally, for at least some of the presenting problems acceptance work actually leads to change, change that could not have been achieved through direct change strategies. There are three ways that acceptance interventions can help couples: by generating greater intimacy with the conflict area used as a vehicle; by generating tolerance; and by generating change.

To return to the concern about gender disparities, our experience thus far has been that our integrative approach satisfies both partners. Wives who are seeking change from intransigent husbands are more likely rather than less likely to get it (by no longer demanding it). When they don't get it, they often get something else that turns out to be more important to them. Finally, they learn, through tolerance and self-care techniques, to be less *affected* by negative behaviors.

Nevertheless, a purely acceptance-based approach would still put change-seekers at risk, since it is conceivable that their presenting complaints would not be addressed. Moreover, from a structural perspective, a purely acceptance-based approach *looks like* it could be oppressive to the change-seeker or is in some sense anti-change. Thus, it is important to point out that, despite the emphasis on acceptance, we have not abandoned any of the traditional change techniques associated with behavior therapy. Partners cannot avoid change by finding a therapist who uses our approach; it does not let them off the hook. We still use BE and CPT, to maintain balance and to ensure that the approach is truly integrative. We have simply *added* the acceptance work to compensate for an imbalance that limited the effectiveness of TBCT with couples. In fact, we believe that any complete approach to couple therapy has to include both strategies for fostering change and techniques for promoting acceptance.

Implications of Integrating Change and Acceptance

The Distinction between Preaching and Facilitating

In our integrative approach, we take no position on how much change or acceptance is desirable for any given couple. We leave that up to the clients. Our job is simply to create conditions in therapy that allow couples to have experiences fostering both acceptance and change. It is a mistake to think of our acceptance work as *preaching* acceptance.

What Are the Implications of an Integrative Approach for Divorce?

The task of an integrative approach is to create conditions allowing couples to decide for themselves whether or not the relationship has a viable future. By creating a therapeutic atmosphere where partners are free to explore both change and acceptance, we assume that we are maximizing their opportunities to make an informed decision about the relationship.

However, among the possible options is the conclusion by one or both partners that the relationship has no viable future and divorce is the best solution. We would not consider this to be a treatment failure, even though such cases must be counted as failures in randomized clinical trials. As therapists working with couples, we believe that our job is to promote the well-being of the two individuals who are sitting before us. In this very important sense, the whole is less than the sum of its parts. An approach that emphasizes the limits of change as well as its potential is bound to lead in some cases to divorce. An integrative approach is not about saving marriages or relationships; rather, it is about helping partners size up their relationship potential so that ambiguities about the future can be clarified.

During clinical workshops we are often asked, "Under what conditions would you *advocate* that two people split up?" This question constitutes the converse of advocating the marriage. The point is that we do not advocate either, except under extreme circumstances such as battering. Moreover, we do not believe that members of our profession are trained to be experts in answering questions that are of a moral, ethical, or political nature. On the one hand, as we have written in other contexts, psychotherapy, including couple therapy, is inherently political (Jacobson, 1983, 1989): the therapist cannot help but convey implicit or explicit moral and political values in the process of maintaining a relationship with clients. Thus, because psychotherapists tend to be trusted authority figures who are in a position to powerfully influence their clients, this potential to influence must be handled delicately. Nevertheless, the training we get and the expertise we acquire in helping couples do not qualify us to influence them intentionally when the decision they are making depends on personal values and moral imperatives. Inevitably, the decision as to whether or not a couple *should* stay together depends upon individual differences in standards for what is acceptable and necessary in an intimate relationship. Our own personal standards are invariably invoked when we are asked for our opinions regarding a couple's future together. By offering such opinions, we are creating a dual relationship: therapist as behavior change (and acceptance) expert and as secular priest. We are not secular priests, ministers, or rabbis. Unfortunately, we cannot count on our clients to recognize that. Therefore, it is our job to make sure we do not obfuscate what is already a complicated relationship by playing the role of moral arbiter.

This does not mean that we cannot answer specific questions when we have some basis for making predictions. For example, many couples are on a path toward divorce, which can actually be predicted with some accuracy (Gottman, 1994). If we see couples on this path and can confidently predict that marital satisfaction will not increase, it is perfectly reasonable to present that information to couples. One of us once told a couple, "You probably won't be any happier in the future than you are now [at the conclusion of unsuccessful therapy], so you have to decide whether your current level of satisfaction is preferable to the uncertainties and risks involved in splitting up and rebuilding your lives without one another." With another couple, one of us once said, "Ten years down the road it is unlikely that the two of you will be together, given what we know about predictors of divorce; however, you may not be ready yet to split up. In my experience, people march to their own beat on this issue, and they make these decisions when the time is right for them. This is one of the most important decisions you will ever make. Even though I doubt whether the two of you will stay together forever, I could be wrong." These comments were both made in response to empirical questions: the first was, "How likely is it that things will get better between us down the road?"; the second, "Do you think we'll eventually split up?" Both questions came at the conclusion of unsuccessful therapy. Neither asked for an advocacy position from the therapist. While it is an abuse of the therapist's position of influence to take a position of advocacy regarding the couple's staying together, the therapist can and should answer empirical questions. Granted, it is always dicey going from prediction formulas based on groups to prediction for an individual couple, and therapists should offer the appropriate caveats when they answer these questions.

But, some will protest, don't we have an obligation to strongly urge couples to work things out, given the negative effects of divorce on children? A thorough discussion of this issue is well beyond the scope of this book. However, we are fortunate in having a long and illustrious research literature to refer to when responding to this question. The answer is no. The original concerns regarding the negative effects of divorce on children came from work that was full of methodological problems. More recent and better controlled studies suggest that many of what were thought to be the negative effects of divorce on children can be accounted for by marital conflict that is associated with divorce. The actual effects of divorce are often small and transitory (Emery & Forehand, 1995; Heatherington, 1989). Still, this is a complicated issue. There are vast individual differences in how children respond to divorce; their age, sex, and personality will all influence their reactions. Also, economic conditions of the parents after divorce dramatically affect the child's well-being. Yet, it is not at all clear that parents are doing their children any favors by staying together just for them, despite severe and unremitting conflict! It *is* clear that children can come through divorce without major effects on their adjustment; in fact, some kids may be better off after divorce. Eleanor Maccoby (Maccoby & Mnookin, 1992) has reported findings suggesting that *if* fathers stay involved subsequent to divorce, and *if* the biological parents can co-parent effectively after the divorce, children may be better off following the divorce than they were living in an environment of marital conflict day in and day out. Thus, a responsible therapist should not urge parents to stay together just for the kids. The impact of divorce on the children is an important consideration for couples but only one of many.

Does Acceptance Mean Accepting All Partner Behaviors?

Another question that is frequently asked of us at workshops is, "Does acceptance mean that people are supposed to accept any negative behavior?" The careful reader already knows the general answer to this question. Our integrative approach carries with it no ideology about what behaviors should and should not be accepted or, for that matter, no commitment to urging acceptance of *any* behaviors. There is no philosophical principle in our approach stating that "acceptance is good" or "acceptance is better than change." We believe that effective couple therapy generates a context where both accepting and

other types of changing will occur. However, we have no stake in selling couples on the notion that one type of change is better than another or that acceptance is something that they "should" try. Although they may become more accepting because of conditions
created in therapy, we accept their insistence on change as much as
we would accept their desire to become more accepting. It is up to
them. Nevertheless, our model does suggest that more couples can be
helped if during therapy the partners become more accepting of one
another.

It is important to note that some behaviors are unacceptable to us.
The most obvious example is battering. When physical aggression is
moderate or severe, or physical or emotional abuse is used as a method
of control, couple therapy is inappropriate (Jacobson & Gortner, in
press): arrest, prosecution, punishment, and, if indicated, gender-spe-
cific treatment for the batterer are all preferable to couple therapy.
Even when couple therapy is indicated, for mild forms of physical
aggression without battering, we insist on "no violence" contracts as a
precondition to therapy and enforce them by discontinuing couple
therapy if the contract is violated. Because of the physical risk involved (usually to the wife), and because of our own moral, legal, and
ethical obligations to potential victims of domestic violence, we are
quite comfortable designating the behaviors associated with battering
as unacceptable. We can do so without in any way creating tension
within the integrative model. An acceptance-based approach does not
preclude the therapists from rejecting particular behaviors for moral,
legal, or ethical reasons.

The Stance of the Therapist

Our integrative model provides a point of departure from many alternative couple therapies, and especially from TBCT, by adopting a non-
didactic format, which emphasizes validation, compassion, and a virtual absence of confrontation. Whereas traditional behavioral couple
therapy is at times confrontational and virtually always didactic and
psychoeducational, our current model emphasizes the same degree of
support and empathy that we would want partners to show toward
one another. The most common mistake among beginning therapists
being trained in our approach is to continue the subtle blaming and
accusatory remarks that characterize many so-called therapeutic interventions. We attempt to create an environment that fosters acceptance and change in part by accepting both partners to the degree that
they might accept one another under ideal conditions. Our emphasis
on validation and nonconfrontation creates the paradox that we have

to accept even their unwillingness or inability to be accepting of one another.

The validating, compassionate stance changes not just the way acceptance work is conducted but also the traditional behavioral techniques. With this model, homework noncompliance is treated as grist for the mill, noncollaborative behavior is taken to be an ideal opportunity for acceptance work, and the unwillingness to practice constructive communication is examined rather than corrected. In fact, some of our colleagues and students have told us that the stance of the therapist is what most differentiates the integrative model from TBCT. This stance permeates the therapy and makes it recognizably integrative regardless of the particular focus of a therapy session.

Pilot Data on the Efficacy of Integrative Couple Therapy

As this book is being written, we are in the process of completing a federally funded pilot study comparing our integrative approach to TBCT. Thus far, sixteen couples have been randomly assigned to either TBCT or to ICT. All couples have been treated at the Center for Clinical Research, Jacobson's laboratory at the University of Washington. Half the cases were supervised by Jacobson and half by Christensen. Five therapists from the Seattle community have been trained in both approaches, with Jacobson and Margolin (1979) serving as the treatment manual for TBCT and Christensen and Jacobson (1991) serving as the manual for ICT. Four of the therapists are licensed psychologists, while the fifth graduated with a master's degree from a training program in marriage and family therapy. All therapy sessions have been taped, so that they can be viewed by supervisors and monitored for adherence and competence by trained and expert raters.

When we initially applied for funds to test the efficacy of ICT, we suggested a large-scale, two-site clinical trial—one site being the University of Washington and the other UCLA. Our funding agency, the National Institute of Mental Health, suggested that we first conduct a pilot study to demonstrate that therapists other than the two of us could keep the two treatments distinct and get promising results from ICT and that observers could truly discriminate between the two treatments. We were not expected to have sufficient statistical power to test for the superiority of ICT over TBCT: that would presumably have to await a large-scale study, assuming that the results of our pilot study were promising.

In data that are thus far unpublished (Jacobson, Christensen, Prince, & Cordova, in preparation), we were able to demonstrate quite convincingly that therapists can keep the two treatments distinct. We developed a system for rating the extent to which therapists were adhering to treatment protocols. Coders were then trained to watch sessions and rate the extent to which particular "change" and "acceptance" interventions were occurring. These coders documented that the therapists did an excellent job of confining "acceptance" interventions to the ICT treatment.

Perhaps more importantly, despite the extremely small sample sizes and the corresponding lack of adequate statistical power to test the relative efficacy of the two treatments, ICT increased couple satisfaction to a significantly greater degree than did TBCT. In fact, the reason that these differences were statistically significant despite the small sample sizes was that the effects were extremely large. Moreover, whereas TBCT performed about as well as it typically does (50% improvement), virtually every couple thus far completing ICT showed significant improvement, and the vast majority (75%) recovered to the point that they were no longer distinguishable from happily married couples on measures of marital satisfaction. These differences appear to be holding up through a one-year follow-up: at that time, three of the eight TBCT couples had separated or divorced, compared to none of the ICT couples.

A skeptic might wonder about the bias of our therapists, given our obvious enthusiasm for ICT. We reasoned that the best protection against accusations of bias would be to have the TBCT tapes rated for therapist competence by an expert who had no other connection to the study. Donald H. Baucom from the University of North Carolina rated our TBCT tapes and found the therapists to be extremely competent: the ratings were "state of the art." Thus, both the outcome of cases in TBCT and the competence ratings from Don Baucom suggest that our findings were not contaminated by bias in favor of ICT.

As a final note on the apparent promise of ICT, Cordova, Jacobson, and Christensen (in preparation) examined therapy process in the two treatment conditions, with specific hypotheses pertaining to how the treatments would differ based on what was supposed to transpire. The hypotheses focused on partner communication. The results were remarkably consistent with the hypothesis that different change processes were occurring in the two treatments, processes consistent with predictions made by the different treatment models.

Of course, any pilot study is extremely preliminary, but even we were surprised at how well ICT performed. Despite numerous workshops over the past few years where we have described the approach to practicing therapists, this was our first piece of concrete feedback on its efficacy. Considering that 50% success seems to be the norm for most if not all currently existing couple treatments (Jacobson & Addis, 1993), we are hopeful that ICT will prove to be more effective than other currently existing treatments.

The rest of this book is devoted to a detailed description of ICT. We begin by describing the analysis of conflict on which ICT is based and follow that theoretical discussion with the case formulation, a central construct within ICT. Beginning in Chapter 4, the focus becomes decidedly more clinical, with a detailed discussion of our assessment processes and procedures. Chapter 5 provides an overview of ICT, both the structure and the process. Chapters 6 through 9 detail the specific therapeutic procedures for promoting both acceptance and change. Chapter 10 focuses on the importance of recognizing group diversity and the implications of group differences (gender, sexual orientation, culture, ethnicity, and class) for ICT. The final chapter takes up a variety of special problems and considerations when conducting ICT.

2

FROM LOVE TO WAR

A couple comes in for therapy and describes their problems. He wants an entirely different kind of relationship than she does. There is a wide divide in their expectations for each other. Furthermore, they are in angry and hurtful conflict about these differences. They seem uniquely suited *not* to be with each other, a match of painfully incompatible partners. The therapist might wonder: was this an arranged marriage? Did some malevolent person force these ill-suited partners to mate? If they did choose each other, it must have been an impulsive decision, after a brief courtship. It is hard to imagine that the partners knew each other well before marriage, fell in love, and then made a free, voluntary, and conscious decision to spend their lives together.

Of course most couples, even those who appear in therapy, have gone through a process of acquaintanceship during courtship, have fallen in love, and have made a voluntary decision to marry. Those couples who end up in separation, divorce, or couple therapy may later rewrite their history together and conclude that they never really loved each other. They were blinded early on by infatuation. They were misled by their partners. They were pressured by their family, their friends, or their circumstances. However, at the time of their commitment, most would have insisted on the integrity of their love, defended their choice, and voiced optimism for the future.

This transition from courtship, love, and marriage to therapy, separation, or divorce is one of the most dramatic that people can experience. At one point, partners are in a state of intense love and commitment, where they tell each other that they are best thing that ever happened to them and pledge themselves "in sickness and in sorrow till death do us part." Then, amazingly, they move to a state of disappointment and anger where they may wish that they had never met, hope to never see each other again, and plan on living the rest of their

22

lives apart. It is important for us to understand this transition from love to war in order to help couples avoid making it.

It is our belief that this painful transition begins with common, garden-variety incompatibilities between partners. The ways partners try to handle these incompatibilities often lead them along this painful path. Understanding how incompatibilities between partners develop, what their consequences are, and how they are managed, we will be in a better position as therapists to help partners accept these incompatibilities and accommodate to them. Since these incompatibilities start from the very beginning of the relationship, our discussion must start with mate selection.

Mate Selection

Theories of mate selection have emphasized *homogamy*, the notion that people tend to marry those who are similar to themselves, and *heterogamy*, the notion that people tend to marry those who are different from themselves. There is evidence for both notions, with evidence favoring homogamy (Surra, 1990).

The key issue is the exchange of reinforcement between the pair. Mate selection is based on the actual and anticipated reinforcement from the relationship. Factors that promote that reinforcement increase the chances that two potential mates will choose each other; factors that interfere with mutual reinforcement decrease the chances that potential mates will choose each other.

Reinforcement can be promoted by both similarity and differences between partners. Consider similarities first. If partners have similar background, values, and interests, they are much more likely to engage in mutually reinforcing conversation. They may both like to talk about sports, politics, or movies. They can make fun of or express admiration for the same kinds of people in their conversation. Similarity, however, leads to much more than easy conversation; it also leads to reinforcing activities. Because of similar interests and values, partners may enjoy going to church together, playing tennis together, going to the opera together, protesting for abortion rights together, or gardening together. Finally, similarity paves the way for joint decisions. Partners who are both fiscally conservative will agree to avoid the risky investment and instead save for a "rainy day." Partners who value family and education will choose a home in a good school district rather than the nicer home in the poorer school district. From a behavioral perspective, it is hardly surprising that people mate with those who are similar to them.

Differences are also a source of reinforcement between partners. Sexual attraction between heterosexuals is based on the differences between male and female bodies and the happy way in which they converge. Conversation can be enlivened by different opinions and points of view. A partner from a different ethnicity or social class can be interesting and exotic. Role differences can facilitate accomplishment of important life tasks. The fact that one prefers to be a house parent while the other prefers to work out in the world may enable partners to manage both raising children and supporting themselves financially. Role differences may also minimize competition and facilitate reinforcement. If Dave is the acknowledged cook in the family, Mary can reinforce him for his skill, not compete with him for attention from others about his cooking, and allow him to have the final say in decisions about what to serve for guests. Similarly, if Mary is the acknowledged decorator in the family, Dave can reinforce her for her good taste, not compete with her for attention from others about her decorating, and allow her the final say in choices about what furniture to buy. Differences in behavior may fill in gaps in couples' lives and enable them to have a more complete and fuller life by being with one another. Consider Jennifer, who has always been earnest and responsible, and Troy, who has always been "fun loving." When they get together, Jennifer is assured some respite from the being responsible while Troy feels certain that he can meet the responsibilities that he knows are his. Or consider James and Anna, who differ greatly on emotional expressiveness. Anna is exciting, provocative, spontaneous, and changeable; James is emotionally steady, dependable, and deliberate. Their union ensures some excitement in James life and some stability in Anna's. Differences and similarities are both a basis of mate selection because they are both a source of mutual reinforcement.

Development of Incompatibility

Similarities, Differences, and Incompatibilities

Similarities and differences, which were the basis of attraction, may over time become a source of incompatibility. Commonly, differences between partners that were initially appealing show a darker and more troubling side. Consider Jennifer and Troy, described above. Jennifer was attracted to Troy because he was so "fun loving." She could laugh with him like she had with no other guy. She could really relax with him and enjoy herself, yet she knew that there was also substance within him. Troy enjoyed making Jennifer laugh, but he also admired her "togetherness." She was organized and had her life under control. Her apartment always seemed organized, clean, and neat, and yet was comfortable and inviting. During their courtship, Troy much preferred to be at her place rather his often dirty, untidy, and chaotic apartment. These qualities that were attractive during courtship gave way to conflict later on in their relationship. Jennifer wanted to save money while Troy was more inclined to spend it; she wanted to have work done before play while he wanted to enjoy life now; she wanted to get a good night's sleep before work while he wanted to stay out late. These conflicts resulted from the very qualities that had served as a source of attraction between the two.

Similarities that were a source of attraction may also become a basis for conflict. Consider Daniel and Joan, who met during their college days in the early 1970s. They had similar, leftist political leanings, and both got involved in peace marches against the war in Vietnam. Antagonistic to materialism and consumerism, after college they became involved in various environmental groups and worked on campaigns for politicians who championed their ideas. Daniel even ran one time for the state legislature. Now in their early forties with two young children, they live in a two-bedroom rented house and get by on a small salary that Daniel makes from his work on a political newspaper. Each has grown cynical about making changes in government; both are unhappy with their current circumstances. Joan gets angry at Daniel for not having gotten a job that could provide better for the family. His reply usually questions her feminist values: why is it just he who is to support the family? She points to his lack of help with the kids and an argument ensues. In fact, their predicament was set in motion when both pursued their political passions, a source of their initial attraction, with little thought for future job and financial security.

As we have seen, some similarities and differences may attract early on in the relationship but repel later. Many other problematic similarities and differences were not a source of attraction but just part of the complete combination of characteristics that made up the two people in the relationship. These qualities were there from the beginning, just part of the package of qualities that comprised each partner. No matter how widely one dates, no matter how thoroughly one surveys the pool of eligibles through friends, singles events, personal ads, computer match or video dating programs, no matter how carefully one chooses a mate, there will always be qualities that the mate has that simply don't fit well.

In a recent paper on their longitudinal research on marriage, Huston and Houts (in press) estimated the probability of subjects in their sample finding a mate whose preferences matched their own. Considering dimensions such as role preferences, they estimated the probability of subjects finding a mate who matched them on *three* separate dimensions to be 17%. The average person in their sample reported dating only five people more than casually before marriage; thus the likelihood of a person in their sample finding a mate whose preferences were compatible on more than a few dimensions was quite low. Incompatibility on some dimensions is a virtual mathematical certainty!

Ill-fitting qualities between partners practically guarantee conflict at some point in the relationship. Consider first some examples of similarities. When Derrick married Jenny he didn't much care that she, like he, couldn't cook and did not want to learn. It was a largely irrelevant quality during their courtship days, when they usually went out to eat. Now, well into the marriage, Derrick is upset that the only way to get a good meal is to go out or order out. He feels that Jenny, as a woman, should have learned to cook a decent meal. The amount of money they spend on eating out bothers him. Jenny replies to his accusations by saying that in this modern world cooking is not just the woman's domain. She reminds him that the world's best chefs are men. Furthermore, he has known since day one that cooking is not her thing.

As another example of a similarity leading to conflict, one that flared up immediately, consider Raymond and Donna. Both are extremely close to their families of origin. This was not a source of initial attraction, in part because it caused conflict from the very beginning. They disagreed on how often to do things with her parents versus his, on where to spend holidays, on whose parents were more enjoyable to be with or more generous.

Conflicts are more likely to be caused by differences than by similarities. Many differences that were not a source of attraction and were barely noticed during courtship can become a source of conflict. Consider Neil and Debra's difference in sociability. Debra is an extroverted, gregarious type who loves to have people around her while Neil is more introverted, preferring a couple close friends to lots of acquaintances. During their early courtship, their intense attraction to each other made both of them exclude others and focus instead on their developing relationship. This tendency was exacerbated by Neil's travel schedule, which often took him out of town on business trips. Neither wanted to share their limited time with other people when he was in town. However, when they moved in together and shared a household, they confronted serious differences in attitudes about how open their home should be to others. Debra wanted friends to come over frequently and liked it if her friends dropped by unannounced.

Neil wanted their home for the two of them; he felt it was rude for people to drop by unannounced.

Potentially conflictual differences and similarities are not likely to create problems early on. The culture of courtship, with its pre-planned events ("dates"), its focus on recreational activities, and its emphasis on impression management (being on one's "best behavior," putting one's "best foot forward"), minimizes the exposure of similarities that don't work or differences that don't mesh. However, as a relationship progresses partners experience more contact with each other; they jointly confront a greater diversity of situations. They experience each other's different moods; they meet each other's friends and family; in short, they get to know each other better. During this time of greater exposure to each other and each other's worlds, partners are likely to encounter preferences, habits, values, and behavior patterns that don't mesh well. Because partners are different genetically and have different learning histories, they will not always want the same thing at the same time in the same way. Whether based in similarities (both partners want to be in charge of decorating the home) or differences (one wants more and different sexual activity than the other), incompatibilities between partners are inevitable. And some of those incompatibilities will be important ones. Partners will not be able to slough them off as insignificant or treat them with indifference. These incompatibilities will arouse emotional upset in one or, more likely, both.

Adding to the complexity and difficulty of these conflicts is the fact that incompatibilities are moving targets. It is not as if partners can go through the process of acquaintanceship, get to know each other well, and thus have a fix on the incompatibilities that will create problems for them. Their shared and individual life experiences will exacerbate some incompatibilities and minimize others. These experiences may even create incompatibilities where none existed before.

Let us consider first examples of how incompatibilities may change through shared experiences. Early on in their relationship, Ben and Melinda argued about the amount of time Melinda wanted them to spend with her parents. Ben felt Melinda's desires for frequent contact were strange and, more importantly, an intrusion on their life as a couple. However, as Ben got to know her parents well and as they adjusted to him, Ben found himself enjoying the visits himself. An incompatibility that both had feared would be a continuing problem in their relationship dissipated completely.

Such a happy outcome as Ben and Melinda's is not likely to occupy the attention of couple therapists. They are more likely to focus on shared experiences that have created or exacerbated incompatibilities.

For example, Jessica and Robert seemed perfectly compatible in their views on children. They planned on how many they would have, when they would have them, and how they would rear them. However, the experience of having a child generated unpredictable and incompatible reactions in them. They both planned that Jessica would return to work soon after the birth, but once the baby arrived Jessica could not bear the thought of turning over her baby's care to another. Robert could not imagine drastically trimming their lifestyle, which would be required with a loss of Jessica's income.

The experiences that the spouses have in their separate worlds may also affect incompatibilities for better or worse. Monica and Rodney fought for years over the priority he gave to his career. However, as he grew disenchanted with his career in middle age, he sought the comfort of a close family life. Their conflicts over this topic diminished as a result. Of course, one can easily imagine the opposite scenario, in which individual life experiences exacerbate or create incompatibilities. For example, Anna and Daren rarely differed on issues of closeness and time together throughout their courtship and early marriage. However, when Anna made an important career change that moved her into a demanding but exciting position, she spent long hours at her office and no longer had the time and interest in Daren that she used to have. Daren felt abandoned by Anna and angry that the pleasures they used to have were so suddenly curtailed. As another example, consider Will and Martha. They got on well with each other's family of origin until Will's mom had a stroke and Will wanted her to move in with them. Martha could not fathom the idea of living with her disabled mother-in-law.

Areas of Incompatibility

Two fundamental dimensions of relationships have to do with the participants' *level of closeness* and *extent of asymmetry* (Kelley et al., 1983). Closeness concerns the extent, diversity, and intensity of interaction between partners. We would say that Joe and Diane have a closer relationship than Bill and Susan because Joe and Diane have more overall contact with each other, over a wider array of situations, and with greater impact on each other than do Joe and Diane. Asymmetry concerns the extent and nature of the differences between the members of the relationship. Joe and Diane have greater asymmetry in their relationship than do Bill and Susan. Joe has a job outside the home, while Diane is a stay-at-home mom; Joe almost always initiates sexual contact while Diane is rarely the initiator; Joe has limited contact with the children, while Diane is very involved with them. In contrast, Susan and Bill both work out of the home; both initiate sexual contact; and their roles with their children are similar. The nature and level of asymmetry between partners determine the roles that they play and affect the power, control, and responsibility each has in the relationship. Joe has the power of initiation in his sexual relationship while Diane has only the power of veto. In contrast, both Bill and Susan share initiation and veto power in their sexual relationship.

To illustrate the importance of these two dimensions, consider how they can be used to distinguish different types of relationships. For example, a friendship differs from a marriage in that the latter usually involves a closer connection. A parent-child relationship and marriage are both typically close but differ in the extent and nature of the asymmetry between the pairs. Usually parent-child relationships, particularly with young children, involve greater disparity in the actions of each than does a marriage. These dimensions can also distinguish between different stages of a relationship. The movement from courtship to marriage typically involves increased closeness between partners. The parent-child relationship goes through stages of decreasing asymmetry. In fact, when the adult child takes care of the aging parent, the asymmetry may be reversed.

These central features of relationships are important to people because they define what the relationship is and who the individuals are. Consequently, incompatibilities often occur along these dimensions. Jane may not feel she really has a relationship with John unless they regularly share their deepest feelings. John may not feel like a "man" in the relationship unless he has the final say in money matters. Yet people are likely to differ in what they want and need along these dimensions. Because of their genetic backgrounds and learning histories, they may want different types and levels of closeness and patterns of asymmetry.

Certainly these two areas do not exhaust the possibilities of incompatibilities between partners. There is probably no content area, however small or trivial, that some couple has not disagreed about. However, issues of closeness and asymmetry are likely to be prominent in many couples' disputes. We will visit these and other areas of incompatibility in the next chapter, when we discuss themes, since the couple's most important incompatibility defines the theme of their conflicts. But now let us turn to the consequences of incompatibility.

Consequences of Incompatibility

Early on in the relationship, we might expect partners to overlook their incompatibilities and accommodate to each other. In their enthusiasm for the relationship and their desire to make it work, they might "paper over" their differences and deny or minimize their incompatibilities. If they sense that their partners may not comply, they may inhibit some of their own desires or express them gently and positively. Each may be willing to make ad hoc compromises to please their partner.

These strategies come at some cost to each. Incompatibilities mean that one or both partners are deprived of reinforcement or exposed to aversive stimulation. If Bart believes that marriage means that both partners end all relationships with previous boyfriends and girlfriends but Claudia feels that her former boyfriends should be able to remain close friends, this incompatibility will mean that either Bart experiences jealousy or Claudia experiences the loss of her friendships: in either case, both will be exposed to painful conflict about the issue. Similarly, if Anna's career takes off so that she no longer has the same amount of time to spend with Daren that she used to and that he values so much, then either she will experience the anxiety of being behind in her work or he will experience the loss of her company; again, both will experience the pain of conflict.

Because these incompatibilities are costly, partners will abide them for only so long. Their patience and tolerance will wear thin. It will become increasingly difficult for them to deny the existence of these incompatibilities. They may grow frustrated with accommodation and compromise. At this point, they may present their conflicting desires openly and negatively. They may demand what they want or forcefully take it. They may criticize each other for not meeting their needs. They may use withdrawal, guilt, or withholding to punish the other for not fulfilling their desires. The result is coercion.

Coercion

Coercive interactions were first described from a behavioral perspective by Gerald Patterson in the 1970s (Patterson, 1975; Patterson & Hops, 1972). In a coercive interaction, one partner applies aversive stimulation until the other responds. The coercive partner then gets positive reinforcement for his or her display of aversiveness (the other responds or gives in), while the other gets negative reinforcement for responding to the aversiveness (the aversiveness stops when compliance occurs). Thus, one has learned that, to get the other to respond, you should be aversive. The other has learned that, to get that aversiveness turned off, you should comply. Consider the early example provided by Patterson and Hops (1972):

Wife: "You still haven't fixed that screen door."
Husband: (Makes no observable response, but sits surrounded by his newspaper.)
Wife: (There is a decided rise in the decibel level of her voice.) " A lot of thanks I get for all I do. You said three weeks ago—"
Husband: "Damn it, stop nagging at me. As soon as I walk in here and try to read the paper I get yelling and bitching."

In this situation, the husband has the wife trained to increase the "volume" in order to get him to comply. She is more likely to resort to shouting next time she needs some change in his behavior. He, on the other hand, has learned that a vague promise will "turn off the pain" (pp. 424–425).

The process gets more complicated by intermittent reinforcement and shaping. Because compliance with the coercive act entails some cost, partners are not always compliant. They provide an intermittent rather than a continuous schedule of reinforcement for coercion. But intermittent reinforcement tends to lead to more persistent responding than does continuous reinforcement. Also, as a result of compliance with coercion, partners unwittingly shape increasing levels of it. They may not respond immediately to the coercive response. Only when the pain of coercion is greater than the pain of compliance do they give in. In this way they train the other to escalate coercive efforts.

An example may clarify these processes. Sharon is more sociable, more of a "party person" than Barry. After a period of time in which she limited her social contact in deference to Barry, she became more overt, definite, and negative about what she wanted. Before one party that meant a lot to her, she criticized and belittled Barry for being "socially isolated" and "unsupportive" of her. He finally agreed to go to the party, thus positively reinforcing her for coercion. At the same time, Barry was negatively reinforced for his compliance (the criticism and belittling terminated once he complied). Thus, on future occasions both repeated their actions. However, because Barry found certain social events uncomfortable, giving in to Sharon terminated her aversive behavior but exposed him to the uncomfortable experience of the party. He refused to comply with certain parties that were particularly aversive to him, but in so doing he put Sharon on an intermittent reinforcement schedule for her criticism and pressure. Furthermore, he unintentionally shaped Sharon's behavior into a pattern of escalating coercive responses. Although early in the relationship he responded with compliance to slight indications of her disapproval at his hesitation to social invitations, later he became habituated to them. He did not comply until she engaged in more and more criticism and belittling, particularly if the social event in question was especially uncomfortable for him.

Sometimes the partner being coerced will use aversive methods to try to control the other's coercion. "Fighting fire with fire," the coerced partner uses coercion as a defense against the other. For example, Barry may at times react to Sharon's coercion by yelling and criticizing her for being so critical and belittling of him. Barry's behaviors may be negatively reinforced by Sharon, if she stops her aversive actions when he begins his. The exigencies of the situation will determine whether Sharon escalates her coercion until Barry complies or whether Barry escalates his counter coercion until she stops hers or whether they escalate to an uncertain stalemate. Such exigencies include the importance of the event to Sharon, Barry's discomfort with the event, and their immediate emotional dispositions toward each other, which may determine whether either is "up for a fight." But often enough, coercion is countered with coercion, because it gets negatively reinforced.

Our discussion and examples up until now have portrayed coercion as starting with one partner, the coercer, who initially uses aversive stimuli with the other, the coercee, who uses coercion only as a counteracting method. However, coercion is rarely so one-sided. Typically, both partners will use coercive strategies to meet their own goals. They may well use different, specific coercive behaviors to meet different ends, but from a reinforcement perspective these behaviors are identical. For example, Barry may withdraw and withhold affection from Sharon when she takes care of their son Ben by bringing him along on her social events rather than giving him the individual attention that Barry thinks is appropriate. Sharon may respond to Barry's coercion in ways that intermittently reinforce that coercion and shape it into greater intensity, just as he does to her coercion. She may counter his coercive efforts with counter coercion of her own. But in this case, the coercion begins with Barry.

Thus, we have two methods for the development of mutual coercion. First, both partners may use their own methods of coercion to meet their own ends, and second, each partner may counter the coercion of the other with coercive efforts designed to terminate the other's aversive behavior. With coercion that goes both ways and escalates in intensity, a relationship may over time become more and more marked by negativity and conflict.

Christensen and Pasch (1993) have suggested three broad behavioral patterns that negative, conflictual interaction can take. In the first, *mutual avoidance*, couples are faced with an incompatibility but anticipate confrontation as being more painful than avoidance so they don't discuss it openly. In the second pattern, *mutual negative interaction*, both partners engage in aversive attacks on the other. One may start the interaction with aversive strategies designed to get the other to change, but the other quickly responds with aversive counter measures. Both get into an angry, critical, blaming, attacking interaction. In the third pattern, called the *demand-withdraw pattern* (Christensen, 1987; Christensen & Heavey, 1993), one partner engages in negative interaction, such as demanding, blaming, and accusation, while the other avoids and withdraws from the interaction. Each of these individual strategies has some immediate reinforcing payoff. By avoidance and withdrawal, partners may protect themselves from the pain of open discussion of an incompatibility. By negative engagement, partners may get some of what they want but the cost of this compliance escalates over time. In demand-withdraw interaction, one seeks the benefits of negative engagement while the other seeks the benefits of withdrawal, but the vicious cycle of interaction that ensues can be costly to each.

Vilification

As partners get deeper and deeper into conflict, they will think about these interactions and try to understand them. They will make judgments about what causes these interactions and who is responsible for them. Based on attribution theory and research (Bradbury & Fincham, 1990), as well as our own clinical experience, we know that partners in coercive conflicts will likely find the cause and responsibility for the conflict in the other. For example, Sharon may decide that Barry is too selfish to rise above his own insecurity to experience new social contacts that could enhance his own life and their life together. On the other hand, Barry may decide that Sharon is superficial and shallow; she pressures him to go to parties with her because of her selfishness. These attributes also explain why she doesn't interact with their son more but merely brings him along to her events. He worries that she will make their son as shallow and superficial as she is. Thus, the differences between them on sociability are now seen as deficiencies. The differences have become vilified.

In our experience, partners are likely to vilify their differences in one of three ways. First, they may interpret their differences as due to badness. It is not that they are just different but that the other is mean, selfish, inconsiderate, thoughtless, stubborn, self-centered, rude, or unloving. Like Sharon and Barry, they will see their differences as arising from moral deficiencies in the other.

Partners who have a bit more psychological sophistication may choose a second way of vilifying their differences: seeing them as arising from deficiencies in emotional adjustment. It is not that we are different, but that you are disordered. You are different from me because you are emotionally immature, psychologically inhibited, mentally unbalanced, hysterical, neurotic, overanxious, depressed, and suffering from several personality disorders.

A third way of vilifying differences spares partners moral condemnation and psychiatric diagnosis but grades them inadequate on personal competence. It is not that we are different but that you are inadequate. You don't know how to treat a man (or woman), or how to love someone, or how to communicate constructively, or how to express your feelings.

These explanations of their differences are not simply material for contemplation as spouses try to understand the causes of their problems. Partners often share their explanations with each other, and with considerable passion. These explanations may look suspiciously like accusations. For example, Sharon and Barry's conflicts about going to social events and maternal contact with their son are filled with accusations of insecurity, selfishness, and inconsiderateness, defenses of oneself against these attacks, and counterattacks. Over time conflicts move beyond the simple level of differences ("I want you to do more of this; I don't like it when you do that") to include conflict about attributions as well ("This means you are a selfish person; No, this means you don't care about my feelings") (Kelley, 1979).

Polarization

As partners become more and more coercive with each other and transform their differences into deficiencies, they may become more polarized in their positions. They begin to look even more different than they really are. This change occurs through deprivation and through specialization. In the context of coercion and vilification, partners are not likely to provide each other their usual positive gratifications. There is too much anger and resentment inhibiting positive encounters. Also, partners may withhold gratifications that they know the other values. Thus, each is likely to experience deprivation from the reinforcers that the other is normally able to provide. This deprivation may intensify each partner's desires for what had, historically, been provided in part by the other. For example, as Sharon is deprived of social events with Barry, those events may become more important to her. She may experience more need for them and develop more elaborate justifications for them. On the other hand, as Barry experiences more and more pressure to go to these events and defends himself more vigorously from Sharon's attacks, he may lose any desire for such social events. It begins to appear as if Barry has no need for social contact while Sharon desires it constantly. Thus, as a result of their coercive efforts to cope with their differences, those differences may grow even greater.

Another process of polarization occurs through the division of labor and specialization that often accompanies incompatibilities between partners. People are usually skilled at what they like to do. They do what they like, and this practice increases their skills. In contrast, people are often unskilled at what they dislike. They don't do what they dislike and therefore don't develop skills for it. In this way, incompatibilities often mask a different set of skills in each partner. The manner of coping with incompatibility may accentuate skill differences. For example, Barry enjoys and is more skilled than Sharon at spending alone time playing with their son Mark. He finds more time to engage with Mark this way and thus increases his ability to relate to Mark in a mutually enjoyable way. Sharon and Barry's conflicts about time with their son are liable to increase this skill disparity. For example, to make up for missing time with Mark, Barry may spend more time than he might otherwise with their son. Sharon's efforts with their son may be no match for Barry's and may be easy for Barry to criticize, all of which may lessen Sharon's activities and her comfort and skill with those activities. Thus, partners can end up looking more different than they were and more different than they needed to be.

The Management of Incompatibility

From our analysis of conflict so far, it may seem as if couples are doomed to incompatibility and its consequences of coercion, vilification, and polarization. It may seem as if there is no hope for couples at all (unless they are saved by integrative couple therapy). Although we believe that all couples will face some areas of incompatibility in their lives together, clearly many couples don't go down the path of increasing coercion, vilification, and polarization. They are able to manage incompatibilities in ways that don't escalate their conflicts or deepen the divide between them. Let us now consider some of the factors that affect how couples manage their incompatibilities.

Level of Incompatibility

Some couples are simply better matches than others. Some couples have fewer differences with which they have to cope than others. Perhaps careful mate selection accounts for some of the variance in how well-suited mates are to each other. Certainly chance must play a large role in who meets whom at the right time and place and how they both traverse their life courses together. Whatever the cause, couples are not all equally suited to each other. Those who have fewer and less serious incompatibilities are less likely, all other things being equal, to go down the destructive paths we have described above. As evidence for this simple notion, Christensen (1987) has gathered data demonstrating a relationship between level of incompatibility on closeness (how close or intimate would each spouse ideally like to be?) and relationship satisfaction: there was a correlation of -.56 between a measure of incompatibility on closeness and scores on the Dyadic Adjustment Scale (Spanier, 1976). Christensen and Shenk (1991) showed that distressed couples (couples who had just started therapy and couples getting divorced) had higher levels of incompatibility on closeness than nondistressed couples.

Attractions

People choose each other as mates, not primarily because they have few incompatibilities, but because there are strong attractions to each other. Some of these attractions relate to the compatibilities between partners. For example, partners are attracted to each other because their similar senses of humor enable them to laugh a lot together. However, other attractions are based on characteristics that are widely valued rather than uniquely meshed. Physical attractiveness, social status, power, wealth, and interpersonal charm are all characteristics that serve as sources of attraction between partners. The higher the level of these attractions, the more likely that partners will put effort into coping with their incompatibilities. For example, a husband may be more motivated to tolerate his differences with his wife if she brings in a large income than he would if she had no income.

Personality

The personalities of the spouses will determine, in part, how incompatibilities are managed. Extensive research has shown, for example, that neuroticism in either partner is a longitudinal predictor of marital dissatisfaction and marital instability (see Karney & Bradbury, 1995, for a review); in fact the longest longitudinal study of marriage in the literature showed that peer ratings of neurotic behavior during the engagement period predicted separation and decline in satisfaction across 40 years of marriage (Kelly & Conley, 1987). Research also suggests that depression in husbands and wives is longitudinally pre-dictive of marital dissatisfaction (see Karney & Bradbury, 1995, for a review). Cross-sectional data have suggested that psychiatric diagnosis is related to marital discord (Hooley et al., 1987).

Because the evidence is strongest in implicating neuroticism as a predictor of marital instability and dissatisfaction, let us consider how neuroticism might affect the resolution of incompatibilities. Neuroticism has been defined as a "propensity to experience negative affect" (Leonard & Roberts, in press). If one or both partners have such a propensity, they are likely to respond to incompatibilities in poten-tially destructive ways. They are likely to overreact emotionally to incompatibilities, to engage in coercive attempts to change their part-ner, to vilify their partner for possessing some incompatible charac-teristic, and to avoid and withdraw from attempts to resolve those incompatibilities. These reactions are likely to polarize partners and make the incompatibility more problematic.

It is not just psychopathological characteristics that affect the reso-lution of incompatibilities between partners. On the positive side, the personality characteristics of agreeableness and conscientiousness in both men and women have been implicated as predictors of marital satisfaction and stability. It is not hard to imagine how agreeable part-ners would accommodate to incompatibilities or conscientious partners would follow through with agreements or be sensitive to partner's differing needs. On the negative side, tendencies to make maladaptive attributions, which tend to maximize the partner's role in negative behavior and minimize the partner's role in positive behavior, are as-sociated cross-sectionally and longitudinally with marital dissatisfac-tion (Bradbury & Fincham, 1990; Karney & Bradbury, 1995). Clearly, attributional tendencies can contribute to what we have called the vilification process that occurs as partners cope with their incom-patibilities.

Conflict Resolution Skills

The most powerful and consistent predictors of marital satisfaction and stability are positive and negative behaviors by husbands and wives and the reciprocity in these positive and negative behaviors (see Karney & Bradbury, 1995, for a review). It is hard to interpret what these data mean, as positive behaviors could result from all the fac-tors listed above, such as few incompatibilities, many attractions, low rates and intensities of neurotic behavior, and being agreeable and conscientious. Similarly, the negative behaviors could result from all the factors listed above (e.g., many incompatibilities, few attractions,

etc.). However, it is likely that the data on positive and negative behavior also reflect the conflict resolution skills of the participants.
Because of their learning history, some partners have been exposed to
models of constructive problem-solving, they have been trained in the
nonaggressive voicing of grievances, they have been shaped into listening to others' points of view, and they have been reinforced for
constructive ways of dealing with differences. These partners bring
into the relationship abilities that will make it easier for them to discuss incompatibilities and to negotiate accommodation to those incompatibilities. Thus, the greater the level of conflict resolution skills
that partners possess, the greater their ability to manage the incompatibilities with which they must deal.

Stressful Circumstances

Major life stressors and daily stressors can both complicate the resolution of incompatibilities. By major life stressors, we mean important
but predictable developmental transitions, such as having a child,
changing jobs, getting promoted, having a parent die, moving to a new
location, and retirement, as well as unexpected and negative events,
such as an untimely death in the family, business failure, disability,
and financial loss. By daily stressors we are referring to long com-
mutes, demanding bosses, persistent work demands, limited financial
resources, and the like. Both kinds of stressors may take a negative
toll on relationships: for example, the transition to parenthood is associated with a decline in marital satisfaction (e.g., Belsky & Pensky,
1988); likewise, the daily workload of air traffic controllers is associated with withdrawal and negative interaction between spouses (Repetti, 1989).

Christensen and his colleagues (Christensen & Pasch, 1993; Christensen & Shenk, 1991; Christensen & Walczynski, in press) have suggested two mechanisms to explain how stress may increase conflict
and dissatisfaction in marriage. First, stressful events place new demands on people that can't be met by typical methods of coping. The
new demands may exacerbate existing incompatibilities and create
new ones. Consider the transition to parenthood. Common incompatibilities about who does household tasks could be easily exacerbated by the increased demands that a new baby makes on the couple.
For example, Sena believes Jacob should do more housework, while
Jacob diagnoses Sena as an "anal compulsive who is obsessed with
orderliness and cleanliness." He does not want to do more housework
and doesn't think she should either. When Sena and Jacob have their
first child and Sena takes on the major role in caring for their child,

she wants more help from Jacob with housework. Jacob thinks that with the demands of the baby they should let many housework responsibilities slide. Sena is opposed to this view. Their conflict over housework increases.

Major stressful events can not only exacerbate old conflicts of interest, but create new ones as well. Consider how illness in the family might create a new conflict of interest. Ron and Sasha are both self-reliant individuals who pride themselves on their independence. They believe they chose each other out of love, not because they needed each other. They each manage their own affairs independently but come together for recreational activities. When Sasha gets into a serious automobile accident, however, she is forced to depend on Ron for many things and he is forced to care for her. At first they both take to these roles easily, as they share an urgent concern for Sasha's recovery. However, during her lengthy recovery, conflicts over dependency and support arise, which were never issues in their relationship before.

A second way in which stress can increase conflict and dissatisfaction is by increasing each partner's need for help and support while at the same time decreasing his or her ability to provide it. First, stress usually creates new demands. These new demands may preoccupy the stressed partner, so that he or she is less available to the other and more needy and demanding. The stress of preparing his company's annual report may occupy all of Joel's attention, make him less attentive to Myra, and make him seek Myra's help in proofing, rewriting, and correcting his work. Second, stressful events can create negative emotions and fatigue in the stressed partner (Repetti, 1989), increasing that partner's need for support and assistance while decreasing his or her ability to provide it. If one spouse has stayed up most of the night with a crying baby, she or he may need comfort from the other as well as respite from usual daily tasks. Finally, stressful events may create distortions in perception (e.g., Jarvis, 1982) and a greater self-focus (e.g., Wood, Saltzberg, & Goldsamt, 1990), which make the stressed partner less able to understand and appreciate the other's point of view. If Frank is preoccupied about losing his job, he might view Nikki's concern about the baby's cold as superficial and distracting.

All of these five factors—level of incompatibilities, attractions, behavioral repertoires, conflict resolution skills, and stressful events—work together to determine how incompatibilities in couples get managed. If partners have few incompatibilities and many attractions, they may be able to work out their differences even in the presence of undesirable personality traits, limited conflict resolution skills, and stressful circumstances. If their incompatibilities are great and the attractions few, even the presence of desirable personality traits, abundant conflict resolution skills, and stress-free circumstances may not ensure a satisfactory and long-lasting union. They may go down the path of coercion, vilification, and polarization that we have described earlier.

Whatever the combination of factors leading to conflict and dissatisfaction in a particular couple, a first goal of the integrative couple therapist is to develop a reasonable, believable, and compelling formulation, based on the analysis described above, for why this couple has come to such a painful outcome. We now move to a consideration of that formulation.

3

THE FORMULATION

The *formulation* is the single most important organizing principle in ICT. In fact, if one were to generate a one-line description of the overarching goal in ICT, it is to get the couples to adopt our formulation, the outcome of the evaluation process described in Chapter 4. If they leave therapy with this formulation as a prominent part of their relationship history, they will in all likelihood have benefited greatly from therapy. On the other hand, if they leave therapy without incorporating the formulation into their lives, chances are that therapy has not helped them much. Hence, the importance of the formulation.

The formulation is not a static concept that is simply presented to couples at a feedback session following the evaluation. Rather, it is a dynamic process that involves continuing dialogue between the therapist and both partners. The beginning formulation will often be altered as time goes on: the "formulating" and "reformulating" of the formulation is an interactional process, and the therapists can be wrong in their initial presentation. However, to say that a formulation is correct or incorrect is to miss one of its essential features: formulations are socially constructed; they are not true or false in an absolute sense. Therefore, it is not so much that the therapist has to get the formulation "right"; rather, the formulation has to be helpful as an organizing concept for the couple. In this instance, "helpful" means aiding them in letting go of a blaming, accusatory stance and opening themselves up to both acceptance and change.

The formulation always consists of three components: a *theme*, a *polarization process*, and a *mutual trap*. The theme describes in shorthand the couple's primary conflict; the polarization process describes the destructive interaction process that is set in motion once conflict ensues; and the mutual trap refers to the outcome of the polarization process, the "stuckness" that prevents couples from reversing the polarization process once it is underway. Let us examine all three components of the formulation in detail.

41

The Theme

It is our belief that for any given couple there is one theme that unifies what seem to be disparate conflict areas. For example, we have described "differences in desired intimacy" (Christensen, 1987) or "conflicts around closeness-distance" (Jacobson, 1989) as common themes in couples, particularly couples seeking therapy. This theme describes a struggle over the optimal level of intimacy present in the relationship. One partner, often the wife, enters therapy desiring more closeness, while the partner, often the husband, seeks to maintain an optimal (for him) amount of distance. Whether the couple is fighting about money, parenting, time spent together, or sex, the closeness-distance theme is always present. In 1989, Jacobson expressed the opinion that virtually all marital conflict could be subsumed under this closeness-distance theme. Over the past seven years, we have come to realize that there are numerous other themes that occur often enough to warrant our attention, even though we still believe the closeness-distance theme to be the most common one.

The theme might be viewed as a label for what contemporary behaviorists refer to as a *response class*, a class of interconnected behaviors that serve similar functions. For example, the function of "demanding" more time together, more intimate conversation, or sexual activity that includes more affection and foreplay is greater closeness. Conversely, the function of seeking time alone and preferring superficial conversation or sex without affection or foreplay is to maintain or create more psychological distance.

In this important sense, the theme can be thought of as identifying the function of each person's behavior in the prototypical conflict. Because behaviors that serve similar functions are often maintained by similar contextual variables; when the context changes to support a shift in one behavior, one often finds that other behaviors in the response class change in a similar manner. In short, one useful function of identifying a theme is that it helps focus on behaviors where a shift in one area can generalize to other areas in the relationship. As we will show, efforts to change the context in which particular conflicts occur are fruitful in both acceptance work and more traditional change interventions.

Another interesting aspect of themes is that they are almost invariably based on differences between the two partners. For example, the closeness-distance theme implies a difference in each partner's definition of an ideal relationship: one defines a relatively close relationship as ideal, whereas the other, when asked, would probably endorse a relationship structure that includes more distance. It is just such differences that eventually become perceived as incompatibilities. Some couples, the ones who seek our help, gradually move from the fact that there are differences to attempts to eradicate them. This is where polarization begins. The attempt to eradicate differences stems from the experience of these differences as intolerable, distressing, and problematic. Furthermore, partners view these differences as indicative of deficiencies in the other person. Closeness seekers view distancers as being "afraid of intimacy"; distancers view closeness seekers as "dependent." The description of their partners' differences as deficiencies may be nothing more than a verbal attempt to justify a behavior that would otherwise be unjustifiable: the attempt to change partners so that the deficiencies disappear and the partners become more alike.

What interests us about the dynamics of the theme is that couples leap from the observation of the differences to the determination that the differences are the problem. The problem is that the partner is a closeness seeker. The problem is that the partner is a distancer. We believe that it is misguided to view differences as anything more than differences: they are not inherently problematic, intolerable, or even distressing. In fact, it is the notion that differences are problematic that has to change if couples are to become more accepting of one another. When couples leave successful therapy, differences no longer imply the existence of distressing or intolerable problems. Differences, at the end of therapy, are natural, inevitable, and perhaps even desirable. They may also be inconvenient and undesirable at times. In any case, the couple's stance toward differences shifts dramatically when ICT has its intended effects; therefore, facilitating the shift away from focusing or dwelling on the unacceptability of differences is a major treatment goal. Here are some examples of common themes among couples seeking therapy.

Closeness-Distance

We have already used this theme as our prototypical example. Although we know from relevant research that the wife is more likely than the husband to be the closeness seeker, we also know that the roles are often reversed. The distancer is usually more reluctant to be in couple therapy, whereas the closeness seeker usually initiates the contact with the therapist. If the distance seeker comes to therapy, it is often either because the closeness seeker has threatened to end the relationship or because the distancer wants to maintain the status quo or differentiate even more from the partner.

It is quite often the distancer who has more power in the relationship, because distancers have resources (unexpressed emotions, intimate behaviors, companionship time, involvement in instrumental tasks) that they control and the partner wants: whenever someone has something that the other wants but can't get, the holder of the resource has power over the resource seeker. Furthermore, since only distancers have the unilateral ability to get what they want (it takes two people to be close, but only one to create distance [Christensen & Heavey, 1993]), in the short run the distancer is often more successful than the closeness seeker at maintaining the status quo.

Sally and Fred initially entered therapy with Fred complaining about the excess of conflict in the relationship. Sally's presenting complaint was that she wanted a second child and Fred was opposed to the idea. Fred was too unhappy with the amount of conflict to make that kind of extra commitment, especially since he felt like the odd man out in the family. To him, the mother and four-year-old daughter were so close that he was excluded in important ways from family activities.

A closer look at the dynamics of their relationship revealed that the "conflict" about which Fred was complaining usually revolved around the theme of closeness-distance. Sally wanted Fred to be more involved in family activities, especially on evenings and weekends. To her, his preference for being alone at these times suggested that the family was not a priority for him. Sally wanted more "cheerful" participation from Fred in family activities. Fred wanted time to himself. He owned a boat and liked to spend time on it. He also was very interested in computers and liked to close the door to his study and engage the computer after dinner, leaving Sally and her daughter with their exclusive relationship. It was an interesting paradox that his distancing led to his feelings of being excluded, whereas her closeness seeking constituted the conflict that Fred wanted to escape.

Henry and Fran also exhibited a pattern that looked like the closeness-distance theme: Fran was the closeness seeker and Henry was the distancer. Fran wanted Henry to initiate sex and affection more often and to respond more enthusiastically to her physical advances. Henry wanted less sex and wanted her to simply accept his lack of interest. To her, his sexual rejection and withdrawal were a sign that he did not really love her. To him, her persistent advances and her seething anger over his lack of interest were both scary and indicative of deeply rooted "dependency needs."

Control and Responsibility

Another common theme has to do with control and responsibility. Couples manifesting this theme argue about who is going to control which domains of married life and who is going to be responsible for those domains where neither wants control. This theme has many permutations. At times, one partner wants the other to take responsibility in a particular domain but at the same time wants to retain control. For example, the husband may want the wife to keep track of finances while he retains ultimate control over financial decision-making. In other instances, the prototypical conflict involves each person's wanting the other to take charge in an area where one person has traditionally been responsible but no longer wants the job. This theme is quite common among couples with peer or egalitarian marriages, where there is no gender stereotype to fall back on. For example, in traditional marriages, women are primarily responsible for housework, while men take responsibility for earning money. With dual-career couples, there is no automatic structure for determining financial responsibility, and each has a legitimate claim to being too busy earning money to take primary responsibility for housework.

Mary was an energetic "take-charge" partner who ran the family business while John made a living as a school teacher. In contrast to Mary, John was a passive, somewhat forgetful man who waited for others, Mary in particular, to take care of family affairs. Their relationship worked well enough until the family business started to crumble. John simultaneously developed some medical problems. In the middle of the business difficulties, he decided, without consulting Mary, to take early retirement from teaching. Mary was angry at John for retiring at a financially stressful time and even angrier about the fact that he made the decision unilaterally. Nevertheless, after the family business went bankrupt, Mary, being a "take charge" person, started a new business, with John as reluctant junior partner. She resented his lack of involvement in the business. He resented being told what to do. When she expressed her resentment, he attributed it to her hysteria. She complained about not having a partner who shared with her both their failures and their successes. He complained that his lack of expressiveness was being mistaken for noninvolvement. Oftentimes, he would be planning to take action, only to be beaten to the punch by Mary, whose energy level was such that she tackled tasks before he got around to them. She insisted that she had no way of knowing that he planned to help, because he was so silent about his intentions. His frequent refrain was, "I love you; that should be enough." Her response was, "I'm glad that you love me, but your love isn't doing me much good these days. I am constantly overworked and overwhelmed; yet, if I didn't take care of business, business would not get taken care of."

You Don't Love Me. Yes I Do. It Is YOU Who Doesn't Love ME.

Anyone who has worked with couples for any length of time encounters this theme: both partners experience the other as unloving, unappreciative, and uncaring. These feelings may not be expressed directly but hidden under a cloud of criticism, disapproval, and withdrawal. Both partners equate love, appreciation, and respect with the behaviors that they engage in, whereas the partners' methods of expressing love are discounted. Neither considers the possibility that they may be expressing love in different ways.

Gary and Bertha were one of these couples. Neither could understand why the other felt unappreciated, although both felt quite justified in feeling that way themselves. Gary experienced constant criticism from Bertha and felt undermined with respect to his parental authority and in his attempts to take initiative with projects around the house. To him, Bertha's criticism reflected a lack of appreciation for his contributions and of respect for his ability to make adult decisions. Bertha felt rejected by Gary sexually. She also felt a lack of interest from him in conversation and in spending time together. To her, the defining characteristics of love were sexual interest and an apparent desire to converse with a partner. She viewed his reaction to her "suggestions" as hypersensitivity and saw them as his excuses for emotional withdrawal. To him, it was perfectly understandable why he would not be interested in closeness of any kind—who could possibly want to be close to someone who was always critical and disapproving? Bertha implicitly defined love in terms of expressions of tenderness and tolerance, while Gary defined love in terms of approval and emotional support.

The Artist and the Scientist

The marital artist believes in spontaneity and play and considers the enjoyment of life to be more important than accomplishing tasks. The marital scientist has a hard time being spontaneous and is not very playful: in fact, to the marital scientist planning for the future, goal setting, and accomplishing tasks constitute the essence of married life.

Patrick was an engineer. Michelle had been a real estate broker, but at the time they sought therapy she was not working outside the home. Her major complaints were that they spent too little time together and that the relationship was not romantic. His major complaints were that their lives were disorganized and that they never set goals so that they could accomplish tasks together. All of their micro-conflicts could be subsumed under this artist-scientist theme. Patrick was compulsive about saving money, while Michelle wanted to use their money in ways that allowed them to enjoy themselves, even if such enjoyment created temporary debt. Michelle was a permissive parent, Patrick a disciplinarian. Even their attitudes toward sex reflected this theme. For Patrick, sex was important for the purpose of drive reduction; he had little use for the creation of a romantic atmosphere. However, he found Michelle extremely attractive and sensual and couldn't understand why she wasn't flattered by his sexual attention. For Michelle, the sexual act was not particularly meaningful in and of itself; it took on meaning only in the context of romance, passion, and a sense of emotional closeness.

Conventionality/Unconventionality

At times, spouses become attracted to one another because they perceive qualities that will help bring out a side of themselves that they experience but do not often express. This attraction to those who are different is a common theme in the marriage literature and applies to many of the themes already discussed. However, we have found it to be particularly striking in a few couples manifesting the theme of "conventionality/unconventionality." People leading conventional lives but longing for adventure often become attracted to those who seem to live on the edge, only to be disappointed when they discover that the other is becoming the opposite of what they thought they were getting. Similarly, people living on the edge but longing for stability often become attracted to those partners who seem to represent conventionality and social conformity, only to be disappointed when that person's unconventional side becomes evident.

When Tanya met Cal, she was in a rut. She had a career in library science but wanted a more exciting life. Cal was a handsome womanizer, someone she figured she would not be able to take for granted, someone who liked to carouse, travel, and seemed to "squeeze the marrow out of life." Little did she know that Cal was tired of being preceded by his reputation and wanted to settle down. He saw Tanya as a perfect person with whom to do this. How disappointed he was when, as he went back to school to get an MBA, she began to manifest manic symptoms, develop a drinking problem, and think that she might be bisexual. How disappointed she was when this handsome womanizer gradually transformed himself into Ward Cleaver before her very eyes.

This list of themes is far from exhaustive. However, it does provide a sense of what issues come up most often and which ones are the most difficult to treat. Remember, these differences do not inevitably become incompatibilities. Nor are these differences necessarily serious marital problems. It is the polarization process that turns these differences into marital problems.

The Polarization Process

When distressed partners enter into conflict over differences pertaining to the theme, there is a tendency for each partner to try to change the other, to bring that partner around to his or her point of view. It is natural, inevitable, and even logical for partners to attempt to change one another. If two people are involved in an intimate relationship and one experiences the other's negative behavior, it is a natural reaction to try to modify that behavior. Often, partners are successful at changing one another—or at least they reach some compromise that is satisfactory to both. Therapists do not encounter the couples who are successful, since these couples resolve their difficulties and do not seek therapy; therapists see the couples who are unsuccessful.

It is not difficult to figure out why the couples we see in therapy are generally unsuccessful in their change efforts. Traditional behavior therapists assumed that the unsuccessful efforts had to do with deficits in communication and conflict resolution skills. However, our position is that failure is inherent in the nature of the theme itself. Since the major conflicts are about differences and incompatibilities between the partners, each change effort directly counters the other's efforts at maintaining the difference. The natural response to attempts to modify fundamental differences is to pull away and maintain the difference. When two people engage in such change efforts simultaneously, the almost inevitable outcome is polarization or an exacerbation of the differences. When polarization occurs, the conflict increases rather than decreases. It doesn't matter how the partners go about trying to change each other: the mere fact that they are attempting to change the other produces a natural counterreaction.

Why is polarization so inevitable? First, it is quite common for partners to infer that the other is wrong when there is conflict. Second, partners tend to see it as their job to correct the other's deficiencies, especially when these deficiencies are causing them pain: they want the other to see the world as they see it; they want to remold the other in a way that is consistent with their idealized view of how the other should behave. Third, when partners have a well-entrenched class of behaviors at the core of their relationship repertoire and they experience their significant other trying to pull them away from those habitual responses, they are bound to push back—by reestablishing, consolidating, and perhaps even exaggerating those responses.

Consider the prototypical closeness-distance conflict. We can safely assume that closeness seekers pull for more intimacy because they do not currently have as much of it as they want. We can also safely assume that distancers seek to maintain the current level of distance because they are not comfortable being in a closer relationship with the partner. Any attempt made by closeness seekers to pull the distancers in will resemble the struggle that ensues when a fisherman tries to reel in a great white shark with a fishing rod. Since the shark does not want to be reeled in, the harder the fisherman pulls on the fishing rod the harder he fights to stay in the water. Of course, the shark will always win. Similarly, closeness seekers cannot force distancers to be closer than they want to be. They might receive promises of greater closeness, which lead to a temporary cessation in the change efforts. They might receive temporary concessions. But as long as distancers are more comfortable maintaining a particular level of distance, they will ultimately pull away again, perhaps even further to protect themselves from the threatening nature of the closeness seeking. In other words, a distancer who is for whatever reason not getting enough "space" will find a way to get it; the more intrusive the efforts to deprive him of space, the more determined he will be to maintain or even increase the distance.

An example of how this process works can be found in the character George Castanza, played by Jason Alexander on the television show *Seinfeld*. George's core problem in relationships is that he only wants them from a distance. Once a woman falls for him, he immediately flees for safety, often to Jerry Seinfeld's apartment. The more determined the closeness seeking girlfriend, the more creative George's efforts to flee. George has engaged in behaviors such as picking his nose, pretending to be gay, convincing male roommates to move back in with his girlfriend, forbidding contact between his girlfriend and his other friends—all with the goal of increasing distance between himself and the hapless girlfriend in the particular episode. The one question never adequately answered on this show is why any woman would want to be with George in the first place.

Both closeness seeking and distancing are common and natural processes. Neither are pathological, weird, or a sign of growing up in a dysfunctional family. When someone wants distance and another is trying to intrude upon it, it is natural to step back. When someone wants closeness and the other is pulling away, it is natural to try to pull them back. Natural, inevitable, and even logical—but self-defeating. Self-defeating because the result of these efforts is polarization. And polarization makes the problem worse, not better. The differences become exaggerated, the incompatibilities evolve into irreconcilable differences, and the pain and suffering multiply.

Let us examine how this process plays itself out, using some of the themes explored earlier in the chapter.

Closeness-Distance

Sally was engaged in a struggle to get Fred more involved in family activities. Fred was engaged in a struggle to carve out more time alone for himself. When he would assert himself and insist upon time alone or when he would join in family activities with a "grumpy" attitude, Sally would get angry. Fred couldn't tolerate conflict, and so when he sensed that Sally was angry with him, he would try various means to reduce her anger. However, if his efforts to reduce her anger at him were unsuccessful, he would get angry and they would have a relationship-threatening argument from which it would take them days to recover. Whoever it was that said "Time heals all wounds" misled us. The passage of time simply provides temporary respite from polarization.

Sally's anger became more and more chronic as Fred continued to exclude himself from family activities. She sought solace in her relationship with her daughter, the only family member who seemed to want to be close to her. Fred felt increasingly excluded from the mother-daughter relationship and became more withdrawn. This incensed Sally even further and increased her desire for a second child, another potential source of closeness, which she wasn't getting from Fred. Fred rebelled against the idea of a second child, because a second child would give him even less free time. As Sally persisted in her requests for a second child, Fred's reluctance grew. At this point, they entered therapy, well along in their polarization process. Fred was hypersensitive to signs of Sally's anger. Sally was extremely threatened by even subtle signs of withdrawal by Fred and intransigent in her demands for a second child. Fred believed that Sally cared nothing for him—she simply wanted his sperm. Sally believed that Fred stayed with her only because his parents' divorce had been very traumatic for him, and he didn't want to repeat the pattern.

Fran reacted to Henry's disinterest in sex by losing her temper and occasionally becoming physically aggressive toward him. Henry had become somewhat afraid of her because she appeared to be out of control at times. Fear is not the world's greatest aphrodisiac. The angrier she became, the less interested in sex he became. As his interest in sex declined further, she became more frequently enraged and more inclined to lose her temper. By the time they sought therapy, they were having sex less than once a month and at least once per week she would "get physical" with him. Her anger had been transferred in part to their children, who provided Henry with an additional "excuse" to avoid sex. She was dangerously close to child abuse.

Control and Responsibility

There is nothing that ignites a power struggle more efficiently than controlling behavior, especially when "control and responsibility" is the couple's theme. Couples who struggle for control feel increasingly powerless as their efforts are thwarted again and again. When power and control become the dominant motivators in a relationship, any attempt to generate more responsibility by one partner just results in more creative ways of shirking responsibility by the other.

Mary and John had been married over thirty years by the time they entered therapy. John had been passive when they married, but after thirty years of polarization, his passivity had reached extreme proportions. Typically he would sleep in the waiting room prior to the sessions and would often appear to be asleep in the sessions themselves. Mary carried around a calendar with not only her appointments on it but also his. He had to consult with her each day to find out his schedule. Although Mary wanted John to help her with the business, she took care of things so quickly that he never had a chance. Not only was she reinforcing his passivity, but she had, for all practical purposes, lost all respect for him. John, retreating to a perversely traditional view of gender differences, proposed the theory that Mary's menopause had resulted in a chronic PMS condition. Needless to say, she did not find this interpretation particularly validating, and in order to keep her from becoming enraged he avoided repeating it. You may recall from the previous section that John said little to begin with, and now he was literally the "silent partner."

All of this was the result of polarization. He was reacting to her efforts to turn him into a "take charge" kind of guy—efforts doomed in the face of his lifelong passivity. Meanwhile, the more passive he became, the less interest she took in him as a man and a husband. She withdrew from him sexually and concentrated her efforts on getting help from him in running the business. But these efforts failed, as his inhibitions generalized to the point where he had become a veritable couch potato watching television. He showed life only when he played golf or lost his temper because she was "overreacting" or "becoming hysterical again." He became interested in a form of Christianity that emphasized forgiveness but used this doctrine to insulate himself from her attempts to change him.

You Don't Love Me. Yes I Do. It Is YOU Who Doesn't Love ME.

We have spoken of Gary and Bertha, who had different ways of expressing love and criteria for feeling loved. What to Bertha was a "constructive suggestion" was to Gary an "insult." What to Gary was an understandable reaction to her disapproval and lack of respect was to Bertha "being ignored and treated as if I'm not there." These two had become so polarized that they had forgotten why they had gotten together in the first place. For them, each day was a struggle; simply avoiding a major argument, keeping the house clean, and getting the kids to bed on time became their raison d'être.

How did it come to this? This is the question they were both asking when they entered therapy. The answer was really quite simple. The more criticism he felt from her, the more disinterested he became in being around her. The more rejected she felt by his disinterest, the more depressed—and bitter and critical—she became. He became so hypersensitive to her criticism that any comment she made about his activities as a parent or husband was interpreted as an intrusion on his autonomy. She became so hypersensitive to his rejection that even neutral actions were interpreted as slights. If he was tired and fell asleep on the couch reading the newspaper, this meant to her that he was avoiding conversation and sex. He became so hypersensitive to her suggestions that he read criticism into her voice tone, her facial expressions, and her body language.

The Artist and the Scientist

Patrick the engineer had grown increasingly frustrated with Michelle during the four years of their marriage because she overspent their budget, their two-year old "ran wild," and she was constantly critical of him for being unromantic. Michelle, who felt there was no quality time in their marriage, did indeed complain quite frequently and accuse Patrick of not wanting to spend time with her. By the time they got to therapy, she had stopped asking. She had become convinced that her husband was incorrigible and had simply withdrawn from him. But this withdrawal was simply a new way of polarizing. Patrick, not being as versatile, simply continued to suggest family meetings to set goals, make plans, and organize their lives. Michelle resisted the structure, because she would be damned if she was going to "waste" what little time they had together "making lists that will just be thrown away." Patrick would simply throw up his hands in frustration or make occasional half-hearted efforts to be romantic. Michelle was unresponsive to these "forced" efforts, thus providing Patrick with ammunition for arguing that "There's no pleasing her." They were like two regiments entrenched in a stalemate battle, each poised with their weapons, waiting for the other to strike. Life was characterized by constant tension. Conversations invariably led to recriminations. Michelle's favorite retort was, "You don't need a wife; you need a financial planner and a secretary." His favorite was, "You wouldn't be happy unless you had a millionaire who could afford to fly off to Hawaii at the drop of a hat."

Conventionality/Unconventionality

Neither Tanya nor Cal was aware of the other's disappointment about how they had turned out. Nor had they verbalized their own disappointment, even to themselves. It was this unarticulated black cloud that followed them around the house. Tanya was drunk most days by 5:00 p.m., had made two suicide attempts within the past year, and was exchanging letters with a female ex-lover in Georgia. In fact, she was threatening to leave the three young children with him and take a year sabbatical to find out whether she was "really" bisexual. He tried hard to be a good father and was making a great deal of money, but the money didn't seem to please her. Neither did his success. The more he focused on traditional family values, the more of a nonconformist she became. The more she drank and the more depressed she got, the harder he worked. He blamed the entire problem on her drinking. She blamed the entire problem on his "air of superiority." Neither of them understood how the increasing divisiveness had been driven by disappointment at who the other had turned out to be. They both thought that they wanted out of the marriage. What they really wanted was the person they thought they had met many years earlier, prior to the onset of polarization.

We have already mentioned that the overarching goal of ICT is to get couples to adopt the formulation. A major portion of this effort is to help them change their focus from the differences themselves, which they define as the problem, to the polarization process, which is really the problem. If they shift their focus from the structure of their conflict to their process of dealing with it, couple therapy has made great progress. Once their focus shifts from the theme to the polarization process, they have implicitly accepted their differences. They have recognized that the differences are not what divides them. This shift constitutes a major part of the acceptance process. However, when they first enter therapy, they are completely and totally stuck. It is this stuckness we have labeled the *mutual trap*.

The Mutual Trap

The mutual trap is the outcome of polarization. When couples feel trapped, that does not signal an end to polarization; in fact, polarization and entrapment typically exist side by side. However, as a therapist, if you interrupt the polarization process with an inquiry about the couple's experience at any point in time, you will invariably hear partners talk about being stuck, being trapped, feeling helpless and desperate.

The mutual trap is an experience that each partner has privately. It is seldom discussed. (Those couples who are capable of discussing their mutual sense of entrapment, and label it as such, usually do not need therapy.) The experience is one of stuckness and futility: if they could articulate the experience, they would put it this way: "I have done everything I know how to do to change this person. Yet the harder I try the worse things get. But I don't know what else to do. If I give up, the relationship is doomed to be at a place where I don't want it to be. Nothing will change. So I see no alternative but to continue my efforts, even though up until now they have been to no avail. Perhaps I just need to be more creative and try different ways of generating change in my partner. But, in my heart of hearts, I don't feel optimistic. So I am stuck. I can't stop, but continuing seems to be, if anything, making things worse."

When the mutual trap is described to most couples for the first time, their typical response is to feel understood but at the same time confused. They feel understood because the therapist has articulated their experience of being stuck; most people in such a situation resonate immediately with the therapist's depiction of their entrapment. What confuses them is that the therapist, who has described one partner's trap so insightfully, goes on to describe the partner as being trapped as well. People know about and experience their own sense of entrapment daily, but they usually do not know that their partner feels trapped as well. They may even be skeptical at first.

A major part of acceptance work is generating empathy and compassion in one partner for the other's sense of entrapment. To the extent that each partner becomes aware of and compassionate toward the other's sense of entrapment, the couple has made a giant step toward the attainment of emotional acceptance. For one thing, it is virtually impossible to be compassionate about a phenomenon of which you are unaware. If you don't know that your partner feels trapped, you can't feel empathy and compassion for his or her sense of entrapment. Furthermore, although compassion does not always lead to acceptance, it is the "royal road" to acceptance. A prerequisite is not just understanding that the partner feels trapped but experiencing the other's stuckness. Finally, the experience of the other's stuckness in and of itself enhances closeness and intimacy. Partners feel understood, whereas they haven't felt that way in the past. The experience of mutual understanding, facilitated by the therapist's ability to put words to that understanding, is a major part of acceptance work.

Now, let us apply the concept of the mutual trap to the couples who we have introduced in this chapter.

Sally and Fred

Fred wanted less conflict and more time to himself. He tried numerous methods to reduce conflict when Sally was mad at him, including initiating sex, saying he was sorry, providing the behavior that she had been mad at him for not providing, and on the negative side, getting mad at her in return. However, none of these methods succeeded in reducing her anger, which seemed to run its course independently of his compensatory actions. In short, there was nothing he could do to reduce her anger. Yet, if he did nothing to try to reduce it, he would have to tolerate and feel helpless in the face of her anger, something that was not easy for him.

Sally wanted Fred to be more of a family man. But whether she asked nicely, got angry, or demanded more of his attention, he refused or complied with such grumpiness that it ruined the activity for everyone. At the same time, her focus on her daughter and her desire for more children simply made Fred feel more excluded and less inclined cheerfully to be part of the family she wanted. If she gave up her efforts, she felt lonely and depressed.

Fran and Henry

Fran wanted to be loved by Henry. She thought he was a good man, but when he showed a lack of interest in sex, she felt unloved. She found herself in the impossible position of demanding love. She experienced herself as not being able to control her anger and her temper.

Even when she was successful in curtailing its verbal expression, steam poured out of her ears. Henry knew when she was feeling unloved and when she was enraged about it. Fran had no idea how to get what she wanted. Similarly, Henry felt unable to control the situation, since the option of having sex without interest didn't work for him. He couldn't feign sexual arousal, and even on those rare occasions when he could, she knew that he was uninterested. Honesty just made her mad. Faking it didn't work, and it made him feel controlled.

Mary and John

Mary wanted John to be a partner, but he seemed to resent her requests for help. If she said nothing, he did nothing. If she nagged him, he got angry and still did nothing. John wanted to be left alone. Yet, even when he withdrew to the point where he was left alone, there was no peace. Mary's anger and resentment permeated the house. She could not get help. He could not find peace.

Gary and Bertha

Neither Gary nor Bertha felt loved. Gary seethed constantly about being unappreciated and not respected. He couldn't turn his seething on and off. He couldn't stop her criticism because she denied that she was critical. Bertha wanted a lover, but he found her suggestions that he be tender and passionate outrageous, in light of the way he felt. She couldn't get any responsiveness from him, however often she bit her tongue instead of "making suggestions," because he would still read criticism into her nonverbal behavior.

Patrick and Michelle

Michelle had given up on the possibility of Patrick placing a priority on time together. She had tried everything she knew how to do; yet, despite numerous promises of change, they still spent a minimal amount of time together. Patrick, however, continued to "hammer away" at financial planning, accomplishing tasks around the house, and creating a proper environment for their son. She had become increasingly withdrawn and depressed, although these bouts of depression alternated with fits of anger and heated arguments between the two of them. Having been married before, she was resigned to her fate. Patrick, however, was simply frustrated, and when he was frustrated, he became more active and agitated. However, he was not getting goals set, money saved, or tasks accomplished. He did not know what to do. Michelle tried to accept his less than intimate, spontaneous, and playful company, but she couldn't shake the low-grade depression.

Tanya and Cal

Tanya's unconventional behavior—the drinking, the suicidal behavior, the bisexuality—did not succeed in loosening Cal up. On the contrary, try as she might to generate the outlaw that she first met, he was becoming more conventional with each act of defiance on her part. Similarly, Cal's attempts at being a good husband and father were clearly not creating for him the family that he wanted. In fact, the more he became a family man, the more his family disintegrated.

The loneliness of feeling stuck in a relationship rut comes in part from not realizing that the partner is sharing in this loneliness. Partners are usually seen as the causes of one's loneliness, not as someone going through a similar experience. The secret sense of entrapment, which each carries, is a primary source of alienation. However, when revealed and understood in therapy as a shared experience, the loneliness can be transformed into a basis for intimacy.

A Unifying Principle in ICT

These are the essential ingredients of all formulations: a theme, a polarization process, and a mutual trap. The formulation provides an organizing principle for both therapist and client. Once therapists have formulations, there is something to refer back to when couples have conflicts either during or between therapy sessions. The therapist understands how the partners turn differences into destructive interaction and how and where they become stuck.

For the partners, the formulation becomes a context for making sense out of a confusing, desperate, hopeless, and painful relationship. Simply having a formulation to explain what goes wrong is often therapeutic in and of itself. It also provides a vocabulary that couples can use to unite against their problems, to create distance between themselves and their problems so that they can experience them together. As time goes on, the therapist expects them to recognize polarization as it occurs and identify particular conflicts as examples of their theme. As they become more knowledgeable and self-conscious about these recurring interactional patterns and their consequences, engaging in the patterns becomes less automatic and more difficult. If they do engage in the patterns, they do so in a fundamentally different way; there will be subtle but important differences in the way they engage one another during conflict. For example, the therapist might notice that they are recovering more quickly from arguments than they were when they first came in. Or the arguments themselves may have a less devastating impact than before.

However, it is not easy as it might sound to come up with a useful formulation. Couples frequently provide example after example of derivative issues, and therapists can come to premature closure about the functional significance of particular themes. For example, our original theme for Sally and Fred was "conflict engagement vs. avoidance." We saw Sally's willingness to engage in conflict and Fred's desire to avoid it as the organizing principle around which they polarized. In fact, it gradually became apparent that their differences around conflict were peripheral to the central theme of closeness-distance. But it took some bumbling and fumbling in therapy before this could be discovered. In particular, when the "conflict" theme did not seem to be producing either change or acceptance, the therapist came up with the alternative formulation, closeness-distance, which immediately paid therapeutic dividends. A good theme is one that works.

We were also thrown at first by Cal and Tanya, who one of us originally misdiagnosed as a closeness-distance couple when in fact the operating principle was conventionality/unconventionality. The closeness-distance theme couldn't explain why Cal's increasing involvement as a family man did not improve the quality of the marriage; in fact, it had the opposite effect. However, the impact of his family values on her was consistent with the conventionality formulation. The real proof came in the responsiveness of the couple to this alternative formulation. Neither had a clue as to the conventionality theme before it was mentioned, but it hit them both like an epiphany when the therapist raised it. And positive developments began to occur in therapy almost immediately.

How do we arrive at a formulation? Through a very particular assessment and evaluation structure. How do we inform couples about our formulation? Through a feedback session that immediately follows our assessment. We now move to a detailed discussion of how we obtain the raw material for our formulations and how we present them to couples.

4

ASSESSMENT AND FEEDBACK

The primary purpose of assessment is to come up with a formulation, which will serve as the basis for a treatment plan. Once the therapist has a formulation and a treatment plan, the couple is presented with both at a feedback session and treatment begins.

In this chapter we describe how we structure assessment, evaluation, and feedback. We recognize that managed care conglomerates often limit the number of client contacts, and that such limitations necessarily demand great speed and efficiency of the therapist. In our final chapter we will address modifications in our ideal approach based on the exigencies of managed care. For now, with a few exceptions we will be describing what we think of as an ideal assessment, evaluation, and feedback process.

This ideal process includes a third goal, in addition to generating a formulation and a treatment plan. That third goal is to have a therapeutic impact during the assessment phase. To the extent that partners improve prior to the feedback session, their commitment to the process will be enhanced. Thus, even though we make a hard and fast distinction between therapy and assessment, in fact our assessment procedures are designed to be therapeutic, as well as to provide the information necessary to formulate and plan a treatment.

Our ideal assessment structure is to have an initial conjoint interview with the couple after they have completed some self-report questionnaires. We like to follow this conjoint interview with individual sessions. Both partners have at least one opportunity to talk to the therapist alone. Then the therapist integrates the three interviews with the questionnaire data and comes up with a formulation and a treatment plan, which is presented to the couple during the feedback session.

In structuring the assessment process this way, we struggle with a basic dilemma: each partner needs to have an opportunity to tell his or her story to an attentive, validating listener; yet, the therapist would like to avoid further alienating the other partner. Very often, during the initial interview, when therapists begin asking about problem areas, the partners immediately start blaming each other for most of them. They may, in other words, attack and counter-attack during the initial interview and as a result leave the therapy session feeling worse than they did when they arrived. In attempting to build a therapeutic alliance with both partners, the therapist risks making a positive impression on no one. As the therapist listens to and validates one person's complaint, the other becomes alienated; then the same process happens with the partners reversed. All too often, the outcome is that the therapist alienates both of them and, more importantly, they are further alienated from another.

We prefer not to spend the initial interview discussing problems in the relationship. Of course, one is forced to deal directly with problems when couples are in crisis: battering, potential homicide, suicide, psychosis, or child abuse would be examples. Generally, ICT therapists have enough information about the spouses from their questionnaires to conduct the initial interview without focusing on problem areas. For some couples, problem areas are best discussed during the individual sessions. First, partners are likely to be more honest, especially with respect to sensitive areas such as sex and violence. Second, during the individual interviews the therapist has the luxury of being totally attentive and validating without alienating the other partner. Consequently, the client is confident that the therapist has heard his/her side of the story and will feel understood when the therapist adopts a neutral posture in subsequent sessions. Lacking this opportunity for one-on-one time with the therapist, clients are likely to give less credibility to reformulations in subsequent sessions, because they may believe that, if only the therapist understood them better, he or she would not be adopting such a neutral posture. Both clients need to know that that therapist has listened to their story and understands their point of view.

When the assessment of problems occurs primarily through questionnaires and individual rather than conjoint interviews, the therapist can concentrate on making the first conjoint interview therapeutic and not worry as much about assessing the couple's problems. With some couples, however, it is impossible or unwise to structure the first conjoint interview as a therapy session in disguise. For these couples, the problems must be assessed immediately; the therapist does not have the luxury of waiting until the individual sessions. For instance, when treatment is limited to six to eight sessions due to managed care constraints, we dispense with both the individual interview and the feedback session. We use the first conjoint session to discuss problems and attempt to end the session with feedback that would normally occur during a separate session: in short, the formulation is presented at the end of the initial interview.

Another time when the initial interview cannot follow our typical structure is when one or both partners object. Some clients want to talk about their problems right away; frustrating their efforts would be not only invalidating but also inconsistent with all other ICT interventions. The therapist can feel the couple out on this issue by beginning the initial interview with its implicit therapeutic intent and letting the partners respond. If it flows smoothly and seems to be having a positive impact, then the session can continue in that vein. However, if the therapist's efforts seem to be frustrating the partners or if they consistently answer questions by bringing the subject back to current problems, the ICT therapist must be prepared to shift gears and allow that discussion to continue.

The Initial Interview as First Therapy Session

With some couples our approach to the initial interview is not much different from that described in the Jacobson and Margolin (1979) book. The basic strategy is to begin the session with a brief discussion of the presenting problems, and then to shift to relationship strengths and courtship history, leaving various assessment interviews and a subsequent evaluation interview with each spouse as the main forums for gathering information about the problems.

The State of the Partners When They Enter the Therapist's Office

Consider the typical couple sitting in the waiting room before the initial appointment with this therapist stranger. Often the clients have already revealed personal aspects of their lives by completing questionnaires sent to them prior to the initial interview. This information is absolutely essential when working under managed care constraints, so that formulations can be generated and hypotheses tested during the initial contact. Even if they have not completed questionnaires prior to their first contact with the therapist, they know that they are about to air their "dirty laundry" to a stranger, something that makes many people uncomfortable, especially those who have not been in therapy before. Moreover, by the time couples seek therapy, their problems have been festering for a long time, perhaps for many years. Because of this, partners are generally not optimistic; many sit in that waiting room feeling hopeless. Because of the first two factors, they are often ambivalent about being in the waiting room in the first place. One cannot assume that because they are there they are committed to therapy; in fact, one or both may have come with great reluctance. They are often confused, because they don't know what to expect. They may have never been in therapy before; or, if they have been in therapy, it has not been couple therapy; or, if it has been couple therapy, it has not been someone with this theoretical orientation. They are uncertain as to how the process works.

In anticipation of this discomfort, the goals of the initial interview should be to: (1) validate their experience of hopelessness, which paradoxically may make them feel more hopeful; (2) honor and respect their ambivalence; (3) make the session as therapeutic as possible; and (4) socialize them into the twin processes of therapy and assessment. They should leave the session feeling better than when they entered, feeling relieved since they have not as yet committed themselves to therapy, and understanding the assessment process that lies ahead.

Socialization. Many states now require that clients be presented with consent forms, which explicate billing procedures, explain "confidentiality," and define the therapist's areas of competence. These compulsory consent forms move the dialogue between therapist and client in the direction of *socialization*: providing clients with information about the processes of assessment and therapy, enough to help them anticipate what will be asked of them in the weeks to come.

In addition to complying with state requirements regarding consent forms, we introduce ourselves to clients in a manner that clarifies the purposes of assessment and explains the distinction between assessment and therapy. Here is an example:

> Let me tell you a bit about how I work so that you can figure out what's in store for you over the next couple of weeks. You have already completed some questionnaires [if relevant], and I really appreciate the time and effort you must have put into them. These questionnaires will help me understand both of you and your relationship and will save me a great deal of time, because I will not have to ask you as many questions. Those questionnaires were the beginning of my evaluation. I set aside a couple of weeks before therapy actually begins to simply collect information. I call this period of time "assessment" or "evaluation."
>
> Today's interview with the two of you is the second step in the evaluation. Then I will meet with each of you alone. During these interviews, I will be collecting information and trying to decide whether or not I can be helpful to you and if so, *how* I can be most

helpful to you. After I have made that determination, I will bring both of you back for a feedback session, where I'll give you the results of my evaluation, tell you whether I think I can be helpful to you, and give you a rough idea of how often we will be meeting and what our treatment goals will be. At that point, during the feedback session, you can decide whether or not the plan sounds good to you. Also, during this evaluation process you will be getting to know me, and you will find out how comfortable you are with me personally.

How does that sound? Does that meet with your expectations, or were you hoping I would be giving you help immediately?

With an opening like this, partners are socialized as to the evaluation process. Even though the difference between therapy and assessment is clear to mental health professionals, it is not intuitively obvious to clients. In fact, even when the therapist takes great pains to explain the distinction to clients, it is not uncommon for them to come back the next week saying, "We don't feel any better yet . . ." The distinction may have to be repeated. Couples need to understand that the evaluation is not intended to be helpful to them, that its primary purpose is to gather information. When asked to what extent this structure meets with their expectations, couples commonly respond that they did not have any expectations. This confirms the value of the socializing statement, since the clients are acknowledging uncertainty about what is to come. In our experience, our credibility is enhanced by thorough assessment, especially when it is explained in this way:

> At times couples are disappointed that we can't start therapy right away. I can certainly understand that disappointment. You are tired of these problems and understandably eager to find out the prospects therapy holds for you. I wish I had the miracle cure that could benefit you without this thorough evaluation. Unfortunately, every couple is different, and any help I tried to give you today would be "shooting from the hip." I would in all likelihood lead you astray. I need the time and contact with you to make informed decisions and to come up with a treatment plan that fits your needs.

Honoring Their Ambivalence. When evaluation and therapy are distinguished, and partners are reassured that they are not necessarily committing themselves to couple therapy simply by showing up for this conjoint interview, they are often relieved. They are allowed—and in fact, encouraged—to buy some time in which to get to know the therapist. They are also reminded that the therapist is not making any commitments until a determination has been made that this approach could be helpful. Thus, couples' understandable ambivalence is normalized and, in fact, built into the structure of the evaluation phase.

Using the Initial Interview to Improve the Relationship. There is a "hidden agenda" when the initial session is designed to be therapeutic: while the therapist takes great pains to emphasize that the evaluation will not be helpful to the couple in the short run, many steps are taken during the initial interview to maximize the likelihood of therapeutic benefit. The problem-focused assessment has begun with their completion of the questionnaires, and there will be more opportunity for discussion of problems during the individual sessions following the conjoint one. A major goal of the couple session is to provide them with some temporary relief—not a "quick fix" but simply some relief from the sense that nothing can be done. While creating such an atmosphere, the therapist also collects valuable assessment information.

During the initial interview, we strive to understand the basis for the partners' attachment to one another. Their current problems sometimes overshadow the reasons they became a couple. We tell our students that generally speaking if a couple's being together does not make sense to us, we have not done our job assessing their developmental history.

As we assess the couple's developmental history and determine the basis for their attachment, the affect in the therapy room often becomes quite positive: hence the therapeutic benefit of gathering this assessment information. Spouses have not reflected on why they became a couple for a long time, since their focus has been on what is wrong with the relationship. It may be that they have never discussed their developmental history together, let alone in front of a stranger.

Some couples use this history-taking period as an opportunity to blame each other for the problems. Instead of thwarting such efforts, we take such blaming statements as a sign that the partner or partners are in too much pain to talk about positive aspects of the relationship and relinquish the goal of making the initial contact therapeutic. Indeed, the validating stance of the therapist is a constant throughout ICT. If the partners are in too much pain to discuss happier times without blaming and accusatory remarks, ICT therapists must be prepared to validate that pain. Thus, the first session would proceed as follows *only* for those couples who are able to talk about the past without using it as a weapon.

How Did They Get Together? As we recommended in Jacobson and Margolin (1979), we spend time during the initial interview finding out exactly how the partners met, and how they evolved into a couple from that initial meeting. We have the partners tell us this story in some detail. which they usually enjoy. Even when they disagree on details like "who hit on whom," they have a good time recounting what for most couples were happier times. Of course, some couples have extremely depressing stories to tell regarding their initial meeting. When the story suggests no basis for attachment, problems from day one, and hatred from the outset, this strategy backfires. But at least the therapists know that they are in trouble early on in the assessment process!

What Was Their Courtship Like? What Was the Relationship Like Before the Problems Began? As a general rule, we approach the couple's basis for attachment by covering the past, the present, and the future during the initial interview. We begin by trying to get a sense of what the relationship was like before the problems began. In addition to the therapeutic benefit of helping couples reexperience this period of their relationship via the interview, this discussion of courtship provides information that is often useful during the acceptance work that will be done once the evaluation phase is over. For example, we are quite interested in why partners were initially attracted to one another, since current conflicts often involve areas of initial strength or mutual attraction. If we can delineate some of the strengths during the initial interview, it may be possible to generate some useful hypotheses regarding the sources of current conflict areas.

How Is the Relationship Different Now on Days When the Partners Are Getting Along? Most couples do not argue or even feel dissatisfied 24 hours per day, seven days per week. Instruments such as the Spouse Observation Checklist (see table for a list of the instruments we typically use) have taught us that, if anything, unhappy couples have more variability in day-to-day marital satisfaction than happy couples (Jacobson, Follette, & McDonald, 1982; Jacobson, Waldron, & Moore, 1980). If we can delineate how things are different on days when marital satisfaction is high, we will have identified possible areas of focus for future treatment sessions.

How Would the Relationship Be Different if the Problems That Currently Exist Were No Longer Present? The last two questions covered the past and the present. This question asks about the future and provides a positive bridge to the individual sessions. Couples are encouraged to describe with as much specificity as possible what they would like to see happen more often, in contrast to the pain that each person

Table

INSTRUMENT	USES
Dyadic Adjustment Scale (DAS; Spanier, 1976)	1. Quantitative index of marital distress 2. Assess commitment to and willingness to work on relationship (last item)
Marital Satisfaction Inventory (MSI: Snyder, 1979)[1]	1. Quantitative index of marital distress; includes specific dimensions as well as global distress 2. Provides normative data on nondistressed, distressed, and divorcing couples
Marital Status Inventory[2]	1. Assess commitment to relationship and steps taken toward separation or divorce
Conflict Tactics Scale (CTS: Straus, 1979)	1. Assess domestic violence
Areas of Change Questionnaire (ACQ)[2]	1. Assess amount and direction of desired change for 34 spouse behaviors
Areas of Change and Acceptance Questionnaire (ACAQ)[3]	1. Assess amount and direction of desired change, current frequency of behavior, and acceptability of behavior at its current frequency for 34 spouse behaviors
Spouse Observation Checklist (SOC)[2]	1. Daily account of positive and negative spouse behaviors 2. Monitor treatment progress 3. Identify spouse behaviors associated with daily marital satisfaction 4. Generate lists to be used in behavior exchange

[1]To obtain this measure, contact: Western Psychological Services, 1-800-648-8857
[2]To obtain these measures, contact: Robert L. Weiss, Ph.D., Oregon Marital Studies Program, Department of Psychology, University of Oregon, Eugene, OR 97403-1227
[3]To obtain this measure, contact: Neil S. Jacobson, Ph.D., Center for Clinical Research, Department of Psychology, 1107 NE 45th Street, Suite 310, Seattle, WA 98105-4631

currently experiences. Once partners have responded to this question, they have described the strengths that originally brought them together, the aspects of the relationship that continue to be good, and the type of relationship they would like to have in the future.

Here is a portion of an initial interview covering certain aspects of the approach described above. Tanya and Cal are the couple who manifested the theme of conventionality/unconventionality. A compromise strategy was used, enabling us not only to emphasize relationship strengths but also to hear about problem areas. In part, this compromise was necessary because the therapist had a limited number of sessions with this couple and wanted to be ready to begin therapy the next session. Nevertheless, there were plentiful opportunities to discuss relationship strengths and generate an atmosphere of hope and playfulness:

Therapist: How long have you been married?

Husband: Six and a half years.

Therapist: Six and a half years. How long have you known each other?

Husband: Nine.

Therapist: Nine. So you met in 1984. How did you meet?

Wife: In a bar.

Therapist: In a bar!

Wife: Of all the odd places, yeah.

Therapist: Tell me more.

Wife: You [to the husband] can tell it, because that way you can say what you want. Or do you want me to?

Husband: I was meeting some friends in a bar for a drink.

Therapist: So you were looking to meet someone that night.

Husband: No. But we just struck up a conversation and developed a relationship over time.

Wife: One of my girlfriends dared me to go and talk to him, so I did.

Therapist: Was it her idea, or did he seem cute to you?

Wife: Both. There were four of us after work having a drink. So I didn't realize anything was going to happen. It was just something to do.

Therapist: Did you also find him attractive?

Wife: He was cute.

Therapist: So you struck up a conversation and would you say there was instant chemistry, or did it take awhile?

Wife: It was fairly instant.

Husband: Um-hm

Therapist: Tell me just a little bit about that. What was it that you found attractive about one another?

Wife: We went for a walk and had a lot more in common than I did with his friend, whom I was supposedly being fixed up with that evening.

Therapist: And what were those things that you had in common?

Wife: I don't know. What would you say [laughs to the husband]? We just seemed to hit it off.

Husband: I was and still am attracted to her mind. She was one of the few people at that time that I knew who actually had a PC and knew how to use it. I thought that was sort of intriguing.

Therapist: PC friendly.

Husband: PC friendly [laughs]. She knew a lot more about computers than I ever did, still does. Had a career that kept her traveling and that was sort of intriguing. Physically attractive. That's probably a lot of the reasons right there. I think her intellectual capabilities were what attracted me the most.

Therapist: So would you say that you were one of those couples who gradually grew from the friendship into a love relationship, or did you sort of fall for each other, or was it somewhere in between?

Wife: I'd say we fell in love. I came home from somewhere that following weekend and he was parked on my front steps so [laughs] he stopped by to see me.

Therapist: And the rest is history?

Wife: The rest is history. Yeah.

Therapist: Let's see, and you've been married for six and a half years and you've known each other for nine. So there's a two and a half year period where you dated.

Wife: I actually moved away for six or eight months.

Husband: Right.

Wife: Moved to North Carolina while he sowed his wild oats.

Therapist. So it wasn't constant involvement. You actually separated for a period of time.

Wife: Yeah.

Therapist: Was the separation your idea?

Wife: It was my idea. He wasn't ready to settle down. And I found it difficult to deal with him going out with other people, so I just left.

Therapist: So you separated for a while, then you got back together. And how did it come about that you decided to get married?

Wife: I told him I would come back up here but only if there was some reasonable, serious commitment. I was approaching 30 and if I was going to be serious about somebody, I wanted it to happen because I was starting to think about kids, and that sort of thing.

And I wasn't going to waste my time on somebody who didn't have the same timeline.

Therapist: And you [to the husband] said?

Husband: I was ready. I missed her. I proposed. I was in love, and absence definitely made the heart grow fonder.

Therapist: Did either of you see anything, in retrospect, that you didn't pick up on at the time, that suggested that you would have problems now?

Wife: I had expected him to be more of a philanderer than what he's turned out to be. He's actually turned out to be a fairly stable husband.

Therapist: So he actually exceeded your expectations in this regard.

Wife: Actually, yeah.

Husband: [to wife] Thank you.

Wife: O my God, a compliment. I'm slipping up [laughs].

Therapist: Better limit yourself to one compliment per session [both husband and wife laugh].

Wife: During our dating he was involved with several other people at the same time he was with me.

Husband: Well, you weren't exactly living in a monastery [teasing tone].

Wife: That's true [laughs].

Therapist: But he's been more faithful and more committed than you might have expected him to be.

Wife: Yes.

Therapist: That's good. That's good to know.

Husband: That's good to hear [laughs]. I take it as something positive, and I'm not used to positives coming from you lately.

Wife: That's true, there have been a lot of negatives.

Therapist: Well, I've gotten enough information about you both to know that there have been some fairly significant problems in recent years. And at this moment there seems to be some positive stuff going on between the two of you. What are things like when the problems aren't there? How are they different?

Wife: We get along pretty well, basically.

Therapist: What does that look like?

Wife: We still enjoy talking to each other when the kids aren't bugging us.

Therapist: What else?

Wife: On those rare occasions when we have privacy, sex is good. And we have some common interests.

Husband: When there's not alcohol in the picture we enjoy each other's company. Either just the two of us, or with the children. It's calm, relaxed, and enjoyable on all fronts at those times.

Wife: It depends on the kind of day I've had with the kids. If they've been fairly good then by 5:00 I'm all right. But if it's been one of the days that everybody's been needy all day, I'm sort of "needed out" by the time he gets home. It doesn't leave me with much to give.

Therapist: So you're pretty exhausted, and short-tempered.

Wife: I've been that way, yes.

Therapist: How would things be different if I could wave my magic wand and transform you into the kind of couple that you want to be?

Wife: That's a tough one. There's been so much anger and resentment. I don't know that I can let go of that. I guess I could, but anyway, if I could, things would be much better.

Therapist: So for you, a big thing would be to find yourself not so angry and resentful.

Wife: Yeah.

Therapist: And what would make you less angry and resentful?

Wife: I don't know if there's anything he can do. But I know that what makes me angry and resentful is when all the problems are blamed on my drinking. I drink because I'm stressed out, angry, and resentful.

Therapist: So, you feel that you would be less inclined to drink if you were not being blamed for the problems.

Wife: That, and if I wasn't drinking, or stressed out, or angry, then we could see how much we still have in common.

Therapist: You've already mentioned a number of times that it's been very difficult for you to have three young kids. And it sounds like you feel it's been pretty much your responsibility to manage them, to deal with them, to parent them . . .

Wife: Well, that's true, except that lately he has been much more involved. He decided to give up some of his outside interests and spend more time at home. He has also been working less. In fact, since I've been in the hospital he's been a single father for the last two weeks. And that takes a lot of time and a lot of energy.

Therapist: And what about that?

Wife: I feel bad for him. Because he's also working. At least I didn't have to work. Sometimes I'd be able to even have an hour or two for myself during the day.

Therapist: So, he's been a good father over the last year and a half, and he's been particularly impressive in the last two weeks.

Wife: He's gone beyond being a good father. He's been both a father and mother for the last two weeks.

Therapist: Uh oh. That's compliment number two.

Wife: [Jokingly] I must be slipping up.

Therapist: You violated my rule of only one compliment per day. We don't want this to go to his head. How are you [to the husband] feeling about what she's saying?

Husband: It's good to hear. I don't want a divorce. But the drinking has to stop.

Therapist: What would a good relationship look like for you, other than her stopping drinking?

Husband: We would be a family. I would come home at the end of the day, she would be sober, we would play with the kids, go out and do things together, you know, like it was all supposed to work out.

In this example, Cal and Tanya were on the brink of divorce at the time of the interview. There were several opportunities to get into discussions of their marital difficulties. The therapist's strategy was to strike a middle ground between using the interview as the "first therapy session" and validating the pain that they were both experiencing. He emphasized both strengths and the severity of their problems. As a result, the partners became at least somewhat playful, and reported at the end of the interview that they were encouraged by some of the things that had been said. Naturally, this outcome does not always occur; when it does, both partners leave their initial contact with the therapist feeling a bit less hopeless and at the same time validated.

Assessment of Problem Areas

In ICT, the assessment of problem areas is organized around the attempt to arrive at a formulation and to come up with a treatment plan that helps sequence change and acceptance interventions. We aim to identify themes, polarization processes, and mutual traps. To help prepare couples for the formulation, the culmination of this assessment phase, we ask them to read the manuscript of the first few chapters of our book for couples (Christensen & Jacobson, 1997). These chapters describe problems and conflicts from the vantage point of ICT in a language easy for couples to follow.

Typically, during assessment, the therapist tries to answer six questions. Each bears on both the formulation and the treatment plan:

1. How distressed is this couple?
2. How committed is this couple to this relationship?
3. What are the issues that divide them?
4. Why are these issues such a problem for them?

5. What are the strengths holding them together?
6. What can treatment do to help them?

The first question, the severity of couple distress, may determine how therapy actually proceeds. If couples are mildly to moderately distressed, the assessment phase can proceed without interruption. However, if the couple is in crisis or cannot tolerate a more leisurely assessment procedure, an immediate intervention may be necessary. Examples include homicide or suicide risks, domestic violence or child abuse, or psychosis.

Level of distress can be ascertained during the conjoint couple interview as well as in the individual sessions. Couples may discuss desires to separate or inform the therapist that they have recently separated. In addition to these content indicators, the manner in which partners discuss their problems can reveal their level of distress. Some partners are so angry at one another that they frequently interrupt and have a hard time listening.

Questionnaires can be used to gain a more precise measure of distress. Couple adjustment scales such as the Dyadic Adjustment Scale (DAS; Spanier, 1976) and inventories such as the Marital Satisfaction Inventory (MSI; Snyder, 1979) provide quantitative indices and normative data for assessing a couple's level of distress. Whatever the couple's level of distress, assessments of violence should also be undertaken. Since couples often fail to report violence during a conjoint interview, and since one spouse (usually the wife) may be in danger, it's best to include questionnaires, such as the Conflict Tactics Scale (Straus, 1979), that partners can complete privately. Interview techniques for detecting violence are discussed in Chapter 11.

Next we ask about the level of commitment. While commitment is often associated with severity of distress (the more committed the couple, the less distressed), there are times when couples are highly committed despite extreme distress; there are also times when couples are ready to divorce even when distress is only mild. While subjective distress tells therapists how difficult it is going to be to help the couple, commitment levels are a good indicator of how much effort the partners are ready to invest in couple therapy.

Self-report questionnaires can be handy adjuncts to the assessment of commitment. For example, there is an item on the DAS that specifically addresses one's desire for the relationship to succeed and willingness to put forth the necessary effort to make sure that it does. The Marital Status Inventory (Weiss & Cerreto, 1980) measures directly the steps that partners have taken to disengage from one another: the higher the score, the closer the spouses are to divorce, and presumably the less committed they are to working on the relationship in therapy. For example, partners who have set up private bank accounts to protect their interests are closer to divorce than those who simply contemplate divorce from time to time, usually after an argument.

The sessions with individual spouses are often helpful in clarifying the level of commitment. At times, during this interview partners reveal that they are on the brink of divorce and see therapy as the final attempt to work things out. Some partners have secretly decided to end the marriage and see couple therapy as a safe haven for their soon to be ex-partner: once safely ensconced in couple therapy, their plan is to announce that the marriage is over. Extramarital affairs may be acknowledged during the individual interview. Infidelity is usually an indicator of low commitment (dealing with infidelity is covered in Chapter 11). To the extent that commitment is low, acceptance interventions are more likely to predominate, especially early in therapy, since couples with low commitment are unlikely to be amenable to interventions requiring accommodation, compromise, and collaboration.

The first step in coming up with a formulation is identifying a theme. In order to identify a theme, it is necessary to determine what issues divide the couple. What do they argue about? What are their positions or points of view in these particular areas? For example, when Harry and Beatriz say they fight about money, we want details. Perhaps Harry is tight when it comes to spending, while Beatriz is willing to assume debt. What are the contextual factors that influence the occurrence of conflict? It may be that Beatriz earns more than Harry and uses that as a rationale for arguing that she should be able to spend as she pleases.

We have already mentioned the common theme of closeness-distance. Perhaps Harry desires more time together, more expressions of affection, more disclosure of personal feelings, while Beatriz prefers to pursue individual interests, doesn't like to talk about personal feelings, and places a premium on privacy. A relevant contextual factor might be that Harry is a writer who works alone all day, whereas Beatriz has a job involving a great deal of social interaction. By the time she gets home, she wants peace and quiet, while Harry, having had his fill of solitude, is looking for a social companion.

Partners are usually aware of the issues that divide them and able to articulate them without much difficulty. In addition, there are questionnaires that probe this area, for instance, the Areas of Change Questionnaire (Margolin et al., 1983), which presents partners with a list of common changes that couples may want in their relationship. Each partner indicates the amount and direction of change they seek, as well as his or her perception of the change the partner seeks. The ACQ targets areas that partners may neglect or be reluctant to mention during the evaluation session (e.g., sexual issues). We have modified the ACQ so that our version assesses not only the desired direction of change (more or less of something) but also how frequently current behaviors occur and how acceptable each behavior is at its current frequency. This Areas of Change and Acceptance Questionnaire (ACAQ; Christensen & Jacobson, 1991) is especially useful with a treatment such as ICT that targets acceptance as well as change in therapy.

The answer to the fourth question, "Why are these issues such a problem for them?", gets directly at the polarization process and the mutual trap. As the partners answer this question, the therapist learns how they react to conflicts when they occur and how they get stuck when reacting to one another. In marital interaction research, there are structured communication exercises that directly assess how couples deal with conflict (Gottman, 1994). There is no reason why these methods cannot be adapted to clinical settings, although the conclusions one might draw from such exercises would necessarily be based on clinical judgment, rather than on the time-consuming and technical observational coding used in research settings. In addition to watching how partners interact during the interview, the therapist asks them to describe typical arguments that occur at home. Do they avoid discussing areas of conflict altogether? Do they complain bitterly to one another and escalate to the point where days of silence follow an argument? Does one try to pressure the other for change while that one withdraws in anger? Consider Harry and Beatriz's interactions around money. Perhaps she goes on spending sprees without consulting Harry. He becomes angry and criticizes her, putting her down and calling her names. When she does mention a possible purchase in advance, he dismisses it as frivolous and unaffordable. Because she has learned that her efforts to negotiate with him in advance are fruitless, and since she does not want to compromise, she may decide to make spending decisions unilaterally and tolerate his subsequent belittling and complaining. Because he is so angry at her for not consulting him, he may not be open to discussion and will much more likely to dismiss her future suggestions regarding purchases.

We learn more about why closeness is such a problem for this couple as the spouses describe their attempts to generate togetherness. He might try to initiate closeness by showering her with affection as a way of "loosening her up" and evoking a loving response. Although she does not want to hurt his feelings, she is not in the mood to be close. But she goes along with it anyway, with accompanying nonverbal behavior that makes it obvious to him that her heart isn't in it. He notices that she appears distracted and seems to be simply going through the motions. When she fails to generate a heartfelt response, he becomes enraged and accuses her of being unloving, or worse. She becomes furious and argues that she has been going along with his initiatives even though she hasn't particularly wanted to—and what does she get but more complaints and criticism? Eventually, she withdraws in anger. Her anger has an effect on him, and he attempts to make amends by apologizing. She forgives him. But the sequence occurs repeatedly, and neither knows how to stop it.

The therapist should be alert to the polarization process that typically accompanies interaction around a controversial issue. In all of the examples above and in Chapter 3, each partner's well-intentioned efforts to solve the problem elicit problematic behavior in the other, in turn eliciting problematic behavior in themselves. Harry's efforts at initiating contact with his wife overwhelm her and make her want to pull back. Her desire not to hurt his feelings leads her to go along with him but in an emotionally dishonest way by being with him only in body. He sees through her efforts and gets hurt and angry. It will be important during the feedback session to give them a new perspective on the problem that paints it as a natural and inevitable vicious circle.

The fifth question often gets answered as a matter of course: What are the strengths that keep the couple together? What are the qualities that attracted them to one another in the first place? Which of these characteristics still operate as a basis for continuing attachment? The therapist can augment this inquiry during individual sessions with the partners. Whether this information comes during the initial conjoint interview, from questionnaires, or from individual interviews, the therapist must be attentive to once attractive features of the two that are now related to their problems. For example, among other things, Harry says that Beatriz's spontaneity and unpredictability attracted him to her, while Beatriz mentions the comfortable, secure "space" that was Harry's house, which she found so attractive. Clearly, Beatriz's spontaneity can be seen in her purchasing habits today, while Harry's orientation toward comfort and security can be seen in his desire to save.

Differences that attract can also repel. In ICT, we try to help couples experience both the positive and negative side of differences, so that those that cannot be changed can be accepted. In the case of Harry and Beatriz, we may want to place their current differences about spending money in the context of their attractive features of spontaneity and security. Therefore, the therapist remains vigilant during the evaluation for material about attraction that can be used later to reformulate current problems.

Variation on the question about strengths is: How did the partners manage to remain together despite the serious difficulties that have brought them into therapy? This is an important question, because it not only speaks to their collective resilience but may also reveal more about their level of distress. Knowing that a couple still shares common, core values about what is important in life or that they are mutually committed to particular goals for their children gives the therapist perspective about their problems and provides information that may inform later interventions. For example, the therapist might ask how their discussions about core values, which are productive, are different from their discussions about finances, which are so unproductive.

The keys to both acceptance and change can often be found in couples' past successes and strengths. To the extent that the therapist can describe what happens when partners are getting along and distinguish it from the interactional sequences producing destructive arguments, he or she has clues as to how partners might interrupt polarization. Often, the BE tasks that work most effectively are those derived from partners' already existing repertoire of reinforcers. Similarly, CPT can be facilitated when the therapist can ascertain how a particular couple works effectively together to solve a problem. Thus, we want to know as much about their positive interactional sequences as we do about how they polarize. Most distressed couples problem solve effectively, at least on occasion; rarely do couples fail every time they are faced with conflict.

The delineation of these success strategies is often at least as important as the rules listed in our communication training manuals. Central to ICT is the functional analysis of each individual case, which emphasizes natural contingencies rather than the rule-governed behavior contained in the previous behavioral books. We care much more about what works for a particular couple than what the rules in the manuals say.

The final question, "What can treatment do to help?", is perhaps the most important. Even if we come up with a brilliant formulation, without goals for treatment and strategies for achieving those goals the therapy sessions will proceed without direction and with little chance of success. The goals of ICT are almost always some combination of acceptance of differences and changes in conflict areas. Change typically involves increases in positive behavior, shaped and reinforced by natural contingencies, and more open, less blaming, and nondefensive communication. The therapist needs to pay attention during the assessment phase to areas where accommodation, compromise, and collaboration are possible, as well as areas where acceptance may be possible.

Consider Harry and Beatriz's money problems. They may be helped by learning to accept their fundamental differences about the value of saving for tomorrow versus spending for today. This process will be facilitated if they are able to discuss these differences without blame and accusation. If Beatriz were to share with Harry her desire for a major purchase before she actually spends the money, and if Harry could listen without dismissing her ideas, they might have a constructive discussion about the problem. A series of open discussions about relevant incidents might lead to more compromises and less resentment. If Beatriz did not feel so controlled by Harry, her genuine desire to please him, her own rational knowledge about the advantages of saving, and her own long-term interests might lead her to be more discriminating in her purchases and save for those that are of highest priority. At the same time, if Harry did not feel so manipulated by Beatriz's secretive purchases and if he could look more closely at their significance to her, his own genuine desire to please her, as well as that part of him that enjoys spending, might emerge. As Harry and Beatriz become less entrenched in their positions, they might be able to negotiate and problem solve about how much to save each month, how much should be left for each to use as he or she pleases, and which purchases require consultation with the other.

When the question is asked, "How can treatment help?", an important component of the answer is each partner's capacity for change and acceptance. In an ideal world, couples would be able to work together on problems, recognize that they need to change themselves if the relationship is going to improve, and recognize the value of compromise and accommodation. This ideal world exists only in our dreams. However, some couples come closer to this ideal than others. At the other extreme are partners who have apparently irreconcilable differences, who believe that they have already accommodated, compromised, and collaborated without the other showing a similar propensity, and who therefore cannot talk constructively about anything that is conflict-laden. Since most couples fall somewhere between these two extremes, it is the therapist's job to propose a plan that leans toward change or acceptance early in therapy. In general, the greater the evidence of collaboration, the more change techniques will be emphasized early in therapy. Conversely, the greater the incompatibilities, the greater the distress, the less the commitment, the more divergent their relationship goals, and the more traditional the marriage, the greater the emphasis on acceptance early in therapy.

Perhaps the most important determinant of whether or not therapy should start with change or acceptance is the extent to which couples enter therapy with a *collaborative set* (Jacobson & Margolin, 1979). This set refers to a shared perspective that they are mutually responsible for the problems in the relationship and that they both need to change if the relationship is going to improve. To the extent that couples bring this set into therapy, change strategies are more likely to be successful. In contrast, to the extent that partners present themselves as innocent victims of the other's oppression and enter therapy hoping that the therapist will convince the other to change, acceptance strategies need to be emphasized. Since only a minority of couples manifest a collaborative set at the beginning of therapy, acceptance work tends to predominate early on. This use of the collaborative set represents an important shift from the Jacobson and Margolin approach. In 1979, we suggested inducing a collaborative set even when none existed at the beginning of therapy. Although this strategy was often successful, we now know that we were usually force feeding change, with the result being rapid relapse following termination from therapy. In ICT, we react to however couples present themselves. If they are not collaborative when they enter therapy, we accept their lack of collaboration and make no efforts to induce such a set.

As we shall see in more detail later, strategies for promoting acceptance always include discussions of the problem with the therapist as mediator. Typically, these discussions occur at four levels: a general discussion of the problem, discussion of an upcoming event that may trigger the problem, discussion of a recent negative incident illustrating the problem, and discussion of a recent positive situation in which either one or both partners tried to "do it better" even if the ultimate outcome was not positive. For certain problems, discussions about upcoming incidents may not occur because such anticipation is impossible. However, general discussions of recent positive and negative incidents are applicable to virtually all couples, while discussions of recent incidents prepare couples for the inevitable and illustrate that the polarization process will be useful.

During the assessment, therapists need to come up with a formulation that is sufficient to provide guidance in: (a) focusing the general discussion and (b) deciding which between-session incidents to inquire about in the therapy session. Suppose that the theme of *control and responsibility* is determined to be fundamental to the formulation with Harry and Beatriz. Perhaps even the closeness-distance issues can be subsumed under this theme. The polarization process has already been described. They are mutually trapped by strategies that emphasize damage control but keep the problem alive and even make them worse. They are each "stuck" in these self-defeating strategies. A recent purchase by Beatriz without consulting Harry or Harry's dismissal of Beatriz's attempt to discuss a potential purchase would illustrate negative instances. In addition, any recent time when Beatriz tried to share her desires more openly would indicate a positive effort, even if it did not lead to a constructive episode. Without regard to their money problems, it may be useful to discuss an upcoming event where Beatriz might desire (or even plan) to purchase something expensive (e.g., a Satellite dish). In such a situation, the therapist has an opportunity to do "in vivo" training of the couple in the presence of a concrete problem.

The Feedback Session

After the evaluation, the therapist provides the couple with a formulation and a treatment plan. With this in hand, the couple can make an informed decision about whether to proceed with treatment.

The six questions we ask during the assessment provide the outline for the feedback session. Therapists go through these questions and their answers with the couple. The answers are descriptive and provide information to the couple; more importantly, they often move the couple in a positive direction.

The feedback session is a dialogue between therapist and client, not a lecture. Notions are presented tentatively, and feedback is elicited. The partners themselves are viewed as experts on what ails them and contribute actively to the working formulation. The purpose is to arrive at a mutually acceptable treatment plan.

Addressing the first question, the therapist indicates to the partners their current level of relative distress. Therapists may tell them their actual scores on relevant instruments (e.g., the DAS or the MSI) and provide normative benchmarks to aid them in their interpretations of the scores (e.g., mean scores of "happy" couples, cutoff scores for distress, mean scores for divorcing couples). At times, it is clinically beneficial to reassure couples, especially those who enter therapy overestimating their level of distress compared to others. At other times, it is important to underscore the seriousness of the difficulties reflected in the current level of distress.

Next the ICT therapist indicates to the partners their general level of commitment to the relationship. When commitment is high, the therapist might say, "I see you two as very committed to the relationship, despite the problems you have mentioned." When commitment is moderate, the therapist might acknowledge both commitment and uncertainty, by saying, for example, "I think both you still want this relationship to work, but the problems have been so severe that you have been seriously considering the possibility of separation or divorce." With low levels of commitment, the therapist focuses primarily on the couple's pessimism: "I think this therapy represents a last ditch effort for the two of you. You are willing to try one more time, but neither of you has much hope." Whatever the level of commitment, the therapist uses information from the questionnaires and the interviews to support his or her observations. The last item on the DAS, mentioned earlier, and all of the items on the Marital Status Inventory are relevant commitment items. The clinical purpose of this feedback, like that on distress, is reassurance for some couples and emphasis of the seriousness of their problems for others. In addition, couples who are not committed are challenged and forced to assume major responsibility for the treatment's success or failure. Do they really want this relationship to work? Are they willing to put forth the effort? The success of this treatment regimen depends primarily on the couple. However skillful the therapist might be, the approach will only work when partners truly want to see the relationship improve and are willing to put forth the effort.

Feedback about the third question, concerning issues, focuses on the theme. First, the therapist describes the theme, for example, "control and responsibility" in the case of Harry and Beatriz. Second, the therapist describes each partner's position on particular issues in ways that validate that position as reasonable but indicate the differences between them summarized in the theme. Whenever possible the therapist adds information to show how these particular examples reflect the theme and how the theme encompasses differences that were once a source of mutual attraction. The clinical purpose of this feedback is to shift them away from a blaming stance toward more acceptance. For example, in giving Harry and Beatriz feedback about their money conflicts, the therapist might say:

> The two of you clearly have a conflict around spending money. I see this problem as reflecting a more general struggle over control and responsibility. Beatriz, you want control over financial decisions, as do you, Harry. You also have different philosophies about whether money should be spent or saved, and you each feel entitled to have your philosophies prevail. Beatriz, you live for today, while you, Harry, prepare for tomorrow. Both positions are reasonable. Neither violates any of the Ten Commandments. Only in the extreme do they become hard to justify. But neither of you would argue that you should never live for today or prepare for tomorrow. It's just a different emphasis. It is interesting to me that this difference that bothers

you now was once a source of attraction for you. You said, Harry, that you were attracted to Beatriz because she was a spontaneous person, and spontaneous people live for today. You said, Beatriz, that you really appreciated the comfortable, secure sense that you got from being in Harry's world. Only people who prepare for tomorrow can provide a sense of security. In fact, all of the things you fight about reflect differences in philosophy, differences that are reasonable. But you each feel that your philosophy has the right to prevail. Whenever you fight, it is about whose philosophy is superior and who will be the philosopher king or queen in this relationship.

Proceeding to the fourth assessment question, the therapist explains the polarization process and the mutual trap. This is the first effort to shift the couple's focus from their differences to their methods of handling those differences. The therapist describes each partner's understandable and often well-intentioned efforts to deal with the differences between them and points out how these actions often generate distress rather than resolution. The clinical purpose of this feedback is to show each partner how he or she is contributing to the problem, as well as suggesting changes that could alleviate the polarization process. At this stage, the therapist emphasizes the understandable feelings fueling this process, so that they can listen to the feedback without becoming defensive. For example, the therapist might say this to Harry and Beatriz:

> This difference between the two of you about the value of saving for tomorrow versus spending for today, which is a common difference between spouses, comes up for the two of you when you, Beatriz, want to purchase something. I think you have tried to talk to Harry about potential purchases at times in the past, but you've found him so resistant to your ideas and, it seems to you, so controlling about money, that you think the only way to have any financial choice in the relationship is to take unilateral action and buy the item. Yes, Harry will find out and get angry at you, but that eventuality, however unpleasant, seems worth it to you to have some power and autonomy in financial decisions. On your side, Harry, you see Beatriz's unilateral actions as shutting you completely out of any role in these financial decisions. Far from feeling in control, you feel unimportant, and neglected besides. So it is not surprising that you get upset when she makes a unilateral purchase or that you are not particularly open to her ideas if she does pass them by you. You assume she may go buy it no matter what you say, and the only way to rein her in is to discourage any purchase in advance.

In discussing polarization, we introduce not only the mutual trap concept, but also two other concepts that are useful with some couples: the *minefield* and the *credibility gap*. For example, consider Erling and Lorna. Erling is extremely sensitive to conflict and would go to great lengths to minimize, eliminate, or resolve it. His "conflict phobia" makes good sense in light of his upbringing, since he was raised in a family where overt expressions of conflict were severely punished. Lorna, who comes from a family where conflict was freely expressed, reports that conflict is helpful to her. When Lorna becomes irritated with Erling, he can't stand it. He tries to talk her out of it, denies what he did that made her angry, or tries to compensate for the anger by making a conciliatory gestures. Yet, she can't turn off her limbic system and so remains angry, at least for a period of time. When his efforts to get rid of her anger are unsuccessful, he becomes angry at her, accusing her of being stubborn, contentious, and unwilling to let go of her anger. From his perspective, she is stubbornly holding onto the anger, thus prolonging the conflict unnecessarily. From her point of view, he is asking her to turn off emotions that are beyond her voluntary control. His pressure actually increases her anger. They are both trapped and cannot extricate themselves.

The minefield refers to those buttons that partners push and that, once pushed, seem to lead inexorably to severe conflict. With Erling and Lorna, one land mine involves money. Anytime he brings up money, she gets furious. A functional analysis reveals that Erling has long used money as a method of control. When he brings up Lorna's spending habits, she bristles because she has never felt control over what she can and cannot spend. To her, money signifies his lack of trust (insisting on a prenuptial agreement), his lack of commitment (he must be planning to leave her some day), and his dominance in the relationship. Thus, no matter how innocent the discussion seems, pushing the money button is likely to lead to an explosion in this relationship.

A credibility gap refers to a point in an argument where an impasse develops because one person's position is simply not credible to the other. Problem-solving is impossible in such situations. With Erling and Lorna, there was a credibility gap when Erling tried to backtrack from a statement that had angered Lorna. When he tried to apologize for, clarify, or minimize a remark that she had experienced as critical, she simply did not believe him. Her disbelief always resulted in his becoming angrier, since she was dismissing his genuine effort to provide her with more perspective on his remark. Mutual traps, minefields, and credibility gaps are often at the core of how people get stuck when they are polarizing around their theme.

Feedback about the sixth assessment question—what treatment can do to help—often follows the feedback about the formulation. We describe for couples the goals of treatment as well as the procedures for achieving those goals. Typically, the goals will be to create conditions in the therapy session where problems can be resolved through some combination of acceptance and change. Therapeutic procedures to achieve these goals include (a) discussion in sessions of the general issue and of particular instances when the problem arises and (b) homework outside the session to further the work of therapy. The clinical purpose of this feedback is to give the partners some notion of what to expect and to orient them toward the goals of change and acceptance through more open communication and alternatives ways of "seeing" their problems. For example, consider the feedback about a treatment plan for their money problem given to Harry and Beatriz.

> How can treatment help this money problem between the two of you? First of all, let me describe what I think the goals of that treatment should be. One goal would be better communication between the two of you about major purchases. That goal may sound desirable and even simple in the abstract, but it would mean that you, Harry, were more open to hearing Beatriz's ideas. Being more open would not mean that you agree to go along with all of her ideas, just that you give her a hearing. Being more open for you, Beatriz, means that you discuss before taking action, but it doesn't mean that you agree to take no action. So neither of you has to give up any of your options by engaging in discussion. However, discussion offers you some hope of accommodation to each other.
>
> Accommodation and acceptance of each other would be the remaining two goals of treatment for this problem. I'm not sure what the mix of the two will work for you, but I'm sure that some of both will be required for successful treatment. The two of you are different in your positions about money, as we have discussed, but both of your positions are reasonable. Therapy can explore whether acceptance of this difference is possible and whether you can stop blaming each other for being the way you are. Therapy may also help you reach compromises, for example, guidelines for the amount to save each month, the amount for discretionary use, and purchase amounts that require consultation with one another.
>
> How will we achieve these goals? Mainly by talking in here with me as a moderator. We will discuss this issue as an example of your "control and responsibility" theme, but more importantly, we will discuss specific instances that come up. I will be interested in discussing positive instances, times when the two of you discuss a purchase more openly, as well as negative instances when you are unable to discuss a purchase and get angry at each other, for example, because, Beatriz, you think that Harry dismissed your idea or because, Harry, you think that Beatriz made a unilateral purchase without consulting you. I may also ask you to try doing some things

outside of this session, such as implementing an agreement that we have reached in here.

In addition to stating the formulation and explaining the treatment plan, the therapist uses the feedback session to begin the intervention stage. In particular, two types of clinical interventions fit nicely into the feedback format. The first pertains to the delineation of strengths. When the therapist spends a substantial portion of time during the session describing strengths, couples often begin to see the solutions to their problem. The feedback itself can change their perspective on their problems, thus stimulating the process of change. While it is important that the therapist, when presenting their strengths, not invalidate their pain, an exclusive emphasis on the pain can have iatrogenic effects, making the problems seem even worse than they were at the time the couple entered therapy.

The second type of intervention employed during the feedback session is the collaborative probe. This probe, which can also be used during the individual sessions, guides the sequencing of change and acceptance interventions. We probe by asking questions such as, "How do you contribute to the problems in this relationship?" and "What are some of the changes that you need to make if this relationship is going to improve?" To the extent that individuals have trouble pinpointing their own shortcomings and changes that may be required of them, the prognosis for a collaborative set decreases. It is important to get specifics when probing. It is one thing to respond in a socially desirable way, for example, "I know that I am not perfect and that I am going to have to make some changes." Most people know enough about pop psychology to acknowledge their imperfections in a general way. It is quite another thing to respond to the probe with specifics as to one's own contribution to the problems and ideas about areas where one needs to change. If the individual's only ideas for self-change involve less reactivity to the partner's obnoxious behavior, the therapist cannot assume a collaborative set.

Conclusion

In this chapter, we have discussed the process of assessment and feedback in ICT. When unconstrained by time limits imposed by third-party payers, we typically have an individual conjoint interview followed by sessions with each spouse alone, concluding with a conjoint feedback session. The first conjoint interview can be either a standard intake interview with the focus on answering our six main assessment questions or an attempt at therapy through emphasizing strengths. Deciding how problem-focused the first session should be depends on a variety of factors, including whether or not a departure from a problem focus would be therapeutic for a particular couple. In any case, the individual sessions are always problem-focused, although there is some discussion of strengths during these sessions as well. We also rely on assessment instruments to aid us in the process; these are becoming increasingly useful as third-party payers limit the number of live contacts therapists can have with couples.

The feedback session is both a summary of the assessment process and the beginning of therapy. It is the first time the couple learns of our formulation: the theme, polarization process, and mutual trap. It is also the time when we present the partners with a treatment plan and decide on goals—usually some combination of acceptance and change.

5

OVERVIEW OF INTEGRATIVE COUPLE THERAPY

Once treatment begins, the ordering and sequencing of interventions vary from couple to couple. There are two major categories of interventions: those designed to promote acceptance and those designed to promote change. Within each of the major categories, there is a series of generic intervention strategies, each of which includes a number of techniques. In Chapters 6 through 9, we will discuss in detail two generic strategies for acceptance work (intimacy-focused acceptance and tolerance) and two generic strategies for change work (behavior exchange and communication/problem-solving training). But first we will provide a theory of therapeutic change, describe the structure of ICT, and discuss the basic sequencing of intervention techniques.

A Theory of Therapeutic Change

Although integrative couple therapy (ICT) represents a return to contextualism (Pepper, 1942), the traditional philosophical roots from which behavior therapy was derived, its approach is a marked departure from traditional behavioral couple therapy (TBCT). ICT places greater emphasis on identifying the controlling variables in marital interaction. TBCT is more modular and technique-oriented; as a result, it places more emphasis on what we call derivative variables. An example will clarify this distinction. Let us assume that for a particular couple, Margo and Dave, a major set of controlling variables for the marital satisfaction of the wife consists of actions from her husband that communicate to her that she is deeply loved and valued. Her childhood history made her question whether she was loved and lovable, so finding a man who was devoted to her was essential for marital satisfaction. For Dave, a major class of reinforcers comprises those things Margo does that let him know she admires and believes in him. Because of his childhood history, Dave is driven to succeed as a writer. He is both embarrassed and dismayed that he must work as a high school English teacher while he struggles with writing during his off hours. The fact that Margo saw talent in him, believed that he could be a writer, and actively encouraged him in that dream was a major facet of his attachment to her.

During the first few years of their marriage Dave and Margo began to take each other for granted, got focused on their own needs, and found the needs of the other annoying and interfering. As a result, Margo missed out on the reassurance that she needed from Dave and Dave missed out on the support he depended on from Margo. Feeling deprived, both began to withhold, not just in the crucial areas of love and support but in other areas as well. They spent less time doing things together. They began to bicker a lot.

ICT would describe the decreases in companionship and sexual frequency and the increase in bickering as derivative problems. These problems came about only because of the decreases in the central areas of love and support. While these derivative problems may have their own dynamics and ultimately achieve a life of their own, they were originally fueled by other factors. For example, an argument over a blouse that Margo chooses to wear may be based on a genuine difference in how Dave and Margo view that blouse; the argument may produce hurt feelings in one or both; and the argument could escalate until one or both take dramatic action, such as ripping up the blouse. However, had Dave not been so angry at Margo over other, more important matters, he would have commented on the blouse in a kinder way or ignored it altogether. Likewise, had Margo not been so mad at Dave over other, more important matters, she could have heard his comments with more objectivity.

With its emphasis on specific, discrete, current, observable behavior, TBCT often focuses on derivative problems such as can be measured with the Spouse Observation Checklist (Wills, Weiss, & Patterson, 1974), and on specific, discrete behavioral changes that are desired, such as will be indicated on the Areas of Change Questionnaire (Margolin et al., 1983). This strategy of assessment, as well as these particular assessment instruments, would likely reveal the lack of companionship, the infrequent sex, and the frequent arguments that characterize Dave and Margo, but they would be unlikely to reveal the lack of love and value that Margo experiences and the lack of encouragement and support that Dave experiences. Thus, TBCT would likely miss major, controlling variables.

Functional Analysis of Behavior

What is the alternative to an assessment focus on specific, discrete, observable behavior or desired changes in that behavior? The hallmark of contextual assessment, a functional analysis of behavior, focuses not on the size of the unit, its specificity, or even its observability. Rather, a functional analysis examines what variables control a given behavior by manipulating conditions that are antecedent to that behavior and conditions that are consequent to it. By observing how the behavior fluctuates in response to these changes, one determines the conditions that control the behavior.

Our ability to conduct a functional analysis of couple interaction is greatly limited in three respects. First, we are not present during most of a couple's time together, so we cannot observe the conditions that precede and follow most instances of marital distress. We are forced to rely on the partners' reports of their behavior and of the conditions that surround it. Although the ability to observe in-session behavior is helpful, it represents only a small and not necessarily representative sample of the couple's interaction.

A second limitation is the idiosyncratic nature of learning histories, which often results in diverse stimulus conditions or even apparently opposite stimulus conditions serving similar functions. Margo may often get distressed when a day goes by without Dave telling her that he loves her. If we were able to gather that information, we might have a good candidate for a controlling variable. If we learn, however, that Margo also gets distressed when Dave tells her that he loves her, we might get confused. However, if Dave's attempts to assure her of his love are done out of obligation, rather than out of a strong feeling of love for her at the time, her similar response to both the absence and apparent presence of a particular condition makes perfect sense.

A third and even more important limitation in conducting a functional analysis with couples is that we have very limited power to directly influence any conditions in their lives. We certainly don't have the luxury of manipulating a series of conditions until we find the true controlling variable. Altering *any* condition in a couple's life may be difficult. If we choose an unimportant one, by the time we have changed it, the couple may be too frustrated or feel too much like a failure to allow us to try another.

For example, if we decided that a lack of companionship was the key to Dave and Margo's unhappiness, we would try to increase their contact with one another. Since it is not the controlling variable and since they are so angry with each other, they might well be resistant to the idea. Even without resistance, they might find it genuinely difficult to make more time for movies, dinners, and the like. Furthermore, the events may produce at best only limited and temporary satisfaction.

These limitations notwithstanding, couples can provide us with information that can aid us in our functional analysis of the variables controlling their distress. First, couples can often articulate something about controlling variables. They are aware of their unhappiness and can frequently voice the reasons for it. These reasons may, unfortunately, be as confusing as they are enlightening. Because the partners are so angry and dissatisfied, their descriptions may sound more like accusations than explanations. Margo may accuse Dave of being selfish rather than describe what she is missing in the relationship. Also, these accusations may be broad, exaggerated, and overgeneralized. Rather than specify the lack of support he feels in his efforts to become a writer, Dave may simply say that "She doesn't support anything I do." Finally, couples may describe not only the controlling variables in their marital distress but also derivative variables. Margo and Dave may be so upset over a recent argument that they focus on that conflict and the derogatory things each said during the conflict rather than on the more important controlling variables in their relationship. Thus, couples can tell us something about their controlling variables, but it requires a skilled clinician to sort out the important from the unimportant and the description from the accusation.

Sometimes partners cannot articulate what is bothering them. They may not be able to put it into words, or they may feel too embarrassed or vulnerable to articulate the exact reasons. Despite this inability to articulate the source of their distress, they may be able to recognize and acknowledge it if the therapist states it, particularly if the therapist does so in a way that doesn't result in their feeling accused, attacked, or defensive.

Affect as a Cue and a Clue

In searching for the controlling variables, the affective expressions of each partner are an important clue. A lack of affect suggests a variable of little importance to the couple. If, when the therapist notes how little time the couple spends in companionate activities, the couple expresses little affect about the apparent loss, the therapist would be wise to search in other areas. Often anger is a clue to an important controlling variable. Partners usually have some idea of what is important to each other and in the throes of distress will attack where it hurts most. These attacks and the anger they generate can reveal a controlling variable. For example, if Margo charges that Dave will never be anything but a high school English teacher, Dave's bristling anger and hurt can be a clue to the importance of his writing career for him and the lack of support he feels from Margo.

While often useful, anger can also be a misleading clue. Couples can sometimes get so frustrated with each other that a variety of unimportant actions or inactions sparks an angry response. Couples can get angry over derivative variables as well as controlling ones.

Perhaps the more important affective clues are softer, sadder expressions. These expressions may reflect the loss that a partner has experienced in the relationship. If the therapist suggests to Margo that she no longer feels valued or important to Dave and Margo nods quietly with tears coming to her eyes, the therapist has some assurance that he or she has made contact with an important factor in the relationship.

Contingency-shaped Versus Rule-governed Behavior

Our contextual approach places great importance on the distinction between contingency-shaped and rule-governed behavior (Skinner, 1966). When behavior is rule-governed, "rule-following" is reinforced, for example, by approval from the therapist; rule violations are punished by either explicit and/or implicit sanctions—importantly, "violating the rule" is the behavior that is punished. The consequences are determined by the extent to which the behavior matches the rule, not by any natural consequences related to the rule. For example, most people who learn to play a song on the piano do so by following the rules specified in the sheet music for that song. In contrast, contingency-shaped behavior is determined by the natural consequences that accrue from that behavior and not from the match of that behavior to a particular rule. For example, those who learn to play a song on the piano "by ear" are shaped by the fit between the sounds from the keys they press and their prior history of practicing the song.

BE and CPT create changes in couples primarily through rule-governed behavior. In BE, couples identify potential reinforcing behaviors and are explicitly or implicitly given the rule to alter those behaviors in a way that promotes increased partner satisfaction. The therapist reinforces the couple for compliance with the rule but also hopes that natural contingencies will maintain those behaviors. For example, the husband increases the frequency with which he compliments his wife based on the BE "rule" developed in therapy. However, the behavior continues only if the natural reinforcement provided by the wife to those compliments (e.g., smiles, laughter) becomes a controlling variable. Similarly, in CPT, a couple defines a problem, negotiates a solution to that problem, and implements an agreement for change. This agreement constitutes a rule. The therapist reinforces the rule but hopes that naturalistic reinforcers will maintain the agreement. For example, a couple might negotiate a schedule for housework, which then becomes a rule. However, the hope is that the schedule will be maintained because it promotes natural reinforcers, such as more harmonious interaction.

Unfortunately, many of the changes that couples desire in therapy do not lend themselves to rule control. Rule-governed and contingency-shaped behavior may look alike but there are some subtle differences between them. From the inside, contingency shaped behavior may feel more "right" or "genuine" than rule-governed behavior. From the outside, contingency-shaped behavior may look more authentic. For example, even though a partner with low sexual desire may engage in the same sexual behaviors as a passionate, loving spouse, the latter feels differently from the former. Furthermore, the sexual act may seem routine to the other partner rather than passionate, if it is a response to a homework assignment rather than an encounter shaped by natural contingencies.

Our approach is based in part on the assumption that changes desired by couples in therapy have to do with the subtleties of contingency-shaped behavior rather than with the bald compliance of rule-governed behavior. Increased trust, greater interest in sex, or greater respect for the partner's achievements are not easily attained through rule-governed behavior. One cannot prescribe them in BE or negotiate them in CPT. Consider Wendel's mistrust of Jody because of her recent extramarital affair. While Wendel would like a promise that she will never do it again, what really disturbs him is that she did it in the first place; he doesn't trust her to keep the promise. Even if she obligingly complied with his request for an apology, a promise, or other acts of contrition, he would still not be satisfied because his distress is based on behavior that cannot be undone as well as unknowns in the future. In fact, her acts of contrition may feel inauthentic to her and be perceived as hollow by him. It is unlikely that anything but a new history of trusting interactions, shaped over time, will actually produce renewed trust.

Therefore, while rule-governed procedures, such as BE and CPT, have a role in ICT, other strategies are used for changes that are not easily brought about by rules. In our view, most of the themes, polarization processes, and mutual traps that bring couples into therapy cannot be altered primarily through rule-governed procedures. Moreover, alternatives to BE and CPT are needed when couples are simply unwilling or unable to accommodate, compromise, and collaborate. When they first enter therapy, this unwillingness is the norm, not the exception.

Basic Categories of Intervention Options

The most basic decision a therapist has to make in ICT is whether the focus at a given moment should be on change or on acceptance. Within those broad, generic categories, therapists have two basic change and acceptance options, each of which includes a number of techniques. Thus, let us begin with these basic distinctions.

Acceptance Interventions

Using acceptance to turn problems into vehicles for intimacy. Some acceptance strategies are designed to turn a source of conflict into a vehicle for intimacy. We aim for such transformations, even though we do not always achieve them. Couples typically enter therapy contending that conflicts must be eradicated in order for the relationship to improve. Since their conflicts are predicated on fundamental differences, it is often difficult, if not impossible, to eliminate the conflict without helping them see their differences in a more constructive way. Ideally, not only will they leave therapy accepting their differences, but they will appreciate these differences and be able to use them to develop a closer, more intimate relationship. Although we are not claiming that this ideal can routinely be achieved, we do believe that it is sometimes possible to turn these differences into sources of strength. When we are successful, not only does it become unnecessary for partners to change one another, but they actually come to appreciate and love each other for the ways in which they are different, not just for the ways in which they are compatible. This is not to say that the differences will never again cause discord or conflict, but rather that the differences, while distressing or inconvenient at times, become yet another vehicle for intimacy.

Tolerance. This is another basic acceptance strategy, which, while not aiming to be transformative, is far better than no acceptance at all. When tolerance techniques are invoked by the therapist, the goal is to neutralize the impact of the partner's negative behavior, so that its effects are less catastrophic than they used to be. When tolerance interventions are successful, clients would still prefer that the conflict not exist, that the negative behavior not occur as frequently, or that the positive behavior occur more frequently. However, the impact of the negative behaviors or lack of positive behaviors is less distressing and the recovery time from the other's undesirable behavior is shorter. The overall impact of undesirable behaviors on the relationship is considerably reduced. Thus, the basic difference between intimacy-focused acceptance and tolerance strategies is that in the former case conflicts contribute to the growth and development of the relationship, whereas in the latter conflicts are still undesirable but more acceptable than they were prior to therapy.

During a typical course of therapy, both intimacy-focused acceptance and tolerance strategies will be necessary. Even when couples are responsive to intimacy-focused acceptance strategies, chances are that for some problems the therapist will have to settle for tolerance. Even in the most responsive couples, not all problems can become vehicles for intimacy. Furthermore, the outcome of intimacy-focused acceptance strategies is often tolerance, despite the lofty goal of intimacy-focused acceptance. In short, it is important to distinguish between the goals of a particular therapeutic strategy and the actual outcomes achieved. These goals are not dichotomies but points on a continuum, where at one extreme we have grudging tolerance and at the other we have spouses embracing those aspects of the partner which at one time they wanted to change. The most typical outcome is somewhere in between these two extremes, regardless of whether the strategy employed is intimacy-focused acceptance or tolerance.

Change Techniques

Behavior Exchange. In Chapter 1, we described behavior exchange techniques as a major part of traditional behavioral couple therapy. We still find behavior exchange techniques quite useful and employ them frequently, although not with each and every couple. Behavior exchange techniques are primarily instigative, in that they are designed to directly change problematic behaviors in a positive direction. Since we have already defined them in Chapter 1, we will reserve further discussion until Chapter 8.

Communication/Problem-solving Training. Since we have largely abandoned the notion that marital problems are primarily the result of skill deficits in communication and problem-solving, the role of formal training in such skills has diminished greatly in ICT. Nevertheless, there are some couples who benefit greatly from the structure of problem-solving training. Furthermore, training couples in more general communication skills, such as "validation," "editing," and "leveling" (Gottman et al., 1976; Jacobson & Margolin, 1979), is often helpful as an adjunct to acceptance work. These techniques teach couples to listen and to express themselves in direct but non-blaming ways; as such they complement the acceptance work. In fact, one way of describing ICT is to say that we are trying to promote an atmosphere where pain can be expressed without blame and accusation and where its expression can be received by the partner in a non-defensive manner. Because of these overarching goals, communication training can be used in the service of promoting acceptance as well as change.

This merging of techniques in the service of a common goal helps define our approach as integrative. As we will show, regardless of the goals of particular techniques, the most efficient interventions serve both change and acceptance. Often, when therapy is going well, the hard and fast distinctions provided in clearly differentiated categories are irrelevant. Acceptance can lead to change, and change can lead to acceptance. And, as we have previously stated, both acceptance and change are forms of change. It is simply a question of the nature of the change and who is doing the changing.

Decisions Regarding the Sequencing of Interventions

The ideal couple for TBCT is relatively young, committed to staying together, emotionally engaged, egalitarian, and sharing the same definitions for what constitutes a good relationship. They also enter therapy with a collaborative set and "buy" the TBCT model, i.e., conceptualize their problems in terms of skill deficits in communication and deficits in behavior exchange. Of course, this ideal is rarely achieved. When we used TBCT, we were able to help approximately 50% of our couples, even though many of them deviated from this ideal in significant ways. Nevertheless, when commitment on the part of one or both partners was low, the collaborative set was nonexistent, and the model did not fit the ideology of one or both spouses, TBCT was rarely successful. Even when it was successful, it would generally take 20 sessions to achieve positive results and there would be at least a couple of major relapses during the course of therapy.

Based on our pilot data as well as our own decade's worth of clinical experience with ICT, there seem to be very few prerequisites to a positive outcome with acceptance work. Success rates have been so high, and relapse rates so low, that on empirical grounds alone it makes sense to start with acceptance work for most couples. However, we don't have to rely entirely on empirical evidence to advocate beginning with acceptance work. First, we have discussed the difference between rule-governed and contingency-shaped behavior. Both BE and CPT are rule-governed and will generalize to the home environment and prove durable over time only to the extent that they come to be controlled by natural contingencies. In contrast, neither intimacy-focused nor tolerance strategies are rule-governed; they rely almost entirely on producing shifts in context, which naturally reinforce behavior that makes the relationship more satisfying for both partners. Because acceptance work is not dependent on rules, the therapist is less likely to worry about generalization: positive developments in the therapy session are more likely to generalize to the home environment and the shifts in context make it highly probable that the improvements will stand the test of time. Second, acceptance work can be more efficient, which of course becomes increasingly important in an era where mental health care is often provided under the auspices of managed care. It usually takes a number of weeks to train couples in CPT skills, whereas acceptance interventions can work quickly with some couples, making brief therapy possible.

In some cases, acceptance work is all that is needed, because once it is complete neither spouse is as dependent on the changes he or she sought when the couple entered therapy. In still other cases, acceptance work actually produces the changes that couples sought without any of the direct change strategies usually associated with TBCT. Once again, although one is tempted to see these changes as spontaneous, they are in fact anything but; rather, they are natural byproducts of changes in the functional relationship between the two persons' interactional behaviors and in the couple's learning history produced by events in and between the therapy sessions. Only some of the time are traditional change interventions even necessary in ICT: they are needed only when increased acceptance has not obviated the need for further change or when those further changes have not occurred as a natural outgrowth of acceptance work. In those instances, either BE and/or CPT may prove to be the icing on the cake. This will, of course, extend the length of therapy. However, both BE and CPT proceed more smoothly when they occur in the context of collaboration, which is in and of itself a natural byproduct of emotional acceptance. Once BE and CPT are conducted within the context of emotional acceptance, they both become straightforward strategies: they are more effective and work more quickly.

Thus, when do we begin with BE or CPT? There are two major types of couples where it makes sense to start with either BE or CPT: first, couples who enter therapy with a collaborative set and meet most if not all of the criteria for responsiveness to TBCT; second, couples who expect or request communications skills training or behavior exchange. We are not referring here to the common situation where one partner (usually the husband) wants a problem-solving approach while the other (usually the wife) wants either an experiential or an insight-oriented approach. We start with TBCT only if *both* partners come to us with articulated goals suggesting that a skills training approach will succeed.

Are there instances when BE and CPT will work when acceptance strategies do not? Occasionally, but not often. On the other hand, it is not uncommon for acceptance work to succeed where BE and/or CPT will not. Why start the couple with a failure experience when the chances of initial success are far greater with acceptance work? Since acceptance work is particularly indicated for difficult, uncommitted, traditional, disengaged, noncollaborative couples, it is highly unlikely that a couple who is unresponsive to acceptance work will respond favorably to TBCT. We have both seen it happen, but not often enough to identify predictors.

Even when the therapist enters a phase where BE and CPT are the primary techniques, he or she should return to acceptance work without hesitation when change techniques are producing conflict. In the 1970s and early 1980s, we would continue with BE or CPT even when intense negative affect over something that happened during the week pervaded or, more generally, when the couple's attention, for whatever reason, was elsewhere. That is no longer our policy. With ICT, we assume that when change strategies generate conflict, or when the couple enters the session in conflict, it is an ideal opportunity to do acceptance work and a particularly bad time to force-feed change via BE or CPT. For one thing, the conflict is probably related to the theme, and when the couple is actually experiencing pain in the room from the theme or the polarization that accompanies it, acceptance work is particularly likely to be beneficial. The therapist may be able to induce an experience where pain is converted into compassion and then acceptance—right in the office! In addition, it is a waste of time to focus on rules for constructive engagement at times when partners are ready to strangle one another.

For example, at the time when the Jacobson and Margolin (1979) book was written, compliance with homework was considered a problem to be overcome. In fact, Jacobson had developed a module during his clinical workshops aimed at teaching therapists strategies for preempting and, if necessary, punishing noncompliance (Jacobson & Holtzworth-Munroe, 1986). Now, when practicing ICT, we see noncompliance as a sign that we chose the wrong assignment and suspect that the theme is operating in some way to prevent compliance. Thus, homework noncompliance leads naturally to acceptance work. Similarly, when a BE task designed to assess or change behavior fails because of an argument that occurred during the week, we immediately attend to the argument; we may not even get to the homework.

Any traditional behavior therapy task has acceptance work as a default option. In fact, one way of looking at behavior therapy tasks is that they are "acceptance probes": if they go smoothly, that may be an indirect sign that the acceptance work was done effectively; if they don't, it probably means that you shouldn't have been focusing on "change" in the first place, since the acceptance work has not been completed.

Another way of looking at this same phenomenon is from the perspective of client resistance. Our definition of resistance hasn't changed much since 1979, but the implications of the definition are different in ICT than they were in TBCT. Resistance is primarily an attempt on the part of therapists to blame clients for not changing or for not complying with the therapist's directives. When clients have a fight, or don't do their homework, or become defensive during therapy sessions in reaction to a remark made by either the therapist or the partner, therapists are severely tested in their ability to do ICT and may resort to the "resistant" label. It is convenient to attribute resistance to the client but it is rarely, if ever, useful.

Structure of a Typical ICT Session

So, what does a typical ICT session look like? Subsequent to the feedback session, they all look about the same. The material brought in by the clients determines the content of the session. We do not begin the session by setting an agenda, the way we did two decades ago. We let couples tell us whatever it is they want to tell us. During the early stages of therapy, the news is usually bad. They had a fight, they had very little interaction, or they bickered all week. All of these descriptions of events during the week lead to the discussion of incidents. The incidents almost invariably reflect the theme and provide an opportunity for the therapist to shift the partners from their "stuckness" over their differences to a consideration of their polarization. This is the essence of acceptance work. If they manage to have a good week early in therapy, the therapist uses this occasion to prepare for slip-ups—not with the goal of preventing them, but rather with the intent of helping the couple handle them when they occur, as they inevitably will. During the latter stages of therapy, once acceptance work has "taken hold," if more change is desired, then we move to BE and/or CPT. But even during these latter stages of therapy, we move in this direction tentatively, prepared to shift back to an acceptance mode at any time if there are indications that the work was incomplete.

When it is time to terminate, we usually reserve a session for recapitulating what went on in therapy, reviewing the formulation, and letting the clients tell us what they have found helpful (if anything). We may lengthen the time between sessions or schedule booster sessions later, with the partners free to call us anytime if they feel that they need to see us. The structure of ICT is really quite simple and, in fact, the technology itself does not take long to teach. But the clinical skills required of an ICT therapist are far more subtle than meets the eye and seem to lag behind the technology learning curve.

Clinical Skills in ICT

Attentiveness to Material Germane to a Functional Analysis

An ICT therapist has to be a good listener. Since the treatment approach is highly idiographic, and since it depends to such a great extent on functional analyses of interactional dynamics, the ICT therapist must be alert to nuances in order to formulate and reformulate. Attentiveness does not just apply to listening. It also applies to awareness of facial, paralinguistic, and bodily cues associated with affect. Although it is possible to code affect nomothetically with good reliability and validity (Gottman, 1994), we take the position that our ability to "read" emotional experience will lead us to varying interpretations of similar topographical cues from couple to couple and that this reading will often determine whether we stay on a particular course or move to a different mode of intervention. For example, a therapist may have learned that, for a particular partner, looking away is the first sign of anger. In the middle of a problem-solving exercise, that cue might lead the attentive therapist to stop the problem-solving action and shift to an acceptance mode.

Attentiveness is particularly important for functional analytic approaches, since with couples the functional analysis is almost always going to be based on indirect rather than direct observation. When observing institutionalized schizophrenics or self-injurious children, or when watching kids interacting with their teachers in school, it is feasible to directly ascertain functional relationships. Although such observation is also possible within limits with outpatients, and particularly with couples (since each is an important part of the other's context), often therapists are relying on verbal reports of incidents that have occurred at home. As Kohlenberg and Tsai (1991) have noted, being able to observe functional relationships as they occur in the session is quite important, whether they be between partners or between a partner and the therapist. We would simply add that deducing functional relationships in the natural environment based on couples' verbal reports requires a different kind of attentiveness, both visual and auditory. It is not easy to teach.

Sensitivity to Context

In ICT, the therapist should always be prepared to shift gears and abandon the prescribed agenda. In order to simplify the complex stimuli present in the room, the therapist may be tempted to develop a game plan, stick to it regardless of alterations in the cues, and miss crucial opportunities. For example, the therapist might be attending to a statement by one partner, only to have the other make a remark that "distracts" the therapist from the original line of dialogue. However, the distraction may indicate that the partner feels left out and misunderstood. The therapist may need to drop the line of inquiry temporarily, shift his/her attention to the one feeling left out, and begin a new dialogue. An ICT therapist is constantly shifting back and forth between the two partners. No overall plan for the session is as important as a partner's most recent remark.

Acceptance

Not surprisingly, it is imperative than an ICT therapist not have an agenda for the couple. There are no "thou shalts" or "thou shalt nots" in this approach. The skilled ICT therapist has to develop the ability to find compassion and sympathy in each person's story, no matter how unsympathetic and contemptible one partner may appear. Our position is that the vast majority of people act badly in relationships because they are suffering—often in ways that they are not aware of. In order for us to create conditions that make it possible for that suffering to be received with compassion by the partner, therapists have to respond in kind. This creates situations not unlike the paradox stated earlier: the ICT therapist has to be accepting even of the partners' inability to be accepting of one another. The ideal ICT therapist responds to even the most provocative behaviors by couples without blame and accusation.

Actually, the "acceptance" required of a good ICT therapist is quite similar to the empathy and unconditional positive regard advocated by Carl Rogers (1951). We certainly don't mean to imply, as Rogers did, that such skills are sufficient for successful couples therapy. However, we have come around to the point of view that they are necessary and certainly conducive to effective ICT.

The Ability to Uncover and Maintain Focus on the Formulation

Readers of Chapters 3 and 4 know the value we put on the formulation, not just as an organizing principle for the therapist but as a shorthand way to produce emotional acceptance and change. What may not be clear is that the deciphering of themes, polarization processes, and mutual traps is not straightforward; it requires a considerable amount of inferring from the raw data originating in the evaluation. Furthermore, maintaining a focus on the formulation, teaching partners to recognize polarization when it occurs, and helping them to incorporate the formulation into their relationship history require tenacity on the part of the therapist. The therapist must be able to distinguish between core and derivative variables and keep couples from going off on tangents.

There are markers the therapist can use to determine whether or not the formulation is becoming incorporated into the partners' way of describing their relationship. You know that therapy is going well if couples are describing their incidents between sessions in terms of the formulation. One might expect this phenomenon to occur gradually during the course of therapy. The therapist can also probe to see whether or not the couple is able to plug a recent incident into the formulation. For example, Jacobson recently asked a couple, "OK, you've both described the fight you had last night. Is there anything about this fight that sounds familiar?" The wife replied, "All of it. It is what we always do." Jacobson then asked, "And what is it that you always do?" The husband replied, "We fight over whether or not to be close. When she is not as close to me as she wants to be, she pressures me into being close, and I withdraw, which leads to more pressure. Of course, sometimes I withdraw before she has a chance to pressure me. In fact, that's usually how it starts. And that's how it started last night." This couple was very close to being ready for termination.

Ability to Maintain a Therapeutic Atmosphere Despite Severe Conflict without Becoming Confrontational

At times, spouses are so angry, blaming, and accusatory of one another that no matter what tactics the therapist uses their defensiveness is virtually impossible to curtail. Yet, allowing it to continue simply establishes the therapist's impotence and contributes to the couple's feelings of hopelessness. The therapist must do something to stop the destructive interaction, but without contributing to the blaming and accusatory language. In other words, the therapist must maintain a nonconfrontational demeanor. The essential clinical skill here is the ability not to be drawn into the blaming and accusation, not to take sides, to remain neutral and calm, and to exert a soothing influence. It is difficult to avoid becoming part of the bickering process, but it is essential in ICT.

When all else fails, separating the partners and having mini-individual sessions is an excellent strategy for interrupting highly charged destructive interaction cycles. Then the therapist can intervene with each spouse separately in the way that he or she did during the evaluation, continuing with attentiveness, sensitivity to context, and acceptance, without further alienating the other partner. Often, after a brief time-out from conjoint contact, the couple is ready to get back to work together.

Skill in Using Language in a Way That "Hits Home"

The skilled ICT therapist uses the right metaphors, ones that are meaningful for the couple, to create vividness and greater understanding of the therapist's points. Choosing the right words requires attentiveness to the partners' use of language. Most couples do not respond positively to social science jargon. Pop psychology terms, such as "dysfunctional family," "co-dependency," and "fear of intimacy," create the illusion of understanding but seldom produce therapeutic breakthroughs.

We cannot emphasize too strongly the importance of language in determining whether or not interventions "hit home." During early sessions, therapists should listen for idiosyncratic uses of speech by partners. Engineering metaphors work well for those who work at Boeing. Acting metaphors hit home with those who work for Disney.

One wife described herself with pride as "loosey-goosey." To her this meant spontaneous and playful. The therapist invoked that word whenever possible in referring to the couple's theme. For many partners, the term would have seemed pejorative, but for this particular wife it was a compliment.

The ability to use humor effectively enhances almost any therapeutic intervention. Making couples laugh at their situation without belittling is a tightrope act. We want couples to know that we take their problems seriously; on the other hand, humor and playfulness form a counterpoint, encouraging them to take their problems less seriously. To the extent that they take their problems less seriously, they will become more accepting of them.

Awareness of When to Stop Therapy

In an approach that emphasizes acceptance as well as change, a great burden is lifted from both therapist and clients. Not all problems have to be solved before therapy is stopped. A lapse or slip-up just prior to a planned termination does not have to disrupt termination, since slip-ups are inevitable and amount to nothing more than "sound and fury, signifying nothing." Knowing when it is time to stop is a fine art: since we have developed ICT, in our own practices we find that therapy rarely ends according to a schedule. Either it tails off because couples don't need us anymore, or we suggest a fading procedure, where sessions become gradually less frequent. Keeping couples in therapy too long or trying to talk them out of terminating because it seems premature is usually a byproduct of misguided instincts originally shaped by superstitious clinical lore. Couples usually know best. Listen to them, and it will usually be clear when it is time to stop. This level of attentiveness is easier preached than practiced; that is why it is easy for us to say, but harder for us to do.

— 6 —

ENHANCING INTIMACY THROUGH ACCEPTANCE

The acceptance strategies described in this chapter attempt to foster a fundamentally new experience of the problem, either as an understandable dilemma that causes both partners pain or as a common external enemy that they face together. Although couples might still prefer not to have the problem, we hope that the problem will become an opportunity for them to be close. Wile (1981) suggests that therapists help couples "build a relationship around a problem"; that is the basic idea.

As a general rule, therapists try at the beginning of ICT to turn problems into vehicles for intimacy, as new sources of strength and closeness, so they start with intimacy-enhancing acceptance strategies. In this chapter, we discuss the two major techniques used to promote such intimacy-enhancing acceptance: *empathic joining around the problem* and *unified detachment*. These notions are also discussed in our book for couples (Christensen & Jacobson, 1997), which partners are asked to read as we begin.

Empathic Joining Around the Problem

When spouses enter therapy, they are usually distressed at each other's actions or inactions because of the context in which these behaviors are experienced. Behaviors are labeled as bad and partners as mean, selfish, inconsiderate, deceitful, or, as one client recently put it, "a filthy excuse for a human being." Alternatively, they may label their partners as mentally or emotionally disturbed—hysterical, compulsive, overly emotional, dependent, afraid of intimacy. If the partners are mental health professionals, the labels may include DSM Axis I or Axis II diagnoses. If they don't experience their partners as bad or label them as emotionally disordered, they may make use of pop psychology language to describe their inadequacies: we can't communicate; I'm co-dependent; he's an enabler; and the like. Acceptance of unpleasant partner behaviors is especially difficult when they occur within the context of this kind of labeling: the partner is not just doing something that is upsetting, but he or she is doing it *because* he or she is bad, sick, or inadequate. Even if such behaviors were to be accepted within this context, an implicit hierarchy would be created: I accept you, despite your evil, sick, or inadequate tendencies; I am OK, but you are not.

To create acceptance through empathic joining, the therapist reformulates the problem and the partner's negative behavior within the context of the formulation. The negative behavior is seen as an example of common differences between people and the polarization process as part of a natural, understandable, and perhaps even inevitable emotional reaction to those differences. Of special importance in this reformulation is underscoring the pain that each experiences and the efforts, however unsuccessful, that each makes to alleviate the mutual pain. We have found this mantra helpful in this process: *Pain plus accusation equals marital discord; pain minus accusation equals acceptance.*

Initially, the therapist simply provides this reformulation during the feedback session. For example, in providing feedback to Cal and Tanya about their conventionality/ unconventionality theme, the therapist might say:

> A major problem that I see the two of you having comes from a difference between you in your desire for a conventional lifestyle. You, Cal, want a conventional family life, and in fact you chose Tanya in part because you thought she would be especially good at providing that for you. You, Tanya, want a less conventional, frequently changing, open lifestyle, and in fact you chose Cal because you thought that he would be well-suited to share that kind of life with you. This is a common difference between people, but it gets the two of you in trouble because of an unpleasant sequence of actions that gets set in motion when you try to deal with this difference. It starts, if you want to go back to the beginning, with the disappointment you felt when you discovered that the other person didn't want the kind of lifestyle that you thought you both wanted. In reaction to that disappointment, at some point, Tanya, you became less conventional and more defiant of family values, while you, Cal, become more conventional and a staunch defender of a socially conforming lifestyle. But it is not just an argument over lifestyle. Tanya, you respond to these differences by what we call "polarizing" or "emotionally escalating": getting depressed, trying

to kill yourself, drinking to excess, and becoming sexually involved with women. And Cal, you actually become more conventional, by investing money in the stock market, getting a degree in accounting, becoming monogamous, and buying suits. The more conventional you become, the more unconventional Tanya becomes. And Tanya, the more rebellious you get, the more your husband acts like one would expect of a conformist. Most recently, you have both escalated: you, Tanya, by becoming a psychiatric inpatient, and you, Cal, by becoming a Republican.

Couples will often agree with this formulation and reformulation when given in the feedback session, but this does not mean that they have achieved acceptance. Having taken this first step, they will need to experience the problem in a different context many times or talk to each other about the problem in a different way over and over before they move substantially toward greater acceptance of each other.

The Language of Acceptance

To promote acceptance, ICT therapists both talk about and guide couples in a different way of talking about problems. At the expressive level, this language of acceptance emphasizes one's own experience rather than what the other partner has done or said. Therapists encourage partners to talk about their own experiences rather than attempting to describe what the partner did or what they think the other feels or thinks. They may prompt partners with statements such as, "Cal, you are providing some interesting ideas about what Tanya may be feeling right before she starts drinking. Would you talk about what is going on with you?" Or the therapist might suggest to the client what is going on with him/her; for example, "Cal, I have no idea what your experience of all this is, but if it were me, I would be scared." (This emphasis on describing one's experience is consistent with the common therapeutic admonition to use "I statements" rather than "you statements." However, we are concerned more with content than with syntax, since syntax can obfuscate content as well as illuminate it. Many a focus on the other has been camouflaged with an "I statement," as in "I feel you are trying to control me.")

When clients talk about themselves, ICT therapists often encourage what we call "soft" disclosures rather than "hard" disclosures. Hard disclosures reveal the self in a stronger, more dominant position vis-à-vis the partner. They often involve expressions of anger and resentment that convey assertion, power, and control (e.g., "I will not let myself be taken advantage of" ; "I will get what I want"; " I won't be controlled"). Soft disclosures reveal the self as vulnerable to the partner. They reflect feelings of hurt, fear, and disappointment or convey doubt, uncertainty, and danger (e.g., "I wasn't sure she cared about me"; "I don't know if I could go it alone"; "I thought he would get upset"; "I wanted to please her"). Hard disclosures are sometimes easier to make because they don't reveal the self as vulnerable, but they are harder for the partner to hear because they imply blame and dominance over the partner. Because of their capacity to generate empathy, soft disclosures are often more likely to promote closeness.

ICT therapists assume that there are soft counterparts to most hard expressions. Hurt usually accompanies anger; disappointment often comes with resentment; fear and insecurity often breed assertion and aggression. When ICT therapists encourage self-disclosure, hard disclosures are most likely to occur first. These disclosures are important because they are accurate reflections of the speaker's experience. However, they are unlikely to produce acceptance unless they are accompanied by and framed in terms of soft disclosures. Cal will not be able to accept Tanya if he sees her as just angry at him for letting others' expectations control his life. However, he may be able to accept her if he sees her fear of "flipping out," her loneliness when she is alone with three young children, and her sadness over the letting go of fantasies that they shared during courtship. Tanya will not be able to accept Cal if she sees him as blaming all of their problems on her drinking, but she may be able to accept him if she sees his nagging as arising from a fear of losing her.

Since the goal of empathic joining is to "soften" the listener, whatever reformulation serves that purpose is appropriate. In ICT, we take a "functional" rather than a "formal" approach to softening. This distinction follows directly from the discussion of functional analyses. A functional approach means that we find whatever formulation promotes acceptance and use it, without assuming that there are universal "softeners."

Although, in general, angry expressions "harden" the listener, some partners soften in response to the other's expression of anger. For example, Alex had avoided any direct expression of feeling for years. Hilda softened toward him during a therapy session when he lost his temper, because at least some emotional expression was occurring. Anger, in other words, will not always be experienced as a hard emotion; it depends on the couple.

Similarly, the so-called soft emotions may not always have a softening impact. Some listeners may respond to expressions of hurt and sadness negatively, seeing such expressions as opportunities to regain or enhance their dominance. To take another example, some listeners soften in response to reformulations involving the family of origin;

behavior that has been thought of as malevolent may be accepted when it is viewed as an inevitable consequence of a traumatic family history. However, not all listeners soften in response to such insight into the childhood roots of their partner's negative behavior. They might say, "It's all well and good that he learned this from his mother, but I want him to get rid of it." In short, couples will respond idiosyncratically to particular reformulations; one that works for a particular couple will not necessarily work for the next.

We try to create a safe atmosphere in therapy where partners can reveal their vulnerabilities. However, these disclosures often do not come spontaneously. Therapists may need to suggest them to the client. When Cal discloses his anger and resolute determination not to be controlled by Tanya's drinking, the therapist might say, "I wonder, Cal, if this anger at Tanya and this determination to hold your own course come from a sense of almost being overwhelmed by her if you don't take a stand." Or, "It sounds like you want to take a strong stand with Tanya. You must fear that, if you don't, you will lose all control of your life."

Until now, we have been discussing the language of acceptance at the expressive level. What do listeners do? If listeners hear the therapist describe the speaker's pain without its accusatory component, or if they hear their partners focus on their own experience, then they may be freed from the demanding task of coming up with defenses, explanations, contrary examples, and counter-attacks. They may be able to listen and understand. Also, as they experience the therapist guiding them away from defenses and explanations, they may be further motivated to listen and understand when the partner is speaking rather than developing rebuttals.

The Pros and Cons of Three Major Tactics

Whenever therapists focus on promoting acceptance through empathic joining, they can choose among (a) trying to teach the couple communication skills in a formal sense; (b) prompting softer disclosures that actually end up being uttered by the client; or (c) simply using their own reformulations to produce acceptance. All three of these methods have costs and benefits. Let us briefly examine them.

Communication Skills Training. One method of producing empathic joining is the traditional skills training method, which teaches couples how to talk to each other like good client centered therapists. This technology was originally applied to couples by Guerney (1977), expanded by Gottman et al. (1976), and made a part of TBCT (Jacobson & Margolin, 1979). The part of communication skills training that focuses on teaching empathy through "active listening" and softening through the use of "I statements," "editing," and " leveling" is directly relevant to empathic joining. For some couples, the structured skills training approach to empathic joining works quite well. More often than not, however, couples have a very hard time engaging the skills in a way that leads to acceptance.

We think that there are two primary explanations for the modest effects of these skill training procedures in promoting acceptance. First, the skills taught in the standardized programs do not represent the ways people naturally talk to each other when they become upset. Whenever Jacobson gives a clinical workshop on ICT, he asks the audience how many of them use active listening when they get angry with their partners. Usually one or two of 200 members of the audience use these techniques in their own relationships. And these are therapists! How can we expect our clients to join empathically through active listening if we mental health professionals don't practice these techniques in our own relationships?

There are good reasons why people don't use "active listening" techniques in their relationships, even if they are mental health professionals. It is simply not natural to actively listen while angry at your partner. It is much more natural to be belligerent, contemptuous, and critical. Gottman's (1979) early interaction research found that even happy couples argue; unlike distressed couples, however, happy couples eventually stop arguing and resolve the conflict. Jacobson et al. (1987) found that couples who were taught CPT in TBCT rarely practiced it by the two-year follow-up; moreover, whether they did or not was uncorrelated with their level of marital satisfaction.

Second, standardized communication skills training programs, including ours, assume mistakenly that there are universal rules for what is good or bad communication in marriage. We are suspicious of all programs that are based on the "rights vs. wrongs" of communication. None of these so-called universal rules apply to all couples. Many partners become annoyed or irritated when their partners "actively listen." "I" statements can and often do leave the listener cold. Consistent with our functional analytic method, we search for the formulations that work for particular couples; those become the pathways to acceptance for that couple—but only for that couple. It is a brand-new ballgame with the next couple. Thus, while communication skills training has some role in our work, it is just one method, and not the most common one, for promoting acceptance through empathic joining.

Prompting Softer Responses from the Speaker. In an ideal world, we would be able to soften listeners by prompting speakers to soften their expressions. If the speaker were able to utter a softening expression, without the therapist's putting words in his/her mouth, the listener would be more likely to experience it as authentic, or so it would seem. However, there is a down side to leaving the softening to the client. The success of the prompt depends on the client's picking up on it and effectively translating the previous response into a softer one. If the speaker either doesn't understand what the therapist is getting at or is stuck in a "hardening" phase, the prompt could actually lead to an escalation of negative communication.

For example, suppose the therapist were to say, "I hear your volcanic rage. Can you tell us what else is going on? What other feelings are you experiencing?" The client might respond by saying, "Nothing else is going on. I want to torture him, humiliate him, tear his manuscript up into little pieces, tell his boss how small his penis is. Does that clarify things for you, doc?" Obviously, the intervention has backfired. When it works, i.e., the speaker responds to the prompt with a softening response, acceptance is often the outcome. But when it does not work and the speaker's response hardens rather than softens the listener, more harm than good has been done.

Leaving the Reformulation to the Therapist. Many individuals find it very difficult to describe their experience in a manner that softens the listener. For still others, the optimal softening statement has to be socially constructed by someone else, since there is nothing in the client's experience that, if properly expressed, would have a softening impact on the listener. Finally, there are people who have it in them to soften the listener but simply can't follow the drift of the therapist's prompts; in these instances, no matter how leading the prompt, the speaker doesn't get it, and the dialogue never goes anywhere.

For these reasons, we have found that it is not always desirable for partners to utter the softening statements themselves. As long as the therapist can effectively reformulate the speaker's behavior in a softening manner, acceptance can occur. When the therapist does the reformulating and the softening, there is no risk that a prompt will fall flat because the speaker says the wrong thing.

Granted, something has been lost when the therapist rather than the client attempts to soften the listener. The listener has more reason to question the authenticity of the reformulation than she or he would if it had come "spontaneously" from the mouth of the partner. How can the therapist be sure of what the speaker's experience is, asks the listener? Nevertheless, something has also been gained. Couples now have something that they did not have before, namely, the therapist's perspective, which becomes a part of their learning history and influences the impact that the problem has on them. Assuming that the therapist has a trusting relationship with both partners, and that the partners have a history of being reinforced for adopting the perspective of trusted authority figures, there is a high likelihood that the therapist's reformulation will be seen as credible.

Whether empathic joining is promoted via communication skills training, an utterance prompted by the therapist but stated by the client, or a reformulation from the therapist, the ramifications are manifold: couples recover from their arguments more quickly; they may debrief the problem in a nonblaming manner, even though the arguments continue; and perhaps most importantly, they may accept the inevitability of these conflicts.

Focus of Therapeutic Conversations

What are the topics of discussion through which therapists promote acceptance? For the most part, we focus on four types of conversations: general discussions of the basic differences between them and their resultant interaction patterns; discussions of an upcoming event that may trigger the problem; discussions of a recent negative incident where the problem occurred; and discussions of a recent positive event where they handled the problem better.

General discussion about the problem can come on the heels of a discussion of a relevant incident or may occur in the absence of any immediate incident. The clinical purposes of a general discussion are to promote a view of the problem as arising from differences between the two and to generate a more sympathetic context for partners' behavior in the face of those differences. Such a discussion may focus on the understandable reasons why partners are different, e.g., personal history, current environmental pressures, and gender-related differences. For example, Cal's family was extremely chaotic with an alcoholic father and an abusive mother. Tanya came from a poor family that pretended to have more money than it did and valued the appearance of being middle class above all else. These differences in family history might explain their different stances toward conventionality. Tanya had three young children and was feeling overwhelmed by the drudgery of being a conventional housewife, especially given her former successful career. In contrast, Cal, who was without direction when he met Tanya, was now on the path toward high career achievement. These differences might help explain their different yearnings regarding a conventional lifestyle. Also, their differences reflect common gender stereotypes: she is rebelling against hers, while he is embracing his.

We do not attempt extensive analysis of personal history, environmental pressures, or gender stereotypes with couples. Rather we use whatever information is readily available to underscore the differences between partners and frame those differences as coming about through common human experience.

During these general discussions, we also try to elucidate the sequence of polarizing interactions that occurs around the theme. We try to reformulate these painful interactions as resulting from understandable reactions and counterreactions of the partners to their differences. Tanya behaves unconventionally partly because she feels trapped in her gender role and partly in reaction to Cal's conventionality. Similarly, Cal is socially conforming in part because he values traditional lifestyles and in part because Tanya is so defiantly nonconforming.

However beneficial these general discussions of the problem might be, focusing on individual incidents is usually necessary to promote acceptance between partners. Looking at an upcoming, potentially problematic incident, therapist and couple can anticipate reactions, develop an understanding and acceptance of those reactions, and plan for recovery from the high-risk situation. For example, Cal and Tanya have to attend a Christmas party connected with Cal's business, but he is afraid that Tanya will get drunk. Tanya has promised not to get drunk but insists on having "a few drinks." This is part of a bigger issue: she is adamant about wanting a controlled drinking program rather than an abstinence-oriented treatment program, while he is equally adamant that only if she stays away from alcohol entirely can she avoid getting drunk. Even before discussing the party, he feels resentful in anticipation of her defiant response. Or Tanya may want to take a trip alone with Cal, leaving the children with a nanny, but she is concerned that Cal will say they cannot both be away from the children for more than a few hours. Already she may be angry about his anticipated response so that her opening comment may be negative. Discussion in therapy of these anticipated events can do much to promote acceptance, as well as allow for some resilience and debriefing afterwards.

Since couples can anticipate only a fraction of their problematic incidents in advance, therapists usually deal with recent incidents rather than upcoming ones. Therapists should seize upon any problem-related incident that went well. If Cal and Tanya were able to agree on how alcohol was going to be handled at the Christmas party, we would want to discuss this in therapy to understand how it happened. Perhaps Cal was especially accommodating to Tanya's insistence on monitoring her own alcohol intake. We may help them discover that his ease in accommodation came about in part because she depolarized a normally polarizing situation by, for example, acknowledging that it was not good to drink in front of the kids. His reaction—cutting her some slack with her drinking when she shows some social conformity—would be underscored in therapy not only for its obvious importance but also because it counteracts a secret fear of Tanya's—that the more concessions she makes, the more conventional and controlling he will become.

Discussions of positive events serve an additional function: they help couples prepare for the inevitability of slip-ups. There is no better time to deal with slip-ups than when things are going well. After the positive events have been thoroughly debriefed, we commonly ask, "What will happen if it does not go as well next time?" This often leads to tolerance interventions (described in Chapter 7) or further discussion of the problem. The question in and of itself communicates that slip-ups are inevitable and helps partners become more accepting of their inevitability. Without such preparation, they are likely to become demoralized when the inevitable slip-up occurs, or when they have their next bad week.

We often don't have the luxury as therapists of dealing with positive incidents, especially early in therapy. Therapists must be prepared to deal with many incidents that have gone badly and generated strong emotions in the couple. In order to promote acceptance, rather than merely replay a bad scene with its plethora of negative emotional expressions, therapists should focus on the initial stages of the incident, even pre-incident material, rather than the middle and closing stages of the incident. Once a negative incident is well underway, exchanges become increasingly aversive, with blaming and accusation running amok. However, in the beginning stages of an argument, each partner's actions may be more understandable and acceptable, at least when elucidated in therapy.

Consider an incident where Michael, a distancer, comes home late from work and Donna, a closeness seeker, greets him with an accusatory, "You don't care anything about me, do you?" Michael gets furious at this attack, especially since his delay was only due to an accident that tied up the freeway. They yell at each other briefly and then retreat into cold silence for the rest of the evening. During the discussion of this incident, the therapist would want to understand what was going on with Donna before Michael came home. Perhaps she became increasingly distressed at the distance between them and this incident of lateness only served as a trigger for the release of her distress. What she was really saying was, "I am unhappy about the distance between us. I fear it means that you don't care much about me. Your being late gives me an opportunity to say this." From Michael's side, he too is aware of the distance between them, but he has no chance to miss it because he is too worried about her reaction to it. To avoid an angry outburst, he tries to be home at agreed upon times. This day, despite leaving at the usual time, he is late. He is distressed by this, but tells himself it is not his fault and any complaint by her would be unjustified. What he might have been saying was, "Yes, we have not been close, but I have been trying to do what I can. I can't stand it when I try and you still criticize me." By focusing the couple on this early material, therapists not only promote acceptance but make it easier for the couple to return to normal after the incident, if they haven't done so already.

It may also be helpful, in debriefing a negative incident, to focus on the recovery process. Often couple's attempts to recover at home fail because the same polarization process that occurred the first time repeats itself. A discussion of these efforts, using softening reformulations, "active listening" exercises, or prompts designed to get partners to soften their remarks, can often promote empathy.

When couples are discussing negative incidents from the previous week, often the feelings that occurred at the time are elicited again in the therapy session. Since ICT puts an emphasis on immediate experience, therapists should shift their focus from the incident being discussed to the feelings that are occurring in the session *right now*. For example, one therapist said, "You seem to be really frustrated now, and out of that frustration you threatened to leave the room. Then he said, 'Go ahead!', because his feelings were hurt. So, you both had hurt feelings and frustration, but neither of you felt the other's pain because it got expressed as a threat or a dare."

Henry and Fran

Let us illustrate "empathic joining" with a transcript from a case treated by one of the therapists on our research project.

When Henry and Fran entered therapy, he complained about her temper, which, according to him, at times led to violence. She acknowledged having trouble controlling her temper but said that his lack of sexual desire was what set her off. Here is an example of an "empathic joining" intervention that produced acceptance by softening the listener, in this case, the husband:

Therapist: What do you mean push the other way?

Husband: I started digging in my heels and became even more opposed to what she was requesting. And it was very frustrating for me. It made me angry.

Wife: Because I told him he had to change, and every time he tries a little bit, he takes a step back and we're back to square one. So he keeps going back. So, basically, I told him that if it doesn't change I'm out of here.

Therapist: So, if he doesn't find a way to be interested in you by the time you get back from your trip you are going to separate.

Wife: Right, and I told him I love him and I still want to be with him but I can't take what's going on. I would rather be separated and I can deal with it.

Husband: And I feel the same way. The frustration, anger, and disappointment are not good for either of us and it's not good for the kids. The reality is that it can't continue this way. It has to move in one direction or the other. Either it has to get better permanently or it has to end permanently because neither of us can handle it in the middle.

Therapist: You had mentioned that you had seen him do some of the things you're asking for. Can you tell him what are some of the positives you saw him doing?

Here, the therapist is trying to help the wife focus on the husband's positive efforts, a standard BE intervention. However, the impact of the question is to send her into an angry frenzy.

Wife: You communicated to me the times when you wanted to make love. You said, "OK, we'll do something about it." And then you followed up on it and it was the way you said things so if I got ticked off at something you would try to calm me down. And there was warmth. And then it would stop [getting angrier]. There's a change and then, all of a sudden—maybe because things get hectic—you forget. It's not part of your routine. So I try to give you time to reconsider. Do you notice that I haven't been bugging you about the toilet seat being down, because you've been doing it on your own?

Husband: It's a matter of becoming a habit.

Wife: Right, but you've done it so often. You start it but don't continue. See with the toilet seat you continued.

Husband: Yeah, because there's nothing emotional about it and you don't get mad about it.

Wife: But I would remind you of it and we had arguments about it. So I stopped and you continued to put the lid down.

Husband: I guess what I'm saying is that the toilet seat is a mechanical deal, putting the seat down.

Wife: But it's still part of a routine. It should be the same thing with having sex with me. It's a routine. You deal with me more than you deal with that toilet seat.

Husband: But the toilet seat still has no explosive content. It's just you make it a habit. That's all it is.

Wife: Then how are you going to make a habit of dealing with me? If you have a routine, how are you going to put me into it?

Husband: Well, I can't do it myself and that's part of it.

Wife: But see, you know that you need a routine. Just like how you remember to put the toilet seat down. OK, whatever you need, do it. But you have to tell me how that's gonna work. You're the only one who knows.

Husband: Right, and I've told you that I'm afraid of you, that I'm shy sexually, and that it's hard.

Wife: Yes, I know, and then you start trying for a week and all of a sudden it stops. I've been trying to hold back. But you have to take the initiative. You have to do it because I don't know your routine.

Husband: But then something happens and I get angry at you.

Wife: Right, and it blows the whole thing. It's like you don't have the capacity to get back on track. You stop and that's it. Nothing pulls you back and say, "Oops, I need to get back on track." That's what pisses me off more than anything else.

By now, the wife is yelling at the husband. His voice is barely audible. Because of the previous history with this client, the therapist hypothesizes that a prompt will work better than a reformulation. The wife responds very effectively to the prompt, thus softening the husband.

Therapist: I can see now what this rage is like. And we know that there is this volcanic rage that comes out. What other feelings are you feeling inside? If you said, "I will try to look behind this rage?" what would you discover? Look within yourself and tune into any other feelings that might be there and try to tell him about those feelings.

Wife: Well, there's a sense of sadness.

Therapist: OK, tell him about the sadness. Try to really tune into it if you could, and try to tell him as close to your heart and as tuned in to that part of you that also feels sad.

Wife: I feel sad that we're always arguing. The other thing I feel is that you don't love me enough. I've worked hard in other relationships, too, but this is the first time that I've had to beg for someone to make love to me. And then I feel inadequate and think it's because I don't have a career. I feel all alone, like I'm in a box.

Interestingly, although the wife is clearly softer in her emotional expression following the therapist's prompt, her tone is a bit flat. It is really the next reformulation that produces the softening response on the part of the wife. The therapist asks the husband to paraphrase what he has heard. The husband paraphrases with a gentle, soft voice, indicating that he has been moved by her most recent remarks. When the wife hears his softening, she softens even more, and there is a profound experience of closeness between them.

Therapist: Can you [to the husband] tell her the feelings you've just heard that she's going through besides the anger? Just try to feed back to her what you've heard.
Husband: I hear her feeling like I'm not putting enough energy into her compared to past relationships. It feels like that. I'm either withholding or don't love you enough or whatever the motivation is the actions aren't there, and so that hurts. I hear that I'm essentially causing you to feel badly about yourself.
Wife: I think the other thing is that . . . [she begins to cry]
Therapist: Go ahead, whatever way you can get it out. Try to get it out.
Wife: [sobbing] I feel guilty because you're a good man and I should be happy and lucky that I have you because of the things you do and the things you put up with, and I feel that I'm asking too much, so maybe I should just be happy with what I have. And I do want to be with you.
Husband: [taking her hand] I don't think you're asking too much.

Although this experience of closeness is a turning point for many couples, for other couples it is just one incident of acceptance through empathic joining. In the worse case scenario, partners may revert to a blaming stance even in the same session. However, even in this scenario, with each incident of empathic joining, the acceptance process becomes more stable.

When doing acceptance work, the therapist often combines the type of empathic joining exemplified with family of origin discussions, as in the following example.

Sally and Fred: Conflict about Conflict

In Chapter 3, we used Sally and Fred to illustrate closeness-distance themes. Sally wanted to have another child, to have Fred be more committed to family activities, and to stop threatening to divorce her every time they got into an argument. Fred was uncertain about his commitment to the relationship and already felt that he was too enmeshed in family activities. Since he was particularly averse to the verbal arguments that occurred at a fairly high frequency, he wanted couple therapy to reduce the level of conflict. Sally was not concerned about the conflict per se, just about his lack of commitment to family. She felt that Fred had a conflict phobia. As might be expected, most of their arguments revolved around family involvement. Or at least that is how they began.

During the two-week period between their fourth and fifth therapy sessions, they had a particularly bad argument on a Sunday, which culminated in Fred's threatening divorce. The argument began when Sally suggested that the family (including Teresa, their four-year-old daughter) go on an outing. Fred didn't want to go, and although Sally got her way, he was grumpy. Sally became angry at Fred for being grumpy during the outing. Fred, upon realizing that Sally was angry, tried various means to make it up to her, but she remained angry. Then Fred became angry, and the ensuing argument led Fred to threaten divorce. When they arrived for the therapy session a few days later, Fred was somber, because he felt that divorce was inevitable, and Sally was irritated with Fred for making such a big deal out of what to her was a relatively trivial incident. Here is an example of an empathic joining intervention from that therapy session:

Wife: I would like him to do things that I would like to do cheerfully.
Therapist: And that is what made you angry on Sunday?
Wife: Actually, in my mind the anger was the least of it.
Therapist: OK, what was important to you about what happened on Sunday?
Wife: What was important to me about Sunday was that I was irritated about an issue that keeps coming up. It was like, "Here we go again." I was irritated about something we had done earlier in the day. It was something that causes trouble between us a lot. I was mad, and Fred decided that he was going to take Teresa to the beach . . .
Husband: As a way to do something positive with the rest of the day.
Wife: Anyway, I was mad. I wasn't going to be very good company and I wanted to stay home and cool off. It seemed to me that this

was a reasonable way to deal with the situation, better than coming along and being mad. He could go off and have a good time
with Teresa, and I would stay home and cool off. But Fred was
mad at me for being mad.

Husband: I was. That's an accurate statement.

Wife: So the length of time I was angry was exacerbated by his not
being willing to have me be mad at him. And then he felt like I
wasn't letting him be himself, in other words, be [laughs] grumpy,
or not wanting to do the things that I wanted to do.

Husband: Yes, she wouldn't drop it. I tried several times after I realized that she was upset to kind of make up for it. It's like one little
slip and, boom! I was nailed!

Wife: And it's true. He was nailed!

Husband: And you weren't going to let me off the hook.

Wife: No, this is a nail that's really big! It has a lot of historical . . .

Husband: Me going along with Sally and doing things that she wants
to do without being grumpy and negativistic.

It had become clear that Fred saw Sally's anger as voluntary, as
something that she was holding over him in order to punish him. The
therapist's goal was to reformulate Sally's anger so that Fred would
realize that, once she became angry, she couldn't just turn off her
feelings at will. If Fred began to see the anger as involuntary, he might
have more compassion for it and be more accepting of it. But it is also
noteworthy that Fred has begun to join with her in "unified detachment" (discussed in detail below). In his last remark he describes for
the therapist what it is that upsets Sally about his behavior, almost as
if it were someone else who is making her angry.

Therapist: So when Fred is grumpy, it sets you off, especially when it
comes to family activities. It makes you very upset. And once you
get angry about it you don't have complete control over when that
anger ends. You can't just say, "OK, now I'm not going to be angry
anymore" and have that anger end, and your feeling is that it's not
OK for you to have feelings that you can't help having. That's an
important piece of this. It feels to you like he's saying, "Enough!"
But you don't know how to turn off the anger. And then, when he
won't let you be angry, then you get even angrier because he
seems to be saying that you are not entitled to your feelings. You
shouldn't have those feelings.

Husband: Boy, that's a good portrayal of it, because I just want it to
end! OK, I made you mad. I'll say I'm sorry. I'll act differently. If
Sally would make some overture toward me at that time, I'd feel

OK about it, but in this case it was going to ruin the rest of the day.

Therapist: So, Sally, you feel trapped because you don't know what to do about being mad at him. You could pretend you weren't mad, but he would probably see right through that. Then, you find yourself getting angrier when you're not being entitled to be angry.

Wife: That's right.

Therapist: But Fred, from your point of view, her anger is an open wound, it hurts to have her angry at you, and you can't feel OK as long as you have her anger hanging over your head.

Husband: Yeah.

Therapist: So, you're trapped too because you don't know how to make it better, and when you can't make it better you end up getting angry yourself. But I can see that her anger is very oppressive to you. It's very hard for you to function as a family when you know that she's got this anger. And [to Sally] perhaps you think that it shouldn't bother him. But the fact is it's like an open wound, and it's very hard for him to act normally as long as that wound is open. So naturally you [to Fred] try to move in and close that wound, but since neither of you has control over Sally's anger the wound remains. What are you supposed to do? I assume that if you [to Sally] could turn off the anger switch at will, you would. This is that mutual trap again rearing it's ugly head. Now, you probably each understand the way you are trapped, but can you see how the other person is trapped too? Can you [Fred] see what the trap is for her and can you [Sally] see what the trap is for him?

Husband: Yeah, in fact I had an experience while you were talking, when you were saying what she must have been feeling, of experiencing it for the first time, what her dilemma was about, how it's not over until it's over for her. She can't make it go away.

Fred's statement was a major breakthrough. The therapist had reformulated Sally's anger as involuntary rather than purposely malevolent, and he softened immediately once he realized that she couldn't just turn it off at will. Having achieved this breakthrough, the therapist then used a different type of reformulation to try to make Sally more accepting of Fred's inability to tolerate her anger.

Wife: When Fred sees there is a conflict he tries to move very quickly to get out of it, because he's uncomfortable with conflict.

Therapist: Yes.

Wife: And then sometimes what he does makes things worse because he's trying to get out of it, sometimes by denying that anything happened.

Husband: Usually if I don't get out of it when I try. Then I get really angry. Because I'm dealing with somebody who'se being unreasonable and I say to myself, "Why won't she let me be human? Doesn't everyone make mistakes?"

Therapist: So Sally is a lot more tolerant of conflict than you are. She has a harder time understanding what it is that hurts about her being mad at you. And one of my questions, Fred, is what is the history of that for you? Is it just Sally that you don't want angry at you?

Husband: No, it's the world.

Therapist: So, where does that come from, do you think?

Husband: I don't know, but it probably comes from my upbringing because my mother was never angry. But when she was it was like she disowned you until who knows what got it to change. You weren't going to reason her out of it. I mean, she was just going to be angry with you until the episode passed. So it seemed like at all costs the mode in my family was, "Don't piss her off."

Wife: And still is.

Both through her nonverbal behavior and her remarks, Sally began to become involved in the discussion. She was starting to look and sound supportive. Thus, it appeared that the notion of Fred being a natural product of an environment that taught him anger was dangerous was softening her.

Husband: And still is. And frankly quite rarely do I piss her off.

Therapist: Yeah.

Husband: It comes pretty easily right now. But I don't piss her off usually. I think in the time you've [Sally] known me I've maybe confronted her about alcohol a couple of times . . .

Wife: I was thinking about what happened when she did get pissed off. Your mom and dad didn't fight, and then he was gone! He was out of there.

Husband: They were married for 20 years and had maybe a couple of fights. It wasn't their way to fight and I wasn't comfortable hanging around tension. And the other thing is that the only time I saw conflict when I was a kid it was pretty severe—some really out-of-control fights and then suddenly my dad was out of the house and they were getting a divorce. And the next time I saw my father he was gong crazy and doing all sorts of weird shit.

Therapist: Like what?

Husband: One time he tried to break into the house when I was younger and she had a gun to keep him from getting in. Anyway, they never had any conflict and then in divorce they were in total conflict.

Therapist: Yeah.

Husband: I did witness that one time, him coming into the house and me letting him in and him breaking every dish in the house while I kind of sat there numb.

Therapist: I'm trying to imagine what I would take out of a history like that. Certainly different from your [Sally's] history.

Wife: My mom and dad don't fight.

Husband: But it looks like war all the time.

Wife: No, it's guerrilla warfare. [All three laugh.]

Husband: But your father says nothing but critical things to anyone in his path.

Wife: That's true.

Therapist: But Sally, you somehow don't come out of your history thinking that conflict is dangerous.

Wife: No, because if you talk with my father you fight with him.

Husband: Yeah, you do.

Therapist: So you got used to it. And you have a hard time putting yourself in his position, but I can see that from his history, he came out with the equation that conflict is dangerous. First of all, you don't have much experience with it and then when it does occur, all hell breaks loose.

Husband: And my idea is that a woman is totally supportive all the time.

Wife: Until she nukes you! [All three laugh.]

Husband: Until you piss her off.

Therapist: So there are understandable reasons why the two of you have different levels of tolerance for conflict, but when you get mad at each other your differences collide and in those moments you don't have much sympathy for the ways in which you are trapped by your histories.

Wife: I also grew up in a large family and there were fights every day. I do have a higher tolerance, and I wish his was higher, but I have to admit that I have been thinking to myself, "I can understand this. So this is why we get into this stuff."

This experience was a breakthrough for Sally. Even though she would prefer that he not have a conflict phobia, she softened toward him during the course of this session once she saw his fear of conflict as a logical lesson that he had learned from his family. The mutual empathy that was apparent in the session generalized to the relationship at home. They had fewer fights, and when they did fight their recovery time was considerably quicker.

Another noteworthy aspect of this session was that they were engaging in "unified detachment" as they discussed what happens to them when they argue. Instead of having the argument in the session, they were talking about having the argument and about what happens when they argue. Let's take a closer look at unified detachment and what the therapist can do to facilitate it.

Unified Detachment

Whereas our first strategy counteracts blame and promotes acceptance by engendering empathy and compassion in each member for the other, our second strategy works for these same goals by promoting a detached, descriptive view of the problem. Rather than eliciting soft emotional expression, this approach engages partners in an intellectual analysis of the problem, or the therapist performs the analysis for them. The therapist engages the partners in a conversation about the sequence of conflict between them, about what "triggers" each other's reactions, and about the interconnection of specific incidents to each other and to their theme. In these discussions the therapist carefully avoids any evaluative analysis that might place blame or responsibility for change on one person. The emphasis is on a detached description of the problematic sequence. The problem is not a "you" or a "me" but an "it."

Humor and metaphor can be useful in promoting a detached analysis of problems, as long as it does not demean, embarrass, or show disrespect for either partner. Consider, for example, a couple, Georgia and Susan, who have a problem coordinating housework and child care. When Georgia is under pressure and feels that Susan hasn't been doing her share, she angrily takes control and orders Susan to do some chores. In response, Susan finds any excuse to get out of the situation, which of course angers Georgia further. If discussion of this problem were to lead to a humorous characterization of the sequence as the General Georgia and the Deserter Susan syndrome, the couple could use this label to see the problem and their own roles in it while maintaining some humorous distance from it. They might even use the label as a means of recovering from a conflict, such as by saying, "Deserter Susan and General Georgia just took over."

Like empathic joining, acceptance through unified detachment can be conducted at each of the four levels described above: a general discussion of the problem, discussion of an upcoming event that may trigger the problem, discussion of a recent positive event relevant to the problem, and discussion of a recent negative incident relevant to the problem. In fact, although we separate the two strategies for promoting acceptance because they have a different conceptual focus, in practice a therapist will often mix the two. With Fred and Sally, for example, although the therapist's interventions were designed to promote "empathic joining," the partners managed to discuss their conflict styles in a unified, detached manner.

Perhaps the two concepts that "unify" detachment interventions are: "description" and "continuity." If work on unified detachment is going well, couples should be increasingly able to experience their themes and prototypical destructive interactional sequences descriptively, with detachment and insight into the interconnectedness of various incidents. To promote continuity, therapists need to remind clients of what happened last week and draw connections between the formulation and incidents being discussed during the current session. Whenever possible, incidents should be related to the theme, and the polarization process. Couples should learn to critique their own enactments of recurring destructive patterns without blame and accusation.

It is important that one of two things happens during the course of therapy. Either the partners develop increased capacity to discuss their problems as an "it" that they share, a cross they have to bear, rather than as adversaries, or they at least change the way they talk about their problems after an argument is over. Over time, it becomes increasingly apparent that they use descriptive and detached rather than accusatory language; at the very least, they learn to talk to each other in a nonaccusatory way about the fact that they are using accusatory language.

We use a number of exercises from time to time in helping couples put the problem outside of themselves. Sometimes, we simply bring in a fourth chair and say, "Let's put the problem in the chair and talk about it. But whenever you refer to it, talk about it as an 'it' sitting in the chair."

Another task is to have the couple imagine that the therapist is present during their arguments at home. Perhaps a chair can be designated for the therapist. Often couples are better able to discuss the problem as an "it" in the therapist's office than when they are at home. Part of the reason is that they are talking, in part, to the therapist. We sometimes encourage couples to turn to the imaginary therapist in the chair at home to explain what's going on, because that is often easier than saying it directly to the partner. This task often gets them to talk about their desire to blame and accuse each other, rather than actually doing the blaming or accusing. The more people talk about their desire to make accusations rather than actually making them, the more acceptance is fostered.

One of the many ironies in acceptance work is that giving up on change strategies often facilitates change. As couples stop trying to solve the problem using their self-defeating strategies, the solution becomes straightforward. For example, when Gus and Jill stopped fighting over how Gus could change his priorities,and instead discussed the difficulty Gus had changing his priorities, they became closer and his priorities ultimately changed. If change occurs in the context of acceptance work, so much the better. But acceptance is far better than nothing. In fact, it is often sufficient. And yet, as the following vignette illustrates, unified detachment can pave the way for effective change interventions.

John and Mary: Don't Tell Me You Love Me; Make Yourself Useful

We discussed John and Mary in Chapter 3 under the theme of control/responsibility. Mary was energetic and controlling, while John was passive and resistant to control. Although these patterns were present from the time they met, as they got older the polarization process took its toll and they became caricatures of the persons they had been many years before. As John chose early retirement during a financial crisis, Mary started a business and worked around the clock to make it work. John functioned as her assistant, but if she could have fired him, she would have. The more frustrated she became with his passivity and forgetfulness, the more he accused her of overreacting. When he became desperate enough, he would fall back on "I love you." When she became desperate enough, she would fall back on "What good do those words do me? I need a partner. Make yourself useful."

During a two-week break between therapy sessions, John and Mary took a car trip. The day before the car trip Mary noticed that the brakes on their car weren't working. She mentioned this to John, who replied, "They're fine! They just take a few blocks to kick in." Mary was not satisfied with that response, and she assumed that he was going to ignore her concerns and put them both in danger rather than getting the brakes fixed. John said nothing to Mary, which led her to believe that he did not take her problems seriously. She often felt as if she were being humored, as if she were a hysterical female who needed to be patronized. In the meantime, John silently went and got the brakes fixed.

As they were driving to their destination the next morning, he mentioned in passing that he had tried the brakes himself and discovered that, indeed, they were not working. She blew up at him when she heard this, because if he had validated her concerns the day before by revealing this information she would not have felt so disqualified. She was furious at him for dismissing her concerns and not even revealing to her his discovery that they were, in fact, valid. He was confused by her anger. After all, he had gotten the brakes fixed. Wasn't that the important thing? Here is how the therapist handled the discussion of this incident.

Husband: The part that I have trouble with is when we were driving down the road and she talks to me about this situation, and as far as I was concerned it was already all taken care of. I went out and did what we needed to do to get the car fixed.

Therapist: You thought you'd solved it. You thought you responded to what she needed. She made it clear what she needed. You did it. You thought, "OK, it's fine now."

Here the therapist is simply describing his thought processes in descriptive, nonblaming language. She describes them as natural, understandable, and even inevitable.

Husband: Right.

Therapist: Do you understand why she was still upset even though you had the brakes fixed?

Husband: Well, I was mulling it through my mind. We had one car that was laid up and this is the other car. Now how are we going to deal with the cars? And I thought at this point, "We really didn't need to fix the other car because the brakes warm up after a little while and I can drive it."

Although the husband did not answer the therapist's question, he provided her with an opening for combining empathic joining with unified detachment. By his use of the term "mulling it over," he was implying that, even though he did not visibly respond to her concerns, he was taking them seriously. He was, according to his statement, "mulling" over the problem. This is exactly where this couple begins to polarize, when his passive behavior is viewed as nonresponsiveness. The therapist's goal is both to reformulate his apparent nonresponsiveness as quiet concern and to describe each of their reactions and counterreactions in neutral, nonblaming language emphasizing naturalness, inevitability, and reciprocal causality.

Therapist: OK, so you're mulling this over.
Husband: So the alternative is that we could get it fixed. But it was Saturday . . .
Therapist: It took you awhile to process all of that.
Husband: Yeah, but then I took care of it and took most of the day to do it.
Therapist: It seems as if you needed time to sort through a dilemma: "Here is the car situation. This one is even worse off. The other one's got this brake problem, but my experience is that it gets better as you drive it. What should we do?" You were mulling all of these facts over in your mind. It was a factual dilemma.

Using terms like "dilemma" and "factual," the therapist emphasizes, perhaps with some hyperbole, the activity underlying the observable passivity. She turns the brake problem into a complex information-processing task requiring a great deal of active problem-solving. As she does this, the wife is listening intently, gradually leaning forward, and becoming less angry at her husband.

Husband: And I was apprehensive about going out to get the brakes fixed because it was Saturday and I would have trouble finding a place. But I found one.
Therapist: So you were concerned that there wouldn't be a place to fix them.
Husband: I went to several places.
Therapist: So you were mulling all that over! You were thinking, "I don't even know if I can get the brakes fixed on a Saturday."
Husband: Yeah.
Therapist: So you were really processing a whole bunch of information inside yourself.
Husband: Yeah.
Therapist: You are kind of thinking the facts through of what can we do to solve this dilemma about the car. You're thinking, "Will it even be open?"
Husband: I even contemplated the possibility of a rental.

Now the husband is making his own contributions to the view that he was engaging in active, complex problem-solving. He is adding the consideration of a car rental as another possibility. Perhaps he is responding in part to the therapist's reformulation: it is probably re-inforcing for him to hear himself described as an active information-processor and problem-solver. That is certainly not how his wife de-scribes him.

Therapist: So you were thinking about a whole bunch of stuff over there. And you're [to Mary] clueless to this. You were thinking that he's just kind of ignoring the situation. This is your fear—that he's ignoring the situation.

Husband: The rental idea was kind of dubious.

Therapist: But you were very actively, busily in your brain trying to solve this problem. Right?

Husband: And decide which was the best solution since it was a Saturday.

Therapist: So you were busy trying to respond to her dilemma, which was, "This car is in bad shape." You heard that, obviously.

Wife: But he didn't believe it because he remembers when he drove it and it wasn't in such bad shape.

Therapist: Well, that was part of his factual analysis. You're right. He was incorporating his memory of last driving it.

Wife: "Oh, she's overreacting again."

Therapist: You [to Mary] felt that he saw you as overreacting, and became understandably irritated, and you [to John] saw her reaction, didn't understand it, and did indeed interpret it as overreacting.

Husband: But then when I went out to drive the car I realized that it really was bad.

Therapist: And that's the part that bothers her, but let's put that aside for a moment. It is really important that you hear her concern, which she thought you discounted.

Husband: I didn't discount it, but I was a little befuddled for a while.

Therapist: You were a little befuddled because you didn't understand why it bothered her so much because your memory of driving it wasn't so bad.

Husband: Yeah.

Therapist: OK, you didn't know until later when you drove it.

Husband: Well, that and the fact that I wasn't quite sure what we were going to be able to do.

Therapist: So you have two dilemmas now. You've got Mary's experi-ence of this car which seems different from yours. And you have to decide what to do about solving the problem: "It's a Saturday. I don't know if I can get the brakes fixed." So you are just process-ing all of this information, but what I think is important for Mary to hear is that there was a whole bunch of activity going on inside you that she didn't know was happening. You don't say a lot of things. But you're saying them now. You were not, as it appeared, ignoring the situation or her. You were processing it. It's just that you were doing it all inside yourself, so it was invisible. Make sense?

Husband: Now it does.

Therapist: OK, so Mary is over here, still anxious about the car, still wondering what's going to happen about it, feeling like she tried to express her concern to you: "I'm scared, concerned about driving this car." And she's looking over at you. She thinks her feelings don't matter to you.

Husband: I kind of figured that out a little bit, but I didn't know exactly what do with it.

Therapist: Exactly. You were actually trying to respond to her need. You heard it. You thought about it. You considered various options. But meanwhile, Mary is over here feeling ignored. She can't see all this activity going on in your head, so she thinks you really don't care. You are just ignoring her, her feelings aren't important, her safety isn't important. She doesn't feel respected, or special. What else, Mary?

Wife: Why isn't he listening to me? Why didn't he tell me that the brakes were as bad as I knew they were? Where do I stand? What am I to him?

Therapist: You are thinking of all of those things, feeling all of those feelings as you watch him and all of the activity inside of him is invisible to you. So you get even more upset. The more you see his inactivity, the more upset you get. Meanwhile, [to John] you're really not inactive. You're really a busy little bee!

At the very end of this excerpt, the therapist mixed in empathic joining with unified detachment as Mary's anger was reformulated as anxiety and fear. There are several additional aspects of this vignette that are noteworthy from an ICT perspective. First, the therapist is successful in making both partners' reactions and counterreactions seem natural, understandable, and even inevitable. Second, she detaches both of them from the interactional pattern and succeeds in getting both of them to look at it from a distance, together facing a common enemy. Third, she injects enough empathic joining into the interaction to reformulate John's ignoring as quiet support and Mary's strong emotional reaction as the inevitable outcome of being ignored, unloved, and not respected.

With John and Mary, it would not be enough to simply achieve acceptance. Mary needed John to become more of a partner. For that to happen, changes were necessary, which in this particular case came about primarily through BE later in therapy. But, from an ICT perspective, such change interventions are much more effective after intimacy-enhancing acceptance has been achieved.

Producing acceptance through empathic joining and unified detachment is not possible for all couples. Even for those couples who respond positively to such interventions, the promotion of tolerance is necessary for some problems, as we shall see in the next chapter.

7

EMOTIONAL ACCEPTANCE
THROUGH BUILDING
TOLERANCE

All organisms, including human beings, find it hard to accept pain. We are wired genetically to do all that is possible to prevent, avoid, or escape from pain. In marriage, part of what makes acceptance difficult is that the partner's behavior induces a great deal of pain. One way to increase acceptance is to increase each partner's tolerance for the other partner's behavior, which means making it less painful. But tolerance can occur only if partners stop their frantic efforts to prevent or avoid each other's behavior by trying to change the partner or escape from the behavior. If they experience the other's behavior without struggling to change it, and then additional contextual shifts occur to decrease the behavior's toxicity, the behavior may become more acceptable. The key to building tolerance is to enable partners to give up the struggle to change each other while inducing experiences in the therapy session that make it easier to "let go."

In this chapter and in other places throughout the book, we refer to the importance of creating contextual shifts during therapy sessions. By contextual shift, we mean a shift in the couple's collective and individual learning histories. At any point in time, spouses' responses to one another result from their individual genetic make-ups, their individual learning histories, and their collective learning history as a couple. These learning histories are not static, but always changing. The component of influence exerted by individual and collective learning histories is what we mean by context. All experiences add to, and change, that context. Certain types of new experience add to learning histories in such a way as to produce shifts. For example, when a mother tells a child that strangers are dangerous, and the child should therefore not talk to them, that warning influences the child long after the warning has been uttered. In the same way, certain experiences in therapy, orchestrated by the therapist, exert an influence on the couple long after the experience in the session, long after the remark by the therapist. When such experiences occur, we call them contextual shifts.

Tolerance training is analogous to an exposure procedure used by behavior therapists to treat anxiety disorders. The key to successful extinction of anxiety is nonreinforced exposure to the feared stimulus. During gradual exposure to whatever it is that scares the client, the therapist controls the context in which the stimulus is experienced. If done correctly, exposure occurs gradually enough that, at each stage of the process, fear or anxiety is extinguished. The end result is that the client can face the stimulus without fear. For example, clients with social phobias might be gradually exposed to socially provocative situations, until they reach the point where they no longer fear the social situations that had once sent them into a frenzy of panic. In the same way, when promoting tolerance the therapist tries hard to expose partners to conflict and each other's negative behavior in a safe environment, with the hope that the negative behavior can be tolerated, and therefore accepted more easily.

Tolerance-promoting techniques can be distinguished from both empathic joining and unified detachment in that the latter are designed to produce a more profound type of acceptance, where intimacy is enhanced *because* of the problem rather than in spite of it. With tolerance interventions, the goals are more modest. Even when a tolerance intervention is successful, intimacy is not necessarily enhanced. Rather, conflict is interrupted, its effects are less severe, or recovery from the conflict is quicker. In fact, even after tolerance is achieved, we would expect that clients would continue to find their partners' negative behavior unpleasant, but less so. Moreover, the consequences are less catastrophic after tolerance has been built. For some couples, and for virtually all couples when it comes to certain problems, increased intimacy will never be the outcome of negative behavior. Some problems will not strengthen relationships, even after ICT. However, tolerance interventions can still greatly enhance couples' ability to cope effectively with negative behavior, even in areas where intimacy-enhancing acceptance is not realistic.

There are four primary strategies for promoting tolerance: pointing out the positive features of negative behavior, practicing negative behavior in the therapy session, faking negative behavior between sessions, and self-care. Let us examine each of these strategies in detail.

Highlighting the Positive Features of Negative Behavior

ICT therapists point out to each partner the positive features of the other's negative behavior. If spouses see the benefits of negative behavior, they may be more able to tolerate it. This strategy is quite similar to that of "positive connotation" in family systems therapy. However, as used in ICT, pointing out positive features differs from positive connotation in two ways.

First, ICT continues to acknowledge the negative features while pointing out positive features. It does not attempt a wholesale reframing of problem behavior into positive behavior. We are skeptical about whether such a complete reframing is possible for couples. Furthermore, such a reframing ignores the reality of the current pain.

Second, ICT seeks positive features that are really there for the couple. It is less strategic than "positive connotation" because ICT is not after just any interpretation that might promote tolerance; the interpretation must reflect some reality for the couple. Jacobson once attended a workshop given by a group of strategic therapists. A taped example involved a small man with a high voice married to a large woman with a low voice. The size discrepancy between them was quite striking, and it drew laughter from the audience. The presenting problem was that the husband did not initiate sex. Here is how the therapist turned that problem into one with a positive connotation: "Don't you [to the wife] see why he doesn't initiate sex with you? He is so afraid of the seething cauldron of passion that would be unleashed, were he to give in to his sexual urges. He is afraid of annihilating you!" Then the camera panned the small husband with the high voice, and the audience burst into hysterics. Why? Because the "reframe" was incongruous. It had not a grain of truth to it. Interestingly, the workshop leaders provided no evidence that this intervention was successful. Our guess would be that such an intervention would be self-defeating.

We emphasize positive features of negative behavior that reflect actual experiences from the past or present relationship, rather than arbitrary strategic reformulations. This does not mean that our positive features are any more real in an absolute sense than purely strategic ones: all reformulations are socially constructed, and their absolute truth is not verifiable in the strictest sense. What is relevant is whether or not the positive features resonate with the couple.

For example, if ICT therapists understood Donna's criticisms as coming from her anger at Michael and her desire to hurt his feelings, they would *not* interpret her criticisms as her positive efforts to help Michael; instead, the therapist might suggest that the criticisms originate from her own deep hurt and her view, however incorrect, that the only way she can get through to him is through criticism. They might note to Michael that these criticisms are not a sign of his own failings but rather a clear indication of how bad Donna is feeling.

This ICT strategy of pointing out the positive in the negative is easiest when therapists can frame that negative behavior as part of a characteristic that originally attracted or now attracts the other. For example, assume that Donna's discussion of her attraction to Michael included information comparing him to other men. While other men pressured her for greater sexual intimacy and expressed their love for her as a means, she suspected, of getting her into bed, Michael was different. He never pushed her for greater sexual or emotional intimacy; in fact, she was the initiator sexually and emotionally, and thus could regulate both. When discussing the current problem of Michael's lack of sexual or emotional initiation, ICT therapists would want to discuss this difference between Michael and other men. For example, a therapist might say to Donna:

> Early on you appreciated Michael's respect for your boundaries and his willingness to let you determine the pace of intimacy. Now you wish he would take more initiative, and you feel bad when he doesn't. He may still be letting you set the pace, as long as it doesn't push him to where he is uncomfortable. This does give you some freedom to express intimacy as you wish and makes it unnecessary for you to put energy in setting up boundaries. But now you are mainly feeling the negative side of this, that you are more the giver than the receiver.

Even if spouses don't provide information that allows the ICT therapist to interpret negative behavior as partly positive, he or she can point to a common function of individual differences, that they create balance in the relationship so it can function more smoothly. For example, a therapist might say to Michael and Donna:

> I'm not surprised that you two got together, because both of you need what the other has. If you, Michael, had gotten together with someone like yourself, both of you would have been so distant that the relationship might have dissolved. On the other hand, Donna, if you had gotten together with someone like yourself, both of you would have been so relationship focused that it might have stunted your growth as individuals. So in this relationship, Donna, you see to it that intimacy is taken care of, while you, Michael, see to it that separateness is maintained.

Framing a couple's differences in terms of a positive balance may facilitate both acceptance and change. The balance suggests that what each gives is necessary for the relationship, while also implying that each needs to move in the direction of the other. For example, in a couple where the wife is very critical and the husband keeps his criticism to himself, the therapist might praise the wife for being so discriminating in her judgment and the husband for being so accepting of others. He or she would then indicate that each characteristic is important in a relationship: their problem is that these positive traits are too one-sided. Therefore, each needs to learn from the other's strength.

Patrick and Michelle: The Scientist and the Artist

Here is an example of the therapist pointing out positive features of negative behavior with Patrick and Michelle, the "artist-scientist" couple we met in Chapter 3.

Patrick was an engineer. He believed strongly in goal-setting, making plans, and living life according to those plans. Michelle believed in spontaneity and play as central forces in her pursuit of happiness. When Patrick would return home from a long professional trip, he had tasks that he wanted to accomplish, goals that he wanted to attain, and lists of unfinished business. Michelle missed Patrick when he was gone and hoped each time when he returned that they would have intimate time together, time to replenish the relationship with romance and passion.

In the following excerpt from one of their therapy sessions, Patrick and Michelle were practicing problem-solving training (see Chapter 9). The problem under discussion was a conflict they found themselves perpetually overwhelmed by: what should their priorities be when Patrick returned home from one of these long trips? They were brainstorming possible solutions to this problem, and during the process of brainstorming, they quickly became angry at one another. The problem, a prototype of their artist-scientist difference, afforded a perfect opportunity for the therapist to digress from a change strategy in order to promote acceptance.

Therapist: Now remember, when you brainstorm you say the first thing that comes to your mind, without censoring anything and without evaluating the merits of the suggestion. Who wants to go first?

Wife: I'll go first. I think I should get the car taken care of while Patrick is gone, so that he doesn't have to do it himself when he gets back.

Husband: I think we should have a meeting the first night when I get back to prioritize what we want to accomplish while I'm in town. For example, during this time we want to paint the rail, get the house ready to be shown (we're selling our house), and if we get those things done, then we'll have time for . . .

Wife: Wait a minute.

Husband: Those would be projects and the rest, say, on Tuesday and Thursday we want to go somewhere and that means we have to structure our time to make sure that tasks get accomplished and we can spend time together not worrying about the tasks.

Therapist: Let me ask you both a question. Is it true that there is a difference between you regarding the importance of getting tasks accomplished?

Here the therapist begins to deviate from the stance he would take during problem-solving training. By pointing to a "difference" between them, he is setting up a tolerance-oriented intervention. He made this decision based on the conflict that was developing, conflict that was centrally related to their formulation.

Wife: Definitely.

Therapist: And also that you [to Michelle] might value spending time together with no goal in particular more than he does?

Wife: Definitely.

Husband: I think our major problem is that we don't prioritize. In other words, right now we are trying to sell a house. How big a priority is getting out of the city of Seattle and getting to the suburbs? If that is a very high priority, then we need to define a goal, work together, and plan the tasks: whether they are farmed out or done ourselves. Now if that is the most important thing then we must weigh those tasks that have to be completed to achieve a goal. Many times she'll say, "Forget about that task. It's a nice day. Let's do something else." But this goal is still hanging out there and we're ignoring it. What is the most important thing we need to focus on today? Now if we have an understanding that every sunny day we are going to go enjoy ourselves, and that's more important than selling our house, that's fine. Now we've prioritized and having fun on a nice day comes first. But if selling the house is the most important thing, then we've got to remember that and make sure that we move forward and accomplish that goal. It's just like retirement. You've got to prioritize what you spend or you won't have any money left when it's time to retire.

Wife: I feel like I just heard a sermon.

Therapist: You have some difficulty with the concept of prioritizing, because it implies a restriction on one's freedom to act spontaneously.

Wife: Yeah, I don't like it.

Therapist: So if you were writing the script for how the two of you would spend your lives, you might say, "OK, selling our house is the top priority. We really want to sell it. But if there is a sunny day, I want to stop and enjoy it."

Wife: Yes.

Therapist: And that might be a difference between the two of you that's quite interesting.

By using the term "interesting," the therapist implies that it is not necessarily a problem, merely a difference. In fact, while the difference implies conflict, the word interesting suggests that it might have a positive component. Moreover, from the initial evaluation, the therapist knows that this "difference" was initially a source of attraction between the partners.

Therapist: Would it be fair to say that you're [to the husband] the kind of guy who is not going to let anything interfere with a goal until it is accomplished?

Husband: I wouldn't say anything but I . . .

Therapist: But you're more that way than she is.

Husband: Well, yeah.

Therapist: So, Patrick, you list your priorities and then you go about your business trying to accomplish them and you basically try not to let other things get in the way. Michelle, you have goals too, but you are more easily diverted, like if it's a nice day. You wish he were more like you, and you [to the husband] wish she were more like you. Given these differences, it is inevitable that the two of you will be in conflict at least from time to time. But it is also a difference that you could both enjoy. For example, having Patrick in your life allows you to push for spontaneity because he is going to make sure that things get done. And having Michelle in your life is a check against your becoming too regimented because if she has a say in the matter there is going to be some spontaneity in your lives. In some ways it is a good thing that you are not exactly alike on this.

Wife: Well, it's certainly not going to change.

Therapist: I agree. You've both been this way for 40 years. It doesn't have to destroy your marriage. While it is inconvenient at times, it can also be a boon. You [to the husband] might live longer because you've got her in your life to drag you out from underneath the car and take you to a picnic. That might be good for you in the long run. And Michelle, you might have some money left when you retire because of him.

Husband: That's one of the things I like about her, and I've always liked that about her. Drag me out from underneath the car. I'll do the car another day. But then let's put the "dragging" on our list of priorities.

Therapist: Unfortunately, her role is to ignore that list from time to time, and your role is to remind her of the list. You are the chief of the list police, and her job is to commit misdemeanors.

After this intervention, Patrick and Michelle returned to brainstorming with less conflict. They came to an agreement by the end of the session in a much more collaborative manner than might have been possible without the tolerance work.

Role-playing Negative Behavior During the Therapy Session

Role-playing or behavior rehearsal is a common strategy for change in traditional behavioral couple therapy (TBCT). Couples practice new communication skills in the session so that they can use them later outside the session. These skills focus on more constructive ways of communicating about each one's needs and desires and don't question the validity of the needs and desires themselves; in other words, the needs and desires themselves are implicitly "accepted" in these communication/problem-solving training (CPT) exercises. For example, Michael and Donna might practice constructive ways of signaling each other that they want time together or time apart. However, change efforts are not directed at Donna's needing less time together (which is what Michael may hope for) or at Michael's needing less time apart (which is what Donna may hope for). Thus, even in these traditional, change-oriented procedures, the therapist promotes acceptance of the couple's divergent needs and desires while trying to change the way they communicate about them.

ICT goes one step further. It promotes acceptance not only of partners' divergent needs but also of their old, ineffective ways of communicating these needs. The ICT therapist explains to spouses that no matter how effective they are at making changes, they will at times slip up and lapse into old patterns. It is essential that the partners be prepared for those slip-ups so that they won't misinterpret a lapse as an indicator that all of their efforts in therapy have been in vain.

With this rationale in place, the ICT therapist asks couples to re-hearse a slip-up in the session. For example, he or she might ask Mary to role-play a situation in which she criticizes John for forgetting to take care of a business responsibility. Or John might be asked to role-play a situation in which he attacks Mary for overreacting. During these role-play situations, the therapist actively reshapes the context in which the discussions occur. For example, he might help the part-ners discuss the feelings and thoughts that arise in them during the role-play, subjects that seldom receive attention when the argument is actually occurring at home. Or the therapist might encourage them to discuss the thoughts and feelings that might arise if this episode were to occur in real life. The therapist's goal is to elucidate the reactions of each, however strong, and to put them in a sympathetic context by showing how understandable they are. The therapist may highlight the dilemma that these reactions create.

For example, after role-playing a scene in which Mary attacks John for being irresponsible, the therapist might say,

> So it seems to me, Mary, that when John forgets to do something, you experience it as neglect. After all, he doesn't apologize, and this isn't the first time he has forgotten. So in this situation, it is hard for you not to attack John with a charge of not caring. It seems like he doesn't care. However, on your side, John, the attack feels so "out of the blue" and so unjustified. You have just been attending to your own business. You had good intentions, and in fact planned to take care of the task. You had just not gotten around to it yet. But now with this attack, your feelings are hurt too. You get defensive, and you don't want to talk about it.

The primary goal of this exercise is to expose couples to likely sce-narios without the destructive forces that usually lead to escalation. With the therapist's assistance, spouses express their feelings in these scenarios rather than acting them out: they have the conversation that they seldom, if ever, have outside the therapy session, the conver-sation that would have averted or minimized the argument had it oc-curred at home.

But the purpose of the therapist's interventions is to "bring out" material that changes the context in which future arguments occur, rather than to prevent the occurrence of such arguments. The distinc-tion between *preparing* for and *preventing* slip-ups is extremely important. The therapist is clearly not trying to prevent slip-ups: this would be an unrealistic goal. Moreover, the generation of therapeutic conversation between the partners, i.e., getting them to have the conversation that they didn't have at home (cf. Wile, 1981), is not expected to generalize to the home environment. Rather, the contextual shifts induced by the therapist's interventions are designed to promote tolerance when such arguments occur in the future, as they inevitably will. In short, the expectation is that couples will continue to slip up; therefore, if they can be prepared for these slip-ups their impact on the relationship will be less destructive.

In addition, the act of role-playing rather than spontaneously experiencing the conflict produces a shift in context. Future arguments that occur at home may change because of the exercise. Ideally, role-playing serves to desensitize couples to actual situations and enables them to face them with greater acceptance in the future. If spouses are not so sensitive and reactive to each other's negative behavior, then they can accept the occasional occurrence of that behavior.

Thus, the exercise serves a number of purposes simultaneously. First, it provides couples with the message that slip-ups are inevitable, so that if and when they occur they will be better tolerated. Second, it allows couples to directly prepare for slip-ups, so that they will recover from them more quickly. Third, practicing negative behavior can be likened to an exposure technique, with tolerance analogous to extinction.

For example, as the therapist inquires as to the thoughts and feelings that accompany these common negative interactions, he or she in effect "ritualizes" them; in other words, the therapist turns contingency-shaped interaction patterns into exchanges about which the spouses are now self-conscious. Furthermore, the labeling or ritualizing of these patterns results in the partners' learning things about each other's behavior that renders that behavior less toxic. Finally, there are times when the process of ritualizing a pattern that was once automatic produces one of the contextual shifts that we referred to above, and the negative behavior actually stops. If it stops, so much the better. But the goal is preparation for slip-ups, not prevention of them. In the following example, both change and tolerance occurred following a role-play in the session.

Randy and Ginger: Is It Me or My Money You Want?

Randy, a skilled laborer, often worked overtime because he was so concerned about the family having enough money. He insisted on a rigid budget and would lose his temper if Ginger exceeded the budget by even a few dollars. He also desired very frequent sex and felt hurt and rejected whenever he wanted sex and Ginger did not. Ginger loved Randy and felt guilty about her lower sex drive. However, she firmly insisted on her right to refuse, and Randy did not question that right. Ginger also acknowledged overspending her budget, but refused to discuss such issues with Randy when he lost his temper, because he used abusive language. When she refused to talk to him, Randy would get even angrier, and the argument would escalate. This pattern stopped during the course of ICT, and the cessation seemed tied to the following intervention.

Therapist: I want you to have your discussion about money as if you were having it at home. Don't try to do it better because I'm here. In fact, do it as badly as you ever do it. Be the lousiest communicators possible.

Wife: Can I do his part?

Husband: No.

Therapist: Do your own parts but let's see it as bad as it gets; in fact, you can even exaggerate it a bit.

Husband: OK, we can do that easy.

Therapist: This better be bad.

Wife: You [to the husband] had a problem with me going over budget by five dollars.

Husband: Well, you can't control your compulsive spending. And then you tell your family that I'm abusive, making it sound like I'm beating you or something. Can't you keep your mouth shut and your wallet closed? You're like a kid when it comes to money. Are you trying to send us to the poor house? Don't you care if your kids have enough money to eat? You're supposed to interrupt me now and change the subject.

Wife: I only went over budget by a few fucking dollars. For God's sake . . .

Husband: A few fucking dollars add up, when it happens every month.

Wife: You're nuts. It hasn't happened in six months.

Husband: Your memory is about as good now as it is when you forget to balance the checkbook.

Wife: You're just being paranoid. You think I spend money and don't tell you about it. Get some help.

Therapist: You two surely can do worse than this.

Husband: It might follow us out of here.

Wife: I'm not really mad at the moment, but that is what it sounds like. When we are tired we often create problems, especially you [to the husband] . . .

Therapist: Are we still doing lousy communicating?

Husband: She always gets the last blow, the last word.

Wife: "Like you always do" is one of my favorites.

Therapist: OK, are you both finished now? I'd like to go over it with you. When you were trying to be lousy communicators, what were you doing?

Wife: Talking and not listening. Being defensive.

Husband: Insulting her about her mouth. She's very sensitive about how much she talks.

Therapist: She called you "paranoid" and "nuts."

Husband: Yeah, those are about the rudest things you [to the wife] can come up with as far as I'm concerned.

Wife: It's a trigger for Randy. I'm questioning his mental health and he really goes off the deep end about it.

Therapist: OK, so one thing you were doing is questioning his mental health. What else?

Husband: I was just getting warmed up. I was trying to get in the mood. Mostly I was just doing what we do.

Wife: Accusing.

Husband: Yeah, accusing, I guess. Thank you, dear.

Therapist: What were you accusing her of?

Husband: Having a big mouth.

Therapist: Blabbing to everybody.

Husband: Sabotaging me with money and with gossip. Telling things out of context that make me look bad.

Therapist: Right, in a loud voice that everyone would hear.

Husband: Um-hum.

Therapist: OK, that was good. But what's it like when you are really in each other's faces, like when you're eye to eye and escalating?

Wife: I stop talking and Randy starts yelling.

Therapist: How would you [to the wife] do it? You would be quiet, but what does your face look like?

Wife: I sneer.

Therapist: OK, could you please just sneer the best you can? Can you [to the husband] rant just for a minute so I can see what your ranting looks like? First, you [to the wife] have to give him your best sneer. So look [to the husband] at her, because I won't be able to judge how good a sneer it is.

Wife: [Demonstrates sneer, combined with flipping her hand upward] All I've got to do is go, "Whatever." That means I don't care, I'm blowing you off.

Therapist: OK, so you have to wave your hand like, "OK, whatever."

Wife: It's an indication that I'm not going to listen anymore.

Husband: Yeah, "whatever" is a trigger.

Therapist: What does her hand movement mean?

Wife: That I'm shutting you out.

Husband: Yeah, that's it.

Therapist: "I flip you off."

Husband: That sort of thing, yes.

Wife: I won't deal with you when you're like that.

Husband: Yeah, I start cussing and the volume goes up. I look for about the meanest thing I can think of at the moment to say.

Therapist: OK, what's the meanest thing he's ever said to you?

Wife: Worthless and lazy are my least favorites.

Therapist: Would you [to the husband] mind doing those?

Husband: [reluctantly] OK.

Therapist: You [to the wife] have to get into your very best dismissive mode. Is that the right face?

Husband: She's getting close.

Wife: Yeah, I don't know if I can create it.

Therapist: So, it has to be provoked?

Wife: It develops naturally.

Therapist: What if he called you worthless and lazy first, would that help you get your face, or does the face come first?

Husband: The face comes first.

Wife: I don't know. I just shut off at some point. I go someplace else if it gets loud. The face means "You're not going to be dealt with unless we can talk about this calmly."

Therapist: OK, so you do the silent dismissal treatment. And so she goes silent. You [to the husband] go loud. How loud? Let's hear it. Could you just call her worthless and lazy as loud as you can? But first she has to give you the face. You [to the wife] have to do your best dismissal.

Husband: I don't particularly want to because I guess I'm ashamed. I wouldn't want anyone else to hear it. It's bad enough that Ginger has to hear it. When it happens, I wonder, "Did just one neighbor hear it? Or did the entire neighborhood hear it? Do the fishermen on the lake hear it? Are the windows open?" OK, here goes. You [to the wife] stupid lazy worthless excuse for a human being! What did you do this time? Where did all the money go? Where did it go? [To the therapist] That ain't loud but that's what I say.

Therapist: OK, but that's the worst of it, calling her names.

Husband: "Stupid" gets her going a whole lot more.

Wife: "Lazy" and "stupid" really get me.

Although the nonverbal body language is lost in a written transcript, during this segment the threesome alternated between playfulness and sheepish embarrassment. The therapist did everything she could to highlight the extreme versions of what happens when their arguments get nasty and to get each of them to provide context. The segment illustrates the ritualization process, which is accomplished through role-playing rather than having the argument occur naturally, facilitation of a contextual shift (getting them to have the conversation that they never have during the argument, but one that might have prevented the argument), and accentuation of tolerance-building emotions (e.g., his shame). All of these factors probably contributed to the interaction sequence stopping subsequent to this session.

Faked Incidents of Negative Behavior at Home

To further promote tolerance by desensitizing partners to negative behavior, we ask couples to fake instances of it at home. That is, partners are instructed to behave negatively at times when they would not otherwise be inclined to engage in such behavior. For example, John may purposely "forget" to accomplish a business-related task, even though he actually remembers that the task needs to be accomplished. Or Mary might react strongly to John's forgetting even though at the particular moment she is not angry at him.

ICT therapists ask couples to fake negative behavior rather than wait until it occurs naturally because a faked behavior is devoid of a negative emotional experience on the part of the faker. Although fakers may feign negative emotion as part of the negative behavior, internally they are calm. This inner tranquillity allows the faker to more clearly observe the partner's pain; it is also likely to prevent the incident from escalating. In fact, the faker is instructed by the therapist to reveal the fake soon after it is initiated to ensure that escalation will be prevented; the couple can then discuss their reactions to the incident.

The instructions to fake are given in front of the partner, so that the partner knows that some negative behavior in the future may be faked. This knowledge may interrupt the partner's stereotypical reactions to negative behavior. For example, if Donna attacks Michael as not caring when she really doesn't feel that way, she can see his upset and defensiveness more clearly, since she is not angry. She may be able to empathize with him. Furthermore, the instructions cast a shadow of doubt over her attacks, which may interrupt Michael's defensiveness.

The powerful aspect of this task is that it can work in so many different ways. By instructing one partner to behave negatively in the presence of the other, the potential recipient of the negative behavior is now going to wonder, every time the behavior occurs, whether this instance is the assignment or a "spontaneous" example of the problem. This aspect of the directive tends to ritualize the transaction and change its function. Lacking its former impact, the problem may go away.

The primary purpose of the task is to build tolerance in the partner who experiences the faked behavior. Generally, the "faking" task makes behavior that was once contingency-shaped rule-governed. Now it is occurring at least in part because the therapist assigned it, rather than as a response to natural events in the environment that "pull" for the behavior. Since rule-governed behavior is often formally as well as functionally distinct from contingency-shaped behavior, this shift in controlling variables can lead to a less emotional or negative response on the part of the recipient. To put it another way, the recipient of the "faked behavior" may respond with greater tolerance to all instances of the behavior, both because of the ambiguity in controlling variables and because the new rule changes the behavioral expression in a way that makes its occurrence more tolerable.

This assignment is similar to the technique of "prescribing the symptom" in strategic therapies. However, the primary goal in "faking" instructions is not to reduce the likelihood of the behavior through a paradoxical directive. If such reduction does occur, we are not displeased. However, our rationale for this assignment is greater desensitization and thus acceptance of inevitable negative behavior. Unlike strategic approaches, this rationale can be shared with the couple. Here is an example.

Michelle and Patrick Revisited: ICT as a Cure for Seasonal Affective Disorder?

By the time this session had occurred, Michelle and Patrick's therapy was winding down. They had come a long way in accepting their differences and making changes. For example, they had agreed to live in Seattle for no more than three years. If Michelle still found herself depressed during the Seattle winters (she had been diagnosed as having a seasonal affective disorder) after three years, Patrick agreed that they would relocate to San Francisco. They agreed to put some money each month into a "sun fund," which Michelle could use whenever she felt boxed in by the Seattle winters. She would take a vacation, and if Patrick could he would join her.

Through a combination of intimacy enhancing acceptance and tolerance interventions, they have also recognized that he will always be a scientist and she will always be an artist. During the current session, they are expressing a readiness to terminate. However, the therapist is concerned about a potentially destructive interaction pattern that he views as both inevitable and imminent. The rainy season is approaching (it is mid-October in Seattle). Michelle complains about the weather in Seattle during the rainy season. Patrick usually responds to her complaints by accusing Michelle of not trying hard enough to enjoy Seattle. This response leads to Michelle's becoming angry at Patrick and accusing him of defensiveness. She also blames him for having brought her to Seattle in the first place. Of course, this makes Patrick even more defensive. The therapist, wanting to prepare them for this inevitable transaction, proposes a homework assignment involving their "faking" negative aspects of this interaction cycle.

Therapist: OK, here's the scenario that I want us to talk about. The scenario is that when you [to the wife] feel blue about the weather, you make a remark that's not necessarily intended to be hostile or blaming. You make a remark about the weather.

Wife: Stating a fact.

Therapist: But also reflecting depression. And you [to the husband] notice that she's depressed. You feel guilty and responsible and then you make a defensive response.

Husband: [to the wife, jokingly] He knows how this works, doesn't he?

Therapist: If you look at that situation, both of your reactions are quite understandable. If you [to the wife] feel blue, you are going to make a comment about the weather and it's understandable why you would get angry at him for being defensive, because you weren't blaming him but he feels blamed anyway and so it's irritating to you that he reacts the way he does. Now in order to change that pattern it would require that you [the wife] recognize that you are feeling blue about the weather, moderate your response, and that you [the husband] recognize that she's not blaming you and not get defensive.

Husband: What if she is? [jokingly]

Wife: I never do.

Therapist: The point is that no matter how hard you work this chain is so automatic and happens so quickly that it's inevitably going to happen, at least occasionally. So, the question is, what can you do to minimize the harm that these exchanges do to the relationship? And Michelle, I would like you to try a little experiment over the next week. I would like to give you a task to do at home. At some point during the week when you don't feel badly about the weather, complain about it anyway. I want you to do this so that you can observe the impact that these complaints have on him at a time when you are not really feeling bad. It gives you a chance to look at his reaction when you are not emotionally involved in the discussion.

Wife: OK.

Therapist: I'm assuming that he's going to have the same defensive reaction he always does but you won't be upset and so you will be able to see his defensiveness. You may be more sympathetic to it because you are not upset. You may see the bind that he gets put in when you feel blue about the weather. Now, shortly after he begins his defensive response, I want you to say, "I was faking. It was the assignment." I don't want it to turn into an argument. And you [to the husband] won't know which behaviors are faked and which are real, so you may not respond as automatically as you usually do. But I'm trying to put Michelle in a situation where she can see your response, because it makes good sense to me, at a time when she's not upset and hopefully she will become more empathic with the bind that you are in during those situations. So, the purpose is not to get you [to the husband] to stop being defensive or to get you [to the wife] to stop making these remarks, but to help you [to the wife] become more sympathetic to him when he reacts the way he does, so you don't get mad at him when he gets defensive. So that's half the assignment. And the other half is something you [to the husband] do.

Thus, unlike symptom prescriptions, the goal of this assignment is to promote tolerance, and there is no investment in changing this pattern. However, the therapist is setting in motion a series of processes that make change possible. Now, whenever Michelle complains about the weather, Patrick is likely to wonder whether or not it is the assignment or not. This may alter his typically defensive response or, at the very least, promote greater tolerance in him for her complaints.

Husband: OK.

Therapist: So, does that make sense to you [to the wife]? Do you think you can pull it off?

Wife: I just don't understand why he can't just do active listening and all of that stuff when I complain. I understand that it's humanly impossible but it sure would simplify the situation.

Therapist: Well, I agree. Presumably, Patrick will try to actively listen, but no matter how good he gets at it he's not going to be successful 100% of the time. So I am trying to prepare you for those times when he is not successful.

Husband: I have gotten better.

Wife: That's true. You have.

Therapist: OK, now here's your [to the husband] assignment. At some point during the week, when you're not feeling defensive about the weather in Seattle, take a weather map and point out to her all of the places where the weather is worse than it is in Seattle.

Wife: He did that this morning.

Therapist: OK, but now do it at a time when you're not really feeling an impulse to defend our climate here in Seattle. Fake it. Do it because it is the assignment. And I want you to observe the impact on Michelle.

Husband: I did that this morning. I couldn't believe it. It was so warm on the west coast and in the Upper Great Lakes, 4–5 inches of snow! And I was just pointing out the extremes, and she got very cold.

Wife: [playfully] Oh, I did not.

Husband: But next time I'll remember to say I was faking.

Therapist: OK, so do you want to point out all the places in the world, or should we just go with the U.S.?

Husband: Let's just go with the U.S.

Interestingly, that winter, and the three winters since, have not produced a seasonal depression in Michelle. We have no direct evidence that this assignment was responsible, but we have asked in detail about this well-established interaction pattern, and it completely disappeared following this homework assignment. Incidentally, they were noncompliant with the assignment. She never did fake the weather-complaining, and he never did show her the map. So, in this example, the assignment apparently produced change as well as acceptance. Once again, if change occurs, so much the better.

Emotional Acceptance through Greater Self-care

It is not uncommon for partners to have difficulty accepting one another when they are feeling especially needy or vulnerable and, for whatever the reason, the partner is unable or unwilling to fulfill their needs or accommodate their vulnerabilities. One avenue toward greater acceptance is to increase each partner's self-reliance, so he or she can manage better when the partner doesn't come through. For example, if Michelle had contingency plans for ways to spend free time when Patrick was unavailable, she could accept his task orientation and goal-setting mentality more easily. Likewise, if Patrick weren't so dependent on Michelle's cooperation in the completion of tasks at the particular time he wants them completed, he could accept her spontaneity and perhaps even value it. Self-care activities are one way of building tolerance in such situations.

Alternative Means of Need Satisfaction

ICT therapists explore with partners alternative means for need satisfaction when the spouse is, for whatever reason, unable or unwilling to respond in a satisfactory fashion. This exploration must be done sensitively because alternative means are likely to be experienced as less than optimal. Yes, Sally could have a good time on weekends with just her daughter, or even with a friend joining them, but what she wants is greater participation from Fred, not time alone with her daughter. Also, the alternatives must be clearly labeled as something to explore only on those occasions when the partner is unable to satisfy needs; otherwise, they could be seen as a way to absolve the partner of responsibility for attending to the wishes and desires of other family members. For example, if Sally sees this exploration as a way of facilitating Fred's freedom on weekends so that he can spend more time on the boat or at the computer, she is bound to look askance at such exploration—and with good reason. However, if most of the attention in therapy is directed at building a closer relationship between Sally and Fred, the self-care techniques are likely to be received more favorably: within the context of a therapy focused on building greater closeness, a tactic that would help Sally take better care of herself when Fred is unavailable makes intuitive sense. Sally is likely to be more amenable to this exploration under such circumstances.

Because ICT therapists are seeking greater acceptance between partners, this intervention can be successful even when partners do not make use of the methods of need satisfaction discussed during therapy sessions. The discussion sensitizes partners to issues related to autonomy and personal responsibility, which form a core component of any intimate relationship. No partner, even in the best of relationships, is always available when he or she is needed. Personal life stresses, work demands, and even responsibilities to previous partners and children all have the potential to hinder the ability of even the most devoted partners to respond as expected in every situation where the partner's need is involved. For example, even if Sally does not plan more weekend outings with just the daughter or friends, this discussion could move her toward acceptance of Fred as having needs which, even in the best of times, might make it difficult for him to be the family man that she wishes he would be. Similarly, even if a self-care discussion never leads to Fred's using his own resources to deal with Sally's anger (e.g., self-talk, exercise, going for a drive), he may come out of the discussion recognizing that managing this anger is not solely her responsibility.

Self-care during Arguments, Polarization Processes, and Other Instances of Negative Behavior

Partners are particularly vulnerable to one another during enactments of their theme: the more trapped they feel, the more they polarize; the more central the issue about which they are arguing, the more they need self-care skills. When Sally accuses Fred of putting his own, selfish interests ahead of his family (something his mother also accused him of), he is challenged to the maximum, because he has to deal not only with her anger but also with a concern that he has had about himself all his life. He is bound to polarize the situation further, because the accusation is too provocative to produce "good communication skills." Of course, his efforts only lead to Sally's polarizing further, since her anger about his disengagement from family life has been part of an intense struggle that has lasted for years. Partners in the middle of such polarization processes need some means of protecting and caring for themselves. If we promote the idea that change efforts, however successful, will rarely eliminate all future occurrences of the problem, then we must prepare couples to face those incidents in ways that are self-protective and minimize escalation.

Common means of protecting and caring for oneself in the face of stress include leaving the situation, seeking solace from others, or acting assertively to alter the situation. For example, in the face of Sally's accusations, Fred could leave the scene of the interaction, call one of his friends for comfort, or tell Sally assertively that he will not sit and listen to attacks on his character.

The self-protective strategy needs to be chosen in part based on the effect it is likely to have on the partner, since the last thing the self-protector wants is further escalation. For example, Sally may react even more strongly if Fred leaves the situation or calls certain friends. ICT therapists help clients explore measures that will protect without further alienating the partner or contributing to further polarization. For some couples, a "time-out" will have dire consequences later, especially if it is unilateral. On the other hand, for couples where there is a high risk of domestic violence, time-outs are preferable. Assertive responses work very well with some couples but simply lead to further escalation with others. The same is true of seeking social support from outside the situation. The functional analysis is all-important when choosing self-care strategies.

Exploring self-care possibilities in the session can promote acceptance even if the strategies are never used. In fact, the discussion can promote tolerance even if the partners can't come up with any effective self-care methods. In particular, the discussion itself promotes two notions that may further acceptance: (1) Provocative behavior will occur at least on occasion even in the best of relationships, and people are better off if they can take care of themselves in these situations; and (2) the provocative behavior does not necessarily imply that the relationship has fallen apart.

Conclusion

In this chapter, we have described four clinical strategies for promoting tolerance: pointing out the positive features of negative behavior, role-playing negative behavior in the therapy session, faking negative behavior at home, and self-care. Although the idealism that is common among couple therapists pulls for techniques with loftier goals, such as empathic joining and unified detachment, tolerance techniques play a vital role in ICT. For many problems, and with many couples, learning to tolerate what was formerly intolerable is a major accomplishment in and of itself. If that is all the partners get from therapy, they will have benefited greatly.

As we have stated repeatedly, ICT has not thrown out the traditional behavior change techniques that formed the core of TBCT. We still use them frequently, and the next two chapters focus on the two primary categories: behavior exchange and communication/problem-solving training.

8

BEHAVIOR EXCHANGE STRATEGIES

Behavior exchange (BE) interventions attempt to instigate change at home directly through instructions. Technically, the instructions come from a variety of theoretical perspectives. For example, a paradoxical directive would be viewed as a behavior exchange intervention if its purpose were to change one or more behaviors in a way that might improve the balance of positive to negative behaviors. A solution-focused intervention, such as, "Pay attention to all of the good things that happen between the two of you between now and the time we meet again," would also qualify as behavior exchange. But the term itself and most of its applications derive from the early days of traditional behavioral couple therapy (TBCT).

The earliest applications of behavior exchange principles were contained in the work of Stuart (1969), Liberman (1970), Weiss, Hops, and Patterson (1973), and Jacobson and Margolin (1979). In Stuart's contingency contracting techniques, couples were taught to use token economy programs in the home. For example, in his initial paper Stuart described the treatment of four couples, where in each case the wife was complaining about insufficient amounts of conversation, and the husband was complaining about insufficient amounts of sex. Husbands earned points for engaging in conversation and these points could be redeemed for sexual favors.

Subsequent to this initial study, Weiss and colleagues (1974) made the distinction between "quid pro quo" and "good faith" contracts. The former was a tit-for-tat contract, such as described by Stuart; the latter was the type of contract where reinforcers and punishers were stipulated in the contract, but, unlike the quid pro quo, target problems were never used as the consequences for behavior change on the part of the other person. Although the pros and cons of these two types of contracts seemed quite important in the early 1970s, Jacob-

151

son (1978a) found that the choice was relatively arbitrary: the types of contracts did not predict outcome.

Moreover, the whole concept of contingency contracting, despite its apparent efficacy (Baucom, 1982), came under critical scrutiny in the late 1970s by behavior therapists (e.g., Jacobson, 1978a, 1978b; Jacobson & Margolin, 1979). Even Stuart himself, the originator of the contingency contract, makes little mention of it in his 1980 text. At this point, for reasons that are well documented in the literature already cited, we do not use contingency contracts; they have fallen into disfavor among other behavior therapists as well (cf. Baucom & Epstein, 1990, for an exception).

To the contingency contracts of the 1970s were added a variety of exchange techniques described by Jacobson and Margolin (1979), Stuart (1980), and Weiss, Hops, and Patterson (1973). All involved attempts to help couples more effectively modify problematic behavior in their own relationships. All relied on homework, and the tasks were only successful to the extent that couples complied with that homework. This included teaching couples how to monitor and reinforce positive behavior in the partner (Liberman et al., 1981; Weiss, Hops, & Patterson, 1973), strategies for contingency management, and various techniques and exercises for instigating increases in positive behavior.

The BE techniques commonly employed by behavior therapists are widely disseminated in the literature. For example, Chapter 6 in the Jacobson and Margolin (1979) book is entirely devoted to these intervention strategies. In Stuart's (1980) text, he discusses "caring days" in detail: this is a technique used early in therapy for helping couples devote time and attention to increased caring. Weiss, Hops, and Patterson (1973) propose a similar task, which they call "love days." Because these change techniques are so widely disseminated, we have chosen not to provide an exhaustive description of BE in this volume. Rather, we have organized our discussion of BE on a conceptual basis, so that the reader will be able to use BE principles creatively within the context of integrative couple therapy (ICT). Once the principles are understood and assimilated within an overall integrative framework, a plethora of intervention strategies is possible. We will discuss reinforcement erosion and how BE can be used as an antidote to such erosion. That discussion will be followed by a brief examination of how BE changes when it shifts from a TBCT regimen to an ICT regimen. Then we will provide a detailed example of a prototypical BE intervention, so that the reader has an opportunity to see how these principles operate. We will conclude this chapter with a discussion of homework compliance, providing the reader with an ICT "take" on the broader issue of homework.

Reinforcement Erosion

The term "reinforcement erosion" was originally defined by Jacobson and Margolin (1979). For our purposes in this chapter, it is important to note that reinforcement erosion is viewed as a natural rather than a pathological process. In all relationships, habituation occurs and, to some extent, behaviors that were once reinforcing become less so. Your partner's favorite jokes, which seemed so pithy, witty, and urbane during courtship, may have begun to sound boorish or obnoxious after you've heard them repeated time and time again. Sexual relationships are often, if not typically, at least somewhat affected by reinforcement erosion: no matter how many manuals one uses, no matter how much variety couples inject into their sexual relationship, and even if they take the extreme step of spending two weeks in St. Louis, the fact remains that part of eroticism is mystery and the body of the partner becomes a bit less mysterious with each episode.

In short, reinforcement erosion occurs to some degree in all relationships. However, some couples take steps to creatively overcome the problem of reinforcement erosion, whereas others believe that love means never having to say "reinforcement." Couples who have been married happily and intimately for a long time discover antidotes to reinforcement erosion without the aid of a therapist. Some discover ways to use variety, fantasy, and playfulness to spice up their sex life. Others figure out that, through continued development as individuals, they not only make their own lives more entertaining but also make themselves more interesting to their partners. "How was your day?" is the question whose absence distressed partners lament. But then, when the partner answers the question, the listener often expresses little interest. We believe that, when partners remain interesting to one another, natural contingencies ensure that interesting conversations will occur: in fact, one of the secrets to a successful relationship is to figure out how to stay interesting!

Still other couples develop new and common interests, avocations, hobbies, and vocations to enhance the quality of their interaction. Finally, although overcoming reinforcement erosion is not the typical reason people give for having children, the fact remains that children often serve that function. Though children have been reported to have a negative impact on marital satisfaction (e.g., Belsky, 1990), it is a small statistical effect with wide variability. Many couples' relationships improve following the birth of children, and the bond formed by the parenting experience can serve as a very effective buffer against reinforcement erosion.

Why all of this attention to reinforcement erosion in a chapter on BE? For two reasons: first, reinforcement erosion, or a couple's inability to counteract it, is often part of the presenting problem in couple therapy; second, BE can be a very effective antidote to reinforcement erosion.

Reinforcement Erosion as Presenting Problem

Rarely do couples enter therapy complaining of reinforcement erosion. In fact, neither of us can recall a single instance of people beginning their explanation of the problem by saying, "Doc, we're here because we've got a reinforcement erosion problem." However, in the process of evaluating the couple, we often become aware that reinforcement erosion is the diathesis that has rendered them susceptible to whatever life stress brought them into therapy. For example, Marla and Peter had a stable but only mildly satisfying marriage. Neither of them thought about their low marital satisfaction much until Marla was offered a job 3,000 miles away. Peter was against the idea of relocating. They began to argue over this issue and eventually entered therapy. This crisis forced them to confront the lack of excitement in their marriage, the lack of attention they had paid to it, and their vulnerability to separation given this attractive career option for Marla.

In contrast, a couple faced with the same dilemma—Jake and Glenda—had a marriage that was full of vitality. Although they had had periods of reinforcement erosion over a 20-year period, they had compensated for it in a variety of creative ways. It was a "given" that, whatever they decided about Glenda's job opportunity, they would be together, and they worked it out without therapy. Incidentally, she took the job, he moved with her, and to the best of our knowledge they lived happily ever after. Thus, reinforcement erosion can place couples at greater risk when life's trials and tribulations provide them with stiff challenges. With such couples, therapists would be remiss not to tackle the diathesis.

BE as an Antidote to Reinforcement Erosion

Although BE techniques are not typically thought of as skills training, they do have the important fringe benefit of teaching couples a method for overcoming reinforcement erosion. Typically, BE provides a number of implicit lessons to couples, which, if learned during therapy, counteract reinforcement erosion. First, BE techniques offer the insight that relationships do not sustain themselves without systematic effort. There is a rather common misconception in our culture that a good marriage should not require sustained effort. We would never expect our portfolios, our tennis games, or our children to grow and develop without attention and systematic effort. Yet somehow love is supposed to be self-sustaining. In reality, intimate relationships are like any other endeavor: they require nurturance in order to flourish. Second, BE techniques provide strategies for monitoring relationship quality on a day-to-day basis. Thus, if BE works, couples leave therapy with an increased capacity for assessing relationship quality, which is necessary but not sufficient for enhancing that quality. Third, BE techniques provide effective methods for couples to improve the quality of day-to-day interactions, which is the key to counteracting reinforcement erosion.

To summarize, BE kills two birds with one stone. It helps couples increase the positive/negative behavior ratio in their relationship, while at the same time providing them with a road map for navigating the troubled territory of reinforcement erosion.

BE as a Component of ICT

Like all of the change-oriented interventions that form the core of TBCT, BE serves an adjunctive rather than a primary role in ICT. BE requires a collaborative set in order to be successful. Couples typically do not enter therapy with a collaborative set. Thus, if one were to begin with BE, in the absence of a capacity for collaboration, compromise, and accommodation, this force-feeding of change would lead to rapid relapse for many couples (Jacobson, 1984). On the other hand, if BE follows acceptance work and the acceptance work has been successful, couples work collaboratively during the tasks and so they are more likely to be successful. The tasks are also more likely to be self-sustaining when they do work. Whereas in TBCT BE was often used in the beginning stages of therapy, in ICT BE occurs later, after acceptance work has run its course.

Moreover, when couples are noncompliant with BE homework tasks, or when the tasks are generating conflict, in ICT the therapist is always ready to move back into acceptance work as the default option. In TBCT, the therapist would occasionally be confrontational and even punitive in the wake of noncompliance. In ICT, even when the goal is change rather than acceptance, the therapist brings the acceptance stance to this work, and responds with compassion and sympathy—especially when clients do not do what they are supposed to do!

A Prototypical BE Task

Here is an example of a BE task that exemplifies the principles described above. We have chosen to describe it in detail because it is one
of our personal favorites, but we do not intend for it to be viewed as
the quintessential BE task. It is simply an example of what BE looks
like. Because we have found it to be one of the most successful BE
tasks, especially when it follows rather than precedes acceptance
work, we recommend that the reader experiment with it. But BE, perhaps as much as any tactic within ICT, depends on the idiosyncrasies
of particular couples and the ingenuity of the therapist in tailoring
tasks to those unique characteristics.

The First Assignment

The task begins with an assignment. Each partner is asked independently to generate a list of all behaviors that would, if done more or
less frequently, lead to greater marital satisfaction in the other. In
other words, the motto behind this assignment is, "Ask not what your
partner can do for you; ask what you can do for your partner." The
husband generates what might be considered his wife's wish list,
without any input from her. His list is his best guess as to all of the
behaviors in his repertoire that have the potential to make her happier
on a day-to-day basis; and his job is to generate this list independently,
without consulting her about it or telling her what is on the list. He is
also asked to refrain from putting this hypothesized wish list into
practice. We don't want him to be inhibited in the generation of items
by the concern that he might be asked to do some of these things. She
will find out what is on his list in due time; in fact, he is asked to
bring the list to the next session. Meanwhile, the wife is asked to
generate her best guess of his wish list.

  Admittedly, there is something counter-intuitive about this assignment; it seems backwards compared to traditional BE tasks. Traditionally, partners are asked to generate lists of what they want from
the other, not what they think the other wants from them. But if the
assignment is given at a time when the partners have adopted a collaborative set—usually after some acceptance work—they are able to
focus on themselves and their own role in determining how successful the relationship is. Although this assignment is only the first step
in the task, it sends a message: both of them have the power to unilaterally affect the quality of the relationship. Instead of perceiving
themselves as innocent victims of the other person's oppression and
passively expecting the other to change, they begin to develop a

broader perspective, one that shifts their focus to their own role in making the relationship what it is.

The Following Therapy Session

If the partners have complied with the initial assignment, then when they come to their next therapy session they have each compiled, but not shared with each other, appropriate wish lists. The primary purpose of the therapy session is for the therapist to talk with one partner, and then the other, to clarify items on their lists and make sure that the lists are comprehensive. Importantly, during this dialogue the potential recipient of the behaviors on these lists is silent: no input at all is allowed! We go so far as to disallow body language, since partners have clever ways of editorializing, by rolling their eyes, shifting in their seats, and sighing. If these behaviors occur despite our admonitions, we take it as a sign that the assignment itself is premature—the couple is insufficiently collaborative and requires more acceptance work.

Why we are so adamant about silencing the potential recipient at this stage will soon become clear. For now, simply consider it as an opportunity for the giver to devote full attention to the potential recipient's needs, without the recipient having to ask for anything. It may be the first time in the couple's history that the recipient has received this kind of unilateral attention from the partner.

The therapist works with each partner, one at a time, while the other simply listens. He or she asks the potential giver to read items from the list, so that he or she can be sure that they are adequately operationalized. For example, one husband wrote that, "She would like it if I were to become more romantic." The therapist wanted to know what that meant: did she want more affection outside the bedroom, more touching and hand-holding while watching TV, more flowers, all of the above, or none of the above? Whatever the outcome of this discussion, the end result is that the item is stated in terms that are observable to the senses, so that it can be objectively determined when it occurs and when it does not. This procedure is repeated with each item on the list. While the therapist is talking to the husband, the wife is simply listening, and while the therapist is talking to the wife about her list, the husband is simply listening.

During the dialogue the therapist also makes sure that each person's list is as comprehensive as possible. Since the recipient is not providing input into the giver's list, the therapist is the only source of feedback regarding the extent to which the giver has included most of the major items from the other's wish list. For example, when Sally and Fred were first given this assignment, Fred came back with a list that did not include any items referring to Sally's wish that Fred be more involved in family activities on weekends. Since the therapist knew that this was a major concern of Sally's, he said, "It seems to me that Sally said something about wanting you to be more of a participant in family activities. Can you think of anything you might do in that area that would make her happier?" Fred responded, "Well, of course, I could initiate more family activities of my own on weekends." The therapist said, "Well then, why don't you add that to the list?" It is important to remember that the therapist is not asking them to *do* any of these things, simply to speculate on what the other wants. The task we are describing now ensures that the list will be as comprehensive as possible without violating our ban on input from the recipient.

By the time the session is over each partner should be armed with a comprehensive list of hypothesized pleasing and displeasing behaviors for the other. Once each partner has successfully developed this list, with the help of the therapist, but without input from the recipient, the couple is ready for the next homework task.

The Next Task

At the conclusion of the session, the therapist presents the couple with the following task, to be undertaken between now and the next session:

> I would like each of you to use your lists to enhance your partner's relationship satisfaction between now and the next session. Specifically, each of you is to go through your lists, pick one or more items that you choose to increase or decrease, and observe the effects of these changes in your behavior on the other's marital satisfaction. So, you [to the wife] pick some items from your list. Don't tell him what items you have chosen. Just implement them, and see what happens. Your goal is to increase his happiness this week. But don't tell him what you are doing or why you are doing it. And you [to the husband] are simultaneously doing the exact same thing with your list. Decide today or tomorrow which items you're going to work on; don't tell her what they are—just do them and see how they work.
>
> Now listen carefully. At no time between now and the next session should you discuss these lists in any way or discuss the assignment. Neither of you is under any obligation to choose any particular item from the list. I don't care what you do, as long as you do something. And most importantly, don't choose any item that will be difficult for you to do. Keep it simple and low cost. That's it.

> Then next week, bring the lists back to the session and we will discuss how things went. Questions? Now let's go over the assignment."

The assignment is handed to the partners in writing, as are most tasks to be conducted between sessions. This assignment to increase the partner's marital satisfaction is the first aspect of the BE task that is explicitly designed to increase the ratio of positive to negative behavior. In the 1970s, when we relied primarily on requests from the recipient rather than suggesting gifts from the giver, we had much less success with BE than we now do. This could be because of the acceptance work that usually precedes it. But we think that its success also has to do with the focus on giving during the early stages of BE. Let us take a close look at the perspective both the giver and recipient are forced to take in implementing this task. We think that it is this perspective-taking that accounts for the often dramatic effect of this assignment.

First, the giver is more likely to comply with the task instructions than with requests for specific behavior changes coming from the recipient. For one thing, there are no requests from the recipient. In fact, the recipient hasn't had any input at all in the generation of the lists. Thus, in a very real sense the giver has chosen the items and also chooses which items to accelerate and decelerate. These choices are made from a wide range of options, thus providing the giver with numerous paths by which to comply with the task. The general nature of the directive, experience of "freedom of choice," and the fact that the requests did not come directly from the recipient conspire to ease the burden on the giver and thus increase the likelihood of both compliance and success.

More importantly, the lack of input from the recipient actually increases the likelihood that the behaviors that are chosen will be well received by the recipient. In other words, to the extent that the giver appears to be choosing the positive behaviors without coercion from either the partner or the therapist, their effects are more likely to be reinforcing.

There are many bodies of literature that we could cite in support of this hypothesis, ranging from attribution theory to the overjustification phenomenon in children (cf. Jacobson & Holtzworth-Munroe, 1986): it is generally true that people experience behaviors from another as more pleasurable when the giver appears to give freely, spontaneously, or because he or she wants to rather than has to. Given the way this BE task has been set up and structured, the recipient is likely to credit the partner with the kind of free choice, spontaneity, and desire that is needed for the behavior to have its maximum reinforcing impact.

When assigning this task, we take care to caution couples against attempting items from their lists that would be self-defeating because they are of such high cost. Giving high cost items might make the partner happier, but it would be unpleasant for the giver and therefore self-defeating. Suppose, for example, an item on the wife's list is, "He would like it if I initiated sex more often." If the wife is currently lacking in sexual desire, her sexual initiations might indeed increase her husband's marital satisfaction, but these would be unpleasant experiences for her, and thus detract from her own marital satisfaction. Couples should focus on only those items from their lists that can be enacted without detracting from their own marital satisfaction.

Of course, there is a down side to this particular method of constructing a BE task. Because the recipient has up until now provided no input, the giver may choose behaviors that are ineffectual or even detract from the recipient's marital satisfaction, despite the best of intentions. This risk is a real one. Givers sometimes do choose the "wrong" behaviors, with negative results. However, as we explain below, couples can be rescued from this eventuality, and no irretrievable harm is done. In fact, at times, even if the wrong behaviors are chosen, the impact on the recipient is reinforcing because of the giver's obvious effort. The effort to please may be more important to some partners than the ability to immediately access the keys to their heart. In any case, we believe that the risk is worth taking, because when the right behaviors are chosen the impact tends to be extremely positive.

The Inquiry Following Partners' Initial Attempts to Increase Marital Satisfaction

Whether or not this assignment has worked is usually obvious as soon as the couple steps into your office. When a good faith effort has been made, even if only partially successful, the spouses are lighter, more playful and immediately start telling you anecdotes about the week. Generally, this assignment either "takes off" or it fails completely. Let us examine how to proceed during the subsequent session under each eventuality.

If the assignment was successful and marital satisfaction was enhanced, the therapist should begin by helping them describe: which items from the list were attempted; of those attempted, which ones were noticed by the recipient; and of those that were noticed, which ones contributed to the increased marital satisfaction. Thus, for the first time, the recipient is asked to provide input on the giver's behavior. Hearing which behaviors contributed to the enhanced satisfaction, the giver finally has some indication from the person who presumably knows best which behaviors are likely to maintain the enhanced relationship satisfaction experienced since the previous session.

We also want to know how "costly" it was for the giver to provide particular positives or decrease particular negatives. At times, partners are able to muster up considerable energy for a week and create a honeymoon effect; when asked, they acknowledge that they do not envision themselves performing at this level on a regular basis. If the experience is a honeymoon effect, or if particular behaviors were performed once, never or seldom to occur again, it is important for the recipient to know that. At other times, providing positives that, in the abstract, seem costly to the giver turn out, in fact, to be easy. Fred, for example, actually enjoyed initiating family activities on Sundays, even though he had thought that he would experience it as an incredible burden. When asked about it in the subsequent session, he told Sally that she could count on his continuing to initiate at least every other week. When behaviors that sound burdensome turn out to be relatively effortless, the positive changes that result can be fairly dramatic.

After the inquiry about what worked and what did not, the next step is to allow for systematic input from the recipient. First we ask the recipient to comment on each item from the giver's list. The recipient designates each item as either a "keeper," a "minor but still pleasing" behavior, or one that is "off the mark." Armed with this input, the giver now has more information that can be used to make the task work even better when it is reassigned for the following week. None of this input is to be interpreted as a prescription for what the giver "should" do. Rather, it is simply information to help the giver in making decisions about how to inject quality into the relationship on subsequent weeks.

Finally, during this session the recipient has an opportunity to suggest items that the giver should add to his/her list. Once again, these items are not requests for increases in specific behaviors, simply missing items that, according to the recipient, would be useful additions to the list. The giver dutifully adds the items, without incurring any obligation to perform any particular one. The input is added to provide the giver with more information, in order to increase the likelihood that successful items will be chosen in subsequent weeks. The homework assignment from the previous week is reassigned, with a higher likelihood of success: even though no specific directives are delivered for changing particular behaviors, now each partner has more accurate information about what the other finds pleasing.

What if the assignment did not work? As it turns out, there are only a few potential explanations for why a task like this would fail. One possibility is that one or both of them did not comply with the task. If the failure to comply was not due to a mistake made by the therapist (discussed later in the chapter), noncompliance probably means that it was a mistake to assign the task in the first place. We would immediately revert to our omnipresent default option, acceptance work. In fact, this BE task can be thought of as a probe, to see whether or not the previous acceptance work has created sufficient collaboration for the self-focus required by this series of interventions.

A second possible reason for failure is that the wrong behaviors were chosen. Each partner tried some behaviors from the list, but marital satisfaction did not change. This problem can be solved by getting input from the recipient about which behaviors would have worked better. Once the task is reassigned following this input, the outcome should be better.

At times, the task falls flat because the couple does not really have a problem with reinforcement erosion. They may have two or three major issues that they brought with them into therapy, but on a day-to-day basis they get along quite well. Nevertheless, it is not always apparent whether or not a BE task such as this will be helpful until it is attempted. There are other instances where reinforcement erosion is a problem, but the major problems are so prominent that until those are dealt with nothing that happens on a day-to-day basis will make much difference.

In any case, assuming compliance, we typically give a task like this two sessions in which to work. The first assignment typically involves unilateral efforts on the part of both partners, without input from the recipient, while the second typically adds such input. Generally, a task like this will work quickly or not at all. There is no need to dwell on any task that is not working. Since BE is a generic category of techniques rather than one in particular, one failure doesn't mean that behavior change strategies should be abandoned. However, if the tasks are creating conflict or relapses are occurring between sessions, that usually indicates that a return to an acceptance mode is necessary.

Homework and Homework Compliance

If resistance is a characteristic of therapists rather than of clients, then homework compliance is the most mistakenly viewed sign of resistance in the psychotherapy literature. In ICT, noncompliance means that either (a) the therapist gave the wrong assignment or (b) the assignment was not delivered properly. We have encountered therapists who are quick to make interpretations like "the couple really doesn't want to change" or "they are just going through the motions so that they can say they tried before getting a divorce." In fact, therapists often sound suspicious of, rather than sympathetic to, their clients around the issue of between-session tasks. Clients are accused of sabotage when there are often much more plausible explanations. Unfortunately, these more plausible explanations often have to do with mistakes made by the therapist, and so it is easier to blame the noncompliance on sabotage or resistance.

We can be confident that noncompliance means that the couple was not ready for the task if they remembered what they were supposed to do, they understood the instructions, the rationale was explained to them, they were involved in the planning of the assignment, and the obstacles to compliance were overcome in the discussion of how the assignment would be completed—but they still did not do it. Unfortunately, tasks are often assigned to clients without an adequate rationale, without a clear explanation, without involvement from the couple, and without any brainstorming with the couple about obstacles to compliance. There are basic skills involved in compliance induction, but they are often not used by therapists when such tasks are delivered. To put these skills in perspective, the reader may recall the once popular notion of a schizophrenogenic mother, seldom discussed nowadays. For those readers old enough to remember this historical theory, the idea was that there are certain things that mothers do that produce schizophrenia in their offspring. This notion was associated with the double-bind theory of schizophrenia (Bateson, Jackson, Haley, & Weakland, 1956), and has been discredited.

However, we have discovered a phenomenon related to the schizophrenogenic mother that we are convinced is real—the noncompliantogenic therapist. The noncompliantogenic therapist is one who gives tasks to couples in ways that practically ensure that they will not be completed. For example, we occasionally use the Spouse Observation Checklist (SOC; Wills, Weiss, & Patterson, 1974) as an assessment instrument, and find it quite useful as an aid to BE. The SOC, in its original form, had 409 items in it, the items consisting of every conceivable thing that could happen in a marital relationship. The 409 items were divided into subgroups: Companionship, Affection, Sex, Consideration, Communication, Activities with others, Children, Finances, Employment/Education, Personal habits and Independence. All items were either "We," as in, "We went out for dinner," or "Spouse," as in "Spouse hugged me." The way we used the SOC, the task involved three components. First, each partner was asked to give a daily marital satisfaction rating (DSR), ranging from 1–9, where "9" indicated pure and utter ecstasy, "1" indicated pure and utter misery, and "5" was neutral. Second, each partner was to peruse the Checklist once per day at a designated time and indicate which of the 409 items had been implemented within the past 24 hours. Third, for those items that had occurred, a rating of "positive," "negative," or "neutral" was included to indicate the impact of the item on the recipient. Thus, at the end of each day, the therapist had a record of the frequency of positive, negative, and neutral behaviors, along with a DSR. Typically, we would have a couple complete this checklist each night for two weeks prior to therapy and for the last two weeks prior to termination.

The SOC provides the therapist with a great deal of information. First, it is the only existing assessment instrument that actually provides a day-by-day account of positive and negative behaviors as experienced by each partner. When a therapist inquires about the previous week or two, a great deal of information will be lost or distorted simply due to memory decay. Even with the SOC and daily recording of partner behavior, there is memory decay (Christensen & Nies, 1980; Jacobson & Moore, 1981). For example, there is one item on the SOC that states "We took a shower together." One would think that showering with a partner within the past 24 hours is something that would produce almost perfect inter-spouse agreement. However, partners agreed on that item only 70% of the time. "We had sexual intercourse" led to only 60% agreement, perhaps because the item fails to specify with whom. Imagine how much disagreement there must be in a week's time if there is so much disagreement even within a 24-hour period. Thus, the SOC provides an account of activities on a day-to-day basis; though not totally accurate, this information is not easy to obtain in other ways.

Second, the SOC provides a handy way to monitor treatment progress. By asking each partner to complete the checklist for 14 days at the beginning of therapy and then again at the end, we get a bird's-eye view of treatment progress, both in terms of DSR and in terms of the ratio of positive to negative behavior.

Third, the SOC provides a relatively empirical method for identifying important reinforcers and punishers in the marriage. Because the therapist has access to each partner's DSR and daily frequency of positive and negative behaviors, it becomes possible to correlate the behaviors that occur on good days (days where the DSR is high) and also identify those that occur on bad days (behaviors likely or unlikely to occur when the DSR is low). These behaviors that correlate with daily marital satisfaction can be hypothesized to be important reinforcers and punishers in the marriage.

Finally, the SOC generates material for BE. The 409 items, along with the hypothesized reinforcers and punishers, can be used in the BE task described above to aid partners in the generation of wish lists, and also in "caring days," "love days," or a variety of other BE tasks (Jacobson & Margolin, 1979). The SOC can provide a comprehensive stimulus for item generation.

Thus, the SOC can be used in a variety of ways. However, getting couples to complete it is not easy. It takes 20–30 minutes per day to complete, and it is not an intrinsically interesting task. Therefore, it provides a stringent test for the therapist. The noncompliantogenic therapist would wait until the couple was out of time for that particular session, and, as they were leaving, hand them each the checklist, adding, "Here's a little something for you to do if you have the time over the next week. You probably won't have time to do it. I probably wouldn't do it if I were in your position." Then, when the couple returns without having completed the task, the noncompliantogenic therapist attributes the noncompliance to client resistance.

In our experience, if the couple is "ready" for the task (i.e., collaborative, self-focused), compliance is largely a function of how the therapist presents the instructions. Here are the factors that we have found to be most important in increasing the likelihood of compliance.

Explain the Rationale and Emphasize the Importance of the Task

Let us use the SOC as an example of a homework assignment, for the purpose of discussing homework compliance. Since the SOC is so onerous for couples to complete, it is a stringent test of the therapist's ability to induce compliance. When we present the SOC to couples, we use the same rationale that we presented above, except we scale the language down to avoid unnecessary jargon. If couples do not understand why they are being asked to do something, they are less likely to do it. Furthermore, the task needs to be viewed as an essential rather than tangential part of treatment. We might point out that, "This checklist functions like a seeing-eye dog for me. It gives me information I can't get it any other way."

Involve the Couple in the Specifics of the Assignment

Couples are less likely to resist tasks when they have been involved in constructing them. We might say to a couple, when introducing the

SOC, "This checklist has 409 items. Help me decide how many of them are relevant to you, how many days you want to do this, and at what time." The more involved couples are in constructing the task, the less likely they will be to experience the task as coercive. Moreover, the more tailored the task is to their individual situations, the more likely they will be to comply with it. For example, it would be easy to generate an individualized SOC, since our experience has been that only about 100 of the 409 items are relevant to any particular couple. A computer program, or just crossing out irrelevant items, could tailor the checklist in a way that would make it seem both less imposing and more relevant.

Exaggerate the Aversiveness of the Task

We might tell couples that, "I apologize for giving you this task. You're going to hate it. I've had couples terminate just because they didn't want to fill out this checklist. It is like that bad-tasting medicine you took as a kid. First, you will find it quite difficult. Then, by the time you've mastered it, you will find it boring. I wish I didn't have to give it to you." After this, couples are often pleased to discover that the task is not as bad as they had anticipated. Sure, it is not fun. But it is not as bad as we made it out to be! They are actually relieved to make this discovery and more likely to complete the task as a result.

Anticipate and Pre-empt Reasons for Noncompliance

Over the years, we have heard hundreds of couples give dozens of reasons for noncompliance. There are certain "reasons" for not doing the task that occur again and again. If we can anticipate and pre-empt those "reasons," we can greatly increase the likelihood of compliance.

For example, by far the most common reason given for noncompliance is "time": "I didn't have time: it was a busy, hectic week." This reason is given so often that, when assigning the SOC, we routinely anticipate the partners' not having time: "You are busy people, and this task is time-consuming. Are you going to have time to do it? When? Let's try to block it out." If the "time" issue has been dealt with prior to the assignment, it is much less likely to be used as a reason for noncompliance at the beginning of the next session.

The second most common excuse is "I forgot." That is another one we anticipate and try to pre-empt: "How are you going to remember to do this? It is not normally part of your routine. What cues can we plant in your environment that will help you remember?"

Surprisingly, the third most common excuse is, "We had a fight" or "We had a bad week." That has always struck us as an odd reason for not doing the task, since fighting and having bad weeks are expected, especially early in therapy. However, this reason is given often enough that we routinely pre-empt it when introducing the SOC: "This task involves a lot of work and may be particularly difficult for you if you are mad at each other or if you argue. But that is when it is particularly important for us to know what goes on. So, please make sure that you complete the checklist, no matter how negatively you are feeling about your partner."

It is impossible to anticipate the myriad of possible reasons couples might give for not doing homework. Although we advocate trying to pre-empt the most common ones, couples will at times come up with creative reasons that could not possibly have been anticipated. In one of Jacobson's first cases as a graduate student in Chapel Hill, the couple went to the mountains for the weekend, had their homework assignment in the suitcase, had the suitcase tied to their car, and had the suitcase loosen while on top of the car and tumble down an 8,000-foot cliff. It would have been hard to anticipate that reason. Nevertheless, when reasons for noncompliance can be anticipated, they should be mentioned explicitly during the instructions prior to sending the couple home with the task. If the reason is pre-empted, it is highly unlikely that couples will generate it as a basis for noncompliance. To the extent that couples lack valid reasons for completing tasks at home, the tasks are more likely to be completed.

Make Sure the Task Is Understood

A surprisingly common reason for noncompliance is that couples simply misunderstood the instructions. Therapists often forget that clients do not process information about homework tasks at the same rate as mental health professionals do, and so they might easily leave therapy with an incomplete or inaccurate idea about what they were supposed to do. We always write down homework assignments. That way, unless couples lose the instructions (which has been known to happen), they have a written record of the task. The written record not only increases the likelihood of compliance but also counteracts the possibility of an iatrogenic effect: the partners may argue about what the task was, and end up be worse off than they would have been without the homework.

Generate Commitments from Couples to Complete the Assignments

There is a literature in social psychology indicating that public commitments enhance compliance. Written commitments are better than verbal ones, but verbal ones are far better than nothing. We ask couples questions like, "Now, just to make sure you know what you are supposed to do, could you each repeat the task, and tell us whether or not you think it is feasible?" The answer to this question kills two birds with one stone: it reassures us that the task is understood, and it also puts them on record as having agreed to complete the task. More generally, during the feedback session we ask couples to make a commitment to completing assigned tasks. Stuart (1980) went so far as to advocate written contracts at the beginning of therapy. We don't go that far, although we don't think it is a bad idea.

Use Homework in the Subsequent Session

When a task is assigned between sessions, one of the most egregious errors a therapist can make is failing to debrief and go over the task in the subsequent session. That is the quickest way to extinguish homework compliance. Couples quickly get the message that the homework is an afterthought, not something that the therapist considers particularly important. You can be sure that, if the couple sees that the therapist is not concerned about whether or not the task was completed, they will not be concerned about task completion. It is imperative that when assignments are given, they form a central part of the subsequent session, unless some emergency intervenes that requires the therapist's undivided attention.

The Ultimate Weapon in Homework Compliance

If the therapist, on a routine basis, explains the rationale for tasks, thus emphasizing their importance, ensures that clients understand what they are supposed to do, gains from them a commitment to doing the task, involves them in the specifics of task construction, anticipates and pre-empts reasons they might otherwise give for noncompliance, and reinforces compliance by making the task an important feature of the subsequent session, then noncompliance will rarely occur. In other words, most acts of client noncompliance result from the therapist's not effectively delivering the task instructions. This assumes, of course, that a collaborative set has been formed and that acceptance work has effectively preceded BE homework tasks.

There is, however, one additional tactic. We hesitate to even mention it, because it is above and beyond the call of duty. This tactic involves calling couples between sessions to check to make sure that the task has been completed. It does not have to be a long telephone conversation, simply a brief, two-minute inquiry: say, during their favorite TV show, the phone rings: "Hey, George, Neil Jacobson calling. Just checking to make sure the task I gave you has been completed, since our session is in a couple of days. [Long pause, 13 seconds seems optimal] . . . George? Are you there? Oh, you haven't gotten to it yet! Hm [another 13-second pause]. Were you planning to get to it before the session? Great! Look forward to seeing you. Can I speak to Ruth for a moment?"

These telephone calls rarely have to be made more than once. Couples find them extremely aversive and will do almost anything to get you to stop calling them, including the homework. The therapist can put the couple on a negative reinforcement schedule, fading the phone calls as compliance becomes strengthened. These phone calls are quite powerful and do not have to appear coercive.

Conclusion

Homework tasks are an important part of BE and communication/ problem-solving training (CPT) and even play a role in acceptance work, especially some techniques for promoting tolerance. We have found that what often appears at first glance to be the result of incomplete acceptance work or client resistance can actually be attributed to faulty technique on the part of the therapist. BE works much more effectively if the therapist can get couples to comply with between-session tasks. If the therapist presents the tasks effectively, and the couple still fails to comply, then it is reasonable to interpret noncompliance as the result of incomplete acceptance work.

─ 9 ─

COMMUNICATION AND
CONFLICT RESOLUTION
TRAINING

Communication and problem-solving training (CPT) has been a major component of traditional behavioral couple therapy (TBCT) since its inception (Jacobson & Margolin, 1979; Liberman, 1970; Weiss et al., 1973). The tradition has always been to split communication training into two overlapping but distinct sets of skills: training in general communication skills that involve support and understanding (Weiss, 1984), and training in how to deal with conflict, which Jacobson and Margolin referred to as problem-solving training (PST). Although research investigations have tended to treat CPT as one module, the two types of communication training are really quite different and can be distinguished both conceptually and procedurally.

General communication training (CT) with couples has its roots in the work of Bernard Guerney (1977) and is aimed at teaching couples how to be better listeners, as well as how to express themselves more directly and in ways less likely to generate defensiveness in the partner. The listening skills came to be known generically as "active listening," while the expressive skills involved using "I" statements rather than "you" statements and following various additional rules that were designed to maintain active listening. One of the key structural aspects to this communication training (CT) was that only one partner would have the "floor" at a time: while one person spoke (using expressive skills), the other "listened" (using active listening skills); the speaker held the floor either until he or she was willing to relinquish it or until the listener requested it, depending on which variation of CT one was using. Then the roles would reverse: the listener became the speaker, and the speaker became an active listener.

CT skills have become so widely used by couple therapists that it is almost impossible to review them comprehensively or to assign credit for particular innovations. In fact, the concepts have so pervaded popular culture that they recently found their way into an episode of *NYPD Blue.* When insisting on a separation from his wife, Detective Metavoy kindly asked her to leave his office. His wife responded, "Come on Greg, when you do something, I feel something." Greg replied, "I don't want to do any of that marriage counseling crap!" Ms. Metavoy (we never find out her first name): "Greg! When you do X, I feel Y. Come on." Greg: "When you quote from our marriage counseling, it makes me want to scream, run under the bed, and divorce you." Ms. Metavoy: "Good! Now don't you feel better?" Greg: "What I hear you saying is that I feel better. What I hear myself saying is, get out of my office!"

When CT has penetrated popular culture to that extent, it is hard to assign credit. However, let us give it a try: in addition to the pioneering work of Guerney (1977), Gottman, Notarius, et al. (1976), in their book for couples, defined active listening skills *(validation)* and expressive communication skills *(leveling*—telling the other what is on your mind—and *editing*—avoiding defense-inducing, provocative means for expressing what is one your mind) in ways that made them accessible to couples without the aid of a therapist. Jacobson and Margolin (1979) added a major component of "feeling talk," where couples use feeling checklists to develop methods for expressing one's affective experience.

In TBCT, PST played a more important role than CT, at least as TBCT was operationalized by Jacobson and Margolin (1979). This was because in the 1970s research seemed to suggest that it was not conflict per se but how conflict was dealt with that determined whether relationships succeeded or failed. A variety of studies supported this view (reviewed in Gottman, 1994). Therefore, it seemed logical to invent strategies for helping couples deal with conflict more effectively. Jacobson's research in the mid-1980s seemed to support this proposition even more strongly, since the training in conflict resolution was such an essential part of the TBCT package. (In this chapter, we sometimes use the term "conflict resolution" instead of "problem solving," since the latter is more generic, and applies also to decision-making that is not conflictual.)

In ICT, training in conflict resolution is still used, but it plays much less of a role than it did in TBCT. Even as a relative contributor to CPT, conflict resolution training is less important to the model than it was to CPT. There are a number of reasons for this.

First, the more generic communication skills of active listening and expressive training have become more prominent, since they lend themselves to both acceptance and change-oriented interventions. As we mentioned in Chapter 6, the therapist may use CT as a way of promoting empathic joining around the problem. For some couples, the structure of CT breaks down barriers and leads to acceptance more effectively than therapist reformulations or ad hoc prompts. Remember that the goal of empathic joining is to soften the listener: when the speaker and listener roles alternate, the goal becomes mutual softening. When the "softer" expressions characteristic of expressive communications skills are combined with the paraphrasing and reflecting inherent in active listening (or, to use the terminology of Gottman et al., 1976, "validation"), greater acceptance can be the outcome. In addition, CT skills can be used to promote change, especially when they are integrated with training in conflict resolution. In fact, CT skills provide an easy transition into the "problem definition" phase of PST. Therefore, the techniques are quite versatile and can be invoked throughout the various phases of therapy.

Second, the value of training in conflict resolution may have been overestimated in previous research because its contribution was not evaluated independently of CT. In support of this suspicion, we found that couples receiving PST tended not to practice the skills in a formal way after therapy ended, and whether they did or not failed to predict long-term outcome (Jacobson et al., 1987).

Third, we question whether deficits in conflict resolution skills are the primary cause of marital distress for all couples. In particular, there is no direct evidence that the skills taught in CPT resemble the strategies used by happy couples in dealing with conflict. In fact, most existing research says that our rules of engagement are quite arbitrary.

Nevertheless, some couples come to therapy asking specifically for a structured approach to dealing with conflict, and others find it useful. Thus, although it is not the primary mode of intervention for the majority of couples, PST continues to have an important role within ICT.

In this chapter, we adopt a similar structural approach to that taken in Chapter 8. Since the techniques for both CT (Gottman et al., 1976; Guerney, 1977; Jacobson & Margolin, 1979) and PST (Jacobson & Margolin, 1979) are described in detail elsewhere, we will emphasize the principles of training rather than specific intervention strategies. Also, in this chapter we have revised the rules we give to couples when conducting PST. We have used these revised rules since the 1984 component analysis study; they were also used in our pilot study, described in Chapter 1, comparing ICT to TBCT.

Instructional Techniques for
Communication/Problem-solving Training

CPT is taught more systematically by behavior therapists than it is in the CT paradigms recommended by other theoretical models. When ICT therapists teach any communication skill—whether it be part of CT or PST—they use a behavioral skills training paradigm that has been widely adopted to train clients in any complex set of social behaviors. This paradigm, described by Jacobson and Margolin (1979), will be described only briefly here. However, we now have evidence that, in formal skills training, the entire paradigm is necessary for skill acquisition to occur (Jacobson & Anderson, 1980). That is, when any component of the skills training paradigm is omitted from the training, skill acquisition does not occur. The paradigm consists of the following components: instructions, behavior rehearsal, feedback and continued practice until mastery, practice at home, and fading therapist control.

Instructions

Any skills training package has a core content. Mastery of the content is a prerequisite to skill acquisition. Since most CPT skills have been discussed in writing, with couples themselves as a targeted audience, we virtually always assign readings to prepare couples for practice in the skills. We also make sure that the material in the readings is understood before moving on to actual practice. For CT, we typically use the first three chapters of Gottman, Notarius, et al. (1976), which describe validation (active listening), leveling (expressive skills), and editing (finding nondefensive ways of expressing oneself). We also use our own manual, which is being developed explicitly for couples in ICT (Christensen & Jacobson, 1997).

Behavior Rehearsal

The heart and soul of CPT is practice in the therapy session. It is not enough to describe the skill. It virtually always sounds easier in theory than it is in practice. The only way to shape the skills that you want to teach is by having the couple practice them in the session. When couples are given reading assignments prior to practice attempts, they should be warned explicitly about the dangers of practicing the skills at home without first mastering them in the session, under the watchful eye of the therapist. Premature practicing of the skills at home is a recipe for disaster.

Typically, couples practice skills in small rather than in large steps. For example, the therapist might say, "OK, let's practice validation. Frank, you have the floor, and your job is to level and edit. But the focus is on you, Cheryl. Your job is to listen, maintain eye contact, and paraphrase. Don't exert your point of view. Just demonstrate that you are listening and that you understand, whether or not you agree."

Even though couples have typically read about these skills, practice sessions are preceded by prompts from the therapist such as the one above. The prompts are designed to minimize mistakes by reminding couples about just those areas where they are most likely to slip up. Thus, the cues offered to one couple will differ from those offered to another. Some people can't state an affective experience without also stating a point of view. For such a partner, the therapist might say, "Now remember, tell him how you feel, not whether he is right or wrong." Others have problems being explicit when defining problems; then the therapist might say, "OK, when you begin, tell him exactly what he does that angers you." In short, the prompts and cues are tailored to the deficits of the particular couple.

Early in the training, the rehearsals themselves should be brief. The structure of the practice session should be designed to minimize failure; and the briefer the rehearsal, the less likely the client will be to forget to do something right or to add something wrong

Feedback and Continued Practice until Mastery

Research conducted subsequent to the publication of Jacobson and Margolin (1979) has confirmed that the process of providing couples with feedback and then having them practice again is essential. Simply providing them with feedback is not enough. For example, when Jane began a communication exercise by saying, "It pisses me off when I come home and the house is a mess. You've got plenty of time to keep the house clean. I don't know what you do with yourself all day except have lattés with your friends," the therapist responded, "Your anger was very direct. That's good. The problem with the way you expressed it was all of that excess baggage at the end. Try it again without accusing him of wasting him time and being lazy. Just tell him about your experience when you come home and the house is messy." In her next effort, Jane said, "I get angry whenever I come home and the house is a mess." The therapist responded, "That was better. You got most of the baggage out of your statement. My only quibble is with the word 'mess.' Although you may feel that the word fits, it is inflammatory. Remember that your job is to make it easy for him to listen, and not be tempted to respond defensively. You are more likely to succeed without that word. Try a different one. Or no word at all." On her third attempt, Jane said, "I find myself getting angry when I walk into the house and it is not as neat as I might have expected or hoped."

As the above example indicates, Jane gets better and better at conforming to the rules with each attempt. Without actually practicing to the point where the response conforms to the rules, Jane is less likely to get it right when she tries to implement the rules at home. It is also important to note that the therapist is constantly teaching when providing feedback. In addition to correcting her, the therapist is reminding her of the rationale for stating her concerns in a particular way. Couples need to be repeatedly reminded of the reasons why they are being asked to say things in a particular way. We even take things one step further. We drive the point home by bringing in the experience of the listener; for example, "Paul, did it make any difference to you how she said it, or did all three statements have the same impact on you?" Paul, being a well-socialized client, responded as expected: "Well, by the third time she said it, I was still bristling from the idea that I sit around and bite my fingernails all day. But if she hadn't done it the way she did it the first two times, and had led with the final statement, I wouldn't have felt this need to defend myself."

In short, feedback includes restating the rationale for your corrective comments. It also includes verifying with the listener that the experience is truly different when the rules are followed.

Practice at Home Only after Mastery Has Been Achieved in the Therapy Session

Couples should be allowed to practice the skills at home only after they have mastered them in the therapy session. They need to be cautioned repeatedly against trying things at home before they are ready. The context of the therapist's office and the presence of the therapist invariably make the task easier in that environment than at home. It is a safe bet that if they haven't done it right in the office, they are not going to do it right at home.

Fading Therapist Control: State of the Relationship Sessions

When conducting any type of communication training, especially PST, the therapist becomes less directive as time goes on, leaving more of the work to the couple. By the time a couple completes training, the spouses should be able to have their own conflict resolution sessions at home. We call these "state of the relationship" sessions. We encourage couples to meet periodically to discuss the state of the relationship and to engage their conflict resolution skills when there are issues to discuss. We also encourage them to avoid trying to solve conflictual issues at other times. The stimulus control provided by the state of the relationship meeting makes it more likely that they will use the skills taught in therapy. If PST is a component of the treatment plan, the successful completion of a state of the relationship meeting is a good sign that the partners have learned the technique.

Subtleties of Communication Training

Although our purpose is not to revisit the techniques of active listening and expressive communication training in this chapter, we do want to make some general points and emphasize some of the subtleties.

Active listening refers to a particular type of "listening," listening that leads to a demonstration that the speaker has been understood. It is a basic tenet of CT that one cannot express and actively listen at the same time. Therefore, during CT exercises there is always a designated speaker and a designated listener. The listener demonstrates understanding by paraphrasing and reflecting the speaker's comments. This is all the listener does until the speaker feels understood. Then the roles switch.

All of this sounds straightforward. However, there are four very different types of active listening, and their impact is likely to vary for a given speaker and from couple to couple. First, there is simply paraphrasing, where the listener attempts to communicate that he or she has been listening by simply summarizing what the speaker is saying. At times, this level of active listening is reinforcing in and of itself, because for some speakers simply knowing that the other is listening is a vast improvement over typical conversations prior to CT. A second and more complicated form of active listening is reflection. Here the listener tries to capture the emotional state of the speaker as well as summarize the content of what he or she is saying. This response is often more gratifying to the speaker than mere paraphrasing. At times, simple paraphrasing or reflecting is insufficient, and "validation" is required in order to reinforce the speaker. Validation refers to demonstrating not only that the listener has understood the speaker but that their point of view is valid and their feelings understandable.

A paraphrase would be "You didn't like it that I invited my mother over without consulting with you first." A reflection would be "You are really angry that I invited my mother over without consulting you first." A more validating response would be "It makes sense that you are upset and angry about my inviting mother over without consulting with you first." A fourth type of active listening is actual agreement with the speaker: "You are right; I screwed up by inviting my mother over without consulting with you first." At times, speakers require actual agreement in order to be satisfied.

Here is where one of the limitations of active listening becomes apparent. Some people are simply not satisfied unless they are validated. But what if the listener does not see the validity of the speaker's point of view? The CT approach capitalizes on the removal of defensive expressions as a means of softening the listener; however, not all listeners are softened by carefully edited, direct expressions of feeling. Moreover, not all speakers are mollified by knowing that their partner listens and understands. They want it to be acknowledged that they have a reasonable point of view. It is not uncommon that, even after achieving a perfect expression followed by a perfect job of active listening, neither partner is happy: the speaker is still waiting for validation, even though the listener does not find any validity in the speaker's point of view; the listener is waiting for the speaker to have a different feeling about the listener's behavior and will react defensively no matter how the complaint is registered. We would not encourage validation on the part of the listener simply to mollify the speaker; however, we would encourage validation to the extent that the listener does see validity in the speaker's point of view but is unable to communicate that validity. Similarly, we would not encourage the speaker to be dishonest in order to pacify a listener; however, we do want speakers to speak in a nonblaming way and emphasize their own experience, to see if the listener will become more "validating" as a result.

The problem is that the primary deficit is often not in communication skills, although these deficits do exist. The primary problem, with many couples, is that the speaker simply doesn't like something about the listener, and the listener finds no validity in the speaker's point of view, no matter how it is expressed. CT cannot solve this problem. In such situations, the therapist has to become much more active in the reformulation process and in creating conditions where differences are acknowledged and efforts are made to cope with the differences without obfuscation.

The problem is even more acute in those instances where even validation is insufficient and the speaker will not be mollified unless the listener actually agrees with him or her. If the listener does not agree, CT brings couples—even couples who communicate perfectly—to an impasse. Similarly, some listeners can't help but be irritated by the speaker's feeling expression, no matter how much editing goes on. In fact, it is natural to be defensive when your partner finds your behavior objectionable. Here again, acceptance work is required to move beyond such an impasse. There are many people who begin therapy saying that all they want is to be heard, understood, or validated. Unfortunately, they do not always know what they want. Many want the other to be remade in a manner consistent with an idealized image of a partner; no matter how much validation occurs, only agreement will suffice. This is why we find CT limited. Some couples communicate quite well, but these skills do not make their differences and complaints any more reconcilable.

When it comes to editing, leveling, and other expressive communication skills, we think that one of the most valuable aspects of the training is teaching couples to "qualify" (Guerney, 1977). Qualification refers to the injection of a tentative tone into the expression, which ends up being the equivalent of "I could be wrong" or "From my perspective . . ." For example, consider the statement, "I am upset that you invited your mother over without consulting with me first." Although it is a direct expression of feeling, a more qualified response might lead to a less defensive listener. An example would be, "The way I am, I can't help but be upset by your inviting your mother over without consulting me." The qualification can function to communicate, "I recognize that there is no universal truth. You see the world based on your life experience and your genetic make-up, as do I. I can only feel what I feel based on that aggregate of experiences. There is no right or wrong here, there is only feeling good or feeling bad, and I feel bad." Of course, spouses don't usually think this way, let alone verbalize things this way. Nevertheless, at times marital interaction breaks down because each is challenged by the other's apparent attempts to impersonate God. It is as if they are heard to be saying, "I am good and you are bad." Or, "I see the truth and you don't." Since that arrogance of apparent certainty can push conflict buttons in some couples, some recognition of the biased perspective can go a long way toward softening, in the case of acceptance work, or producing a nondefensive listener, when CT is used to promote change. Of course, partners should not be encouraged to qualify if they believe that their perspective on reality is objective, categorically correct, or otherwise indisputable. For such couples, impasses are created with CT, similar to the ones described above. CT is unlikely to get to the root of the problem with such couples.

More generally, CT is limited by the extent to which the spouses can communicate according to the rules without distorting their actual positions. To the extent that they must distort how they really feel in order to communicate properly, CT exercises actually create emotional distance rather than increased closeness. This would be counterproductive from the perspective of ICT.

Subtleties of Problem-Solving Training

The Role of PST in Marital Communication

PST is designed to teach not generalized communication skills, but rather skills of a highly specific nature: how to resolve conflicts through direct interaction. Most of the rules of PST do not apply to other modes of marital communication. In short, this is a specialized form of communication training. We would not expect, nor would we even recommend, that couples communicate in this way about conflict if their goals were something other than solving the problem.

This is important, because couples in conflict often have little interest in resolution. The partners' goals might be to be proven right, to have the other acknowledge that they are right, to obtain revenge, to hurt the other person's feelings, or to vent their own feelings. These are all inevitable, natural, and understandable reactions to conflict, and we do not blame people for having them. But none of these reactions is compatible with solving the problem in such a way as to eliminate the conflict. If the goal is to resolve the conflict, then PST is indicated. However, if the goal is something else, anything else, then PST is contraindicated. Thus, one function of PST is to help couples identify their goals when a conflict arises and to create a permissive atmosphere about a range of goals.

We don't want couples to attempt PST when their goals are to vent, hurt, get revenge, or win. When couples learn the rules of PST but can't stick to them, it is a sure sign that their goals are not to resolve the conflict. Then it is time to stop problem-solving and use acceptance-oriented interventions to deal with alternative goals. We don't want couples to fight or argue in the guise of problem-solving. PST helps us teach them that important discrimination.

Not All Problems Are Amenable to PST

Only behaviors to which the perpetrator has direct access can be targeted for problem-solving or conflict resolution. Typically, one has direct access to engaging in a shared activity (assuming the requisite skill), being considerate, communicating in a certain way, spending or not spending money, working around the house, going to work, parenting, and performing this or that personal activity. These are all behaviors that are under voluntary control. They are perfectly reasonable areas about which to problem-solve. However, one cannot directly control one's degree of sexual desire or how trusting one feels. Behaviors that are not under voluntary control make poor candidates for PST. One cannot legislate or access at will trust, sexual desire, love, or any kind of affective experience. This explains why PST tends to work better when applied to the more instrumental aspects of marriage. Unfortunately, some of the most important areas of marriage are not instrumental. Most people do not marry in order to divide up money, keep house, or negotiate schedules. The "scut work" of marriage simply comes with the territory. The passion, romance, intellectual stimulation, trust, comfort, and self-esteem that people seek from their partners cannot always be provided on demand. This limits the range and applicability of PST.

The range and applicability of PST are further restricted by the requirement that a range of solutions or resolutions is possible for a given conflict. Where compromise is impossible, PST tends to break down. Conflicts with only two possible solutions, such as whether to have a child or whether to take a particular job, don't leave room for brainstorming, negotiation, and cost-benefit analyses that dominate the solution phase of problem-solving training.

Distinguishing between the Definition and Solution Phases of PST

PST has two distinct phases, a definition phase and a solution phase. Couples are supposed to keep those phases distinct. They are not to solve a problem before it has been defined, and once a problem has been defined they are to focus exclusively on solutions, without moving back to the definition phase.

The reasons for keeping these phases distinct are twofold. First, one major mistake that couples make is to try to solve problems before they have been adequately defined. As a result, there is a great deal of miscommunication, some of which is due to their discussing different problems without knowing it. Second, if left to their own devices, couples actively avoid the systematic focus on solutions by continuously moving back to the definition phase. The rules of engagement prevent that from happening. One of the main reasons for problems not getting resolved is that there is literally no systematic focus on resolution prior to therapy. In order to ensure that this phase of the process will be utilized productively, we require that they stay in it once the problem has been defined.

The Rules for PST

All couples who live together over a long period of time face conflicts now and then. Even in the most ideal marriage, periods of discord are inevitable. One of the hallmarks of a successful relationship is the ability to resolve these disputes smoothly and in a way that is satisfactory to both parties.

Success at solving problems means success in bringing about change. A relationship problem usually involves the desire for some kind of change on the part of at least one partner. The couple that can successfully make changes when they are called for is likely to maintain a flexible, satisfying relationship over a long period of time.

Problem-solving is a specialized activity; it is not like any other type of conversation. Therefore, it is not expected to be spontaneous, natural, relaxing, or enjoyable in the way that regular communication is. This is not to say that problem-solving cannot be fun; on the contrary, once couples reap its benefits and become efficient at it, they often report it as an enjoyable activity, something that brings them closer together and creates warm loving feelings. At first problem-solving is difficult, complicated, frustrating and, in and of itself, not rewarding. It seems stilted and unnatural. However, once couples learn the skills, they find that working together and successfully resolving conflicts can be very rewarding. Communication is improved and better understanding between the two people is fostered.

Let us define problem-solving as structured interaction between two people designed to resolve a particular dispute between them. Usually, but not always, the dispute is a complaint by one person concerning some aspect of the other's behavior. The complaint may be that the spouse is doing too much of something, for example, smoking too much or going out with his or her friends too often. Or problems might arise because the partner is not doing something often enough, like showing affection or taking responsibility for household chores. At other times, one spouse will be making costly efforts to please the partner, yet the partner ignores or even puts down those efforts. An example would be the wife who wanted her husband to talk about his feelings more often; yet when he did express his feelings on a given occasion, the wife responded with, "You shouldn't feel that way—that's crazy!" She failed to give him credit for his efforts.

Some marital disputes involve mutual complaints where both partners object to the other's behavior in a particular situation. For example, when a couple gets together with their friends the husband may complain that his wife withdraws from the conversation, while the wife might counter that her husband talks too much at these gatherings. Or, there is a "communication gap" between the two people, whereby each person has different (unspoken) expectations of the other. They get into trouble not because their expectations are different from one another, but because they find out about the differences too late. For example, one couple failed to discuss the mother-in-law's visit before she came and ended up constantly bickering about what to do, when to leave, etc. In sum, there are many different aspects to problems and causes of problems, and any one problem might be characterized by any or all of these various aspects.

Problem-solving Setting

Problem-solving is structured interaction. As such, it should occur only in certain settings and not in others. The first thing couples should be advised to do to when problem-solving is to set aside a time and a place in which discussions will be conducted. Usually, couples like to hold problem-solving sessions at night, after children are either in bed or absorbed in an activity. This way they are less likely to be distracted by either the children or the telephone. Couples should be alone when problem-solving.

There should be an agenda. Couples should not attempt to resolve their disputes at the scene of the crime. When a dispute occurs, they should wait until the next problem-solving session before trying to resolve it. Trying to resolve a grievance when the grievance occurs is usually ill-advised: when partners are emotionally aroused, as they are bound to be when the other does something negative, they are not at their best; they are unlikely to problem-solve in a rational manner. Discussing the issue at a neutral time, like during a prearranged problem-solving session, makes it more likely that it will be dealt with effectively. Tackling difficult relationship problems during structured problem-solving sessions brings new skills to bear on these issues. The rules discussed below, if followed, will make some apparently insoluble problems solvable. Later, when problem-solving skills are well developed, they can be transferred to the scene of the crime when minor, everyday irritants come up. Major problems should always be reserved for scheduled problem-solving sessions.

Problem-solving sessions should be relatively short. If one problem is being discussed, 60 minutes should be the maximum. Couples should never attempt the resolution of more than one problem in a single session. Problem-solving is difficult; couples should avoid exhausting themselves.

Partners should buy a notebook and record the important elements of each problem-solving session. At the top of the page, they should write the date. Underneath, they should record the problem discussed, along with the agreement reached.

Problem-solving Attitude

The purpose of each and every problem-solving session is to improve the relationship. Each time a relationship problem is solved, the relationship improves, and each partner becomes that much happier. It is in the interest of both partners to collaborate during these sessions. Each problem discussed is viewed as a mutual problem. Typically, when distressed couples deal with conflict, the event takes the form of a power struggle. If the wife has a gripe about the husband, he adopts a rigid posture and regards her gripe as a threat. He thinks that if he agrees to change he becomes less powerful in the relationship, and he loses face. He blames his partner for the problem and waits for her to change first. It is easy to see how couples reach stalemates with this view.

The rigid posture adopted by distressed couples makes some sense. After all, in the short run, a partner who agrees to make a change in his or her behavior is sacrificing something. Such changes are costly, particularly if they are not reciprocated by changes on the part of the partner. However, after couples have completed a regimen of acceptance work, and the acceptance work has been successful, they are much more likely to be collaborative. They are much more likely to adopt the view that the refusal to change is self-defeating for their own personal happiness. As long as the relationship remains distressed, they will both be unhappy. By "giving in" and making some changes the partner wants, they usually find that the short-term cost will be more than outweighed by the advantages of an improved relationship. Partners will respond more positively because they are happier and in the process will provide natural reinforcement that often exceeds anything they got out of the old behavior.

To take a simple example, consider the wife who asked her husband to take over the responsibility of playing with their three-year-old son between 5:30 and 6:30 every evening. This was when the husband first came home from work, and he looked forward to this time to relax, read the paper, drink a beer, and unwind. The thought of having to spend this time interacting with his rambunctious son was aversive to him. In the short run, it is clear that he would have been giving up an important period of leisure time by assuming this re-

sponsibility. Thus, it is not surprising that he was reluctant to agree
to her request. Now add to this the dynamics of this couple's power
struggle. They entered therapy plagued by conflict and discord. He
had assumed that most of the problems were her fault. Why should he
agree to her request when it would make his already miserable existence a bit more miserable without her prior commitment to changing in ways that he would find desirable?

The answer is that the positive changes expected of them in PST
were preceded by acceptance work, and they no longer blamed one
another for the negative behavior in their relationship. Some of it
made them closer, and some of it was simply more tolerable. In either
case, they recognized that further change would be beneficial to both
of them. If the husband agreed to his wife's requests, she would experience some relief from the rigors of child management. Not only
would she be more relaxed as a consequence, but she would also be
more loving and appreciative of him. This restructuring of the couple's child responsibilities would probably have repercussions for the
rest of the relationship. Her increased relaxation would probably make
her a more pleasant person to be around. Finally, she might very well
reciprocate by making some changes in her own behavior to accommodate his wishes. All in all it adds up to a more pleasant existence
for the husband as well as for the wife, despite the short-term costs.

Again, since all potential marital problems have implications for
both partners, every problem is a mutual problem. Collaboration is in
the interest of both parties; therefore, each change agreed to by the
partner will make his/her life more pleasant in the long run. Collaboration pays off, and for this reason it is the essence of problem-solving.

The necessity for collaboration does not mean that partners must
always agree to behave in a way that is satisfying to one another.
Some requests for change seem unreasonable; at times the problem
may be in the mind of the person who registers the complaint more
than in the behavior of the person who acts as the object of the complaint. The method simply depends on each partner's remaining open
to the possibility of behavior change in response to the other's wishes.
A readiness to consider changing to make one's partner happier can
more easily be viewed in terms of its long-term benefits, rather than
its immediate costs, if PST was preceded by successful acceptance
work.

Problem Definition versus Problem Solution

A problem-solving session has two distinct, nonoverlapping phases: a
problem definition phase and a problem solution phase. During the

problem definition phase, a clear, specific statement of the problem is produced, a definition that is understood by both parties. No attempt is made to solve the problem until both understand exactly what the problem is. Then, during the solution phase, discussion is focused on generating and talking about possible solutions to the problem, and, finally, on the formation of an agreement designed to resolve the problem.

This means that initially no solutions will be proposed. Until both partners have agreed on a definition of the problem the task is confined to the production of a mutually acceptable definition. Then, once the next phase has begun, returning to the definition phase is undesirable, unless the couple concludes that the PST process should be abandoned. For example, if, during the process, either the therapist or the partners feel insufficiently collaborative to continue, then the "default option" of acceptance work should be exercised and PST should be abandoned, at least temporarily. Otherwise, once discussion has turned to how to solve the problem, couples are better off focusing on solutions and not reverting back to the definition phase.

The distinction between phases is important because couples' problem-solving communication tends to be chaotic and ambiguous. Focused discussion tends to be more efficient. More importantly, perhaps, discussing solutions is positive and forward-looking, whereas problem definition is more apt to be negative and backward-looking. The spirit of collaboration and compromise is dampened by focus on past misdeeds. While an element of this latter focus may be necessary during the definition stage, it should not intrude into the elaboration of solutions, unless the partners decide that they are not ready for PST.

Rule 1: In Stating a Problem, Try to Begin with Something Positive. The way a problem is first stated sets the tone for the entire discussion. If one partner is about to be critical of the other, he or she needs to say it in a way that is least likely to result in the other's becoming defensive. The complainant wants to maintain the other's cooperation and collaborative spirit.

It is difficult for all of us to accept criticism. Most of us immediately want to defend ourselves when we are criticized. This response is natural, and partners should not be blamed for becoming defensive. However, if they are to continue in PST, they should be ready to respond nondefensively, especially if the complaint has been prefaced with something positive.

One very effective way of doing this is by beginning the statement of the problem with a positive remark, such as an expression of appreciation. Partners might be encouraged to mention something about the other that they like before mentioning the problem that is currently upsetting them. To illustrate what we mean, below are lists of initial problem statements without and with positive beginnings (+):

Without a +	With a +
1. I feel rejected by you because you are seldom affectionate.	1. I like it when you hold me when we watch TV, but I feel rejected when you aren't affectionate in other situations.
2. Lately you haven't expressed much interest in hearing about my day.	2. I often look forward to coming home because I can unload all of my tensions on you by telling you what a rough day I had. I have always felt close to you at those times because you are such a good listener. But lately you haven't expressed much interest in hearing about my day.
3. It concerns me that you spend so little time with Sheila on week-nights.	3. You and Sheila get along so well, and you are very good with her. It concerns me that you spend so little time with her on week-nights.
4. I am angry that you are coming home late without letting me know.	4. I love you even though sometimes I get so mad at you. The thing that I'm angry about now is the way you've been coming home late without letting me know.

The differences between the above statements with and without expressions of appreciation are readily apparent. People tend to take the positive qualities of their partners for granted. They assume that their partners don't need to hear about them. Nothing could be further from the truth! Human beings need praise; we all need to know that people recognize and appreciate our positive attributes. This recognition is particularly important when we are being criticized; without such recognition, the natural response is to feel attacked. The positive remark reminds the partner that there is care and appreciation, even though certain behaviors are distressing and objectionable. This kind of specific criticism is much easier to accept than criticism that does not include a positive component. If the partner is able to accept criticism, he or she will remain in a collaborative spirit; otherwise, a counter-criticism or a statement of self-defense is likely to follow. In this case, the problem-solving session can quickly deteriorate.

Ideally, the behavior that is being praised will be directly related to the behavior being criticized. In the first three examples, the expression of appreciation deals with the same behavior about which the partner is dissatisfied. However, it is not always possible to praise someone for something related to the problem. Rather than being phony and inventing a compliment, we recommend that partners express appreciation in a more general way in such instances by reminding the other person that they are loved and appreciated and that the criticism of his/her behavior does not signal total rejection. Example 4 illustrates such an expression of appreciation.

We do not recommend phony praise. Most couples do not need to invent expressions of appreciation. By the time couples get to this phase of therapy, they probably appreciate many things about each other, although they may not feel the need to express them. We are merely suggesting that a problem-solving session is an opportune time to express this appreciation. Actually, telling others what we like about them is a good thing to do frequently. If expressions of appreciation occur with some frequency in a relationship and not just during the problem-solving sessions, they are more likely to be accepted at face value when they occur at the beginning of a problem definition.

Rule 2: Be Specific. When defining a problem, partners are advised to describe the behavior that is bothering them. They are asked to state their needs and their gripes in terms of specific words and actions. What is it exactly that the partner does or says that is disturbing? The problem should be described in such a way that its presence or absence can be clearly determined by an observer. In other words, one should be able to either see it or hear it. Notice the contrast below between vague and specific problem definitions.

Vague	Specific
1. I get the feeling you aren't interested in what I do.	1. You seldom ask me questions about how my day was.
2. You don't want to sleep with me me anymore.	2. Most of the time I initiate sex.

3. We don't seem to make contact.	3. We talk about day-to-day happenings, but rarely do we talk about how we feel.
4. You don't know me very well.	4. You talk to me while I am cooking and I can't do two things at once.

Notice that in each of the vague examples, it is unclear what the problem is. The partner who is being criticized cannot be certain what it is that leads the other to the conclusion that he or she is uninterested, not desirous of sex, out of contact, or unknowing. It is very difficult to get anywhere when the problem is defined in terms of the other's internal state. When the complainant is specific, on the other hand, the other person will know exactly what the referent is and communication is much clearer. The key to understanding the feelings and reactions each has for the other is identifying specific words and actions that bring out these feelings. Learning to pinpoint the relationship between behavior and feelings is an important skill in PST.

There are many pitfalls in defining a relationship problem, many ways to be vague and imprecise and thereby confuse the communication.

Derogatory Adjectives and Nouns. One way is to use derogatory labels as substitutes for descriptions of the negative behavior. Consider the following examples:

1. You are inconsiderate.
2. You are lazy.
3. You are cold.
4. You are dogmatic and intolerant.

In none of these examples do we know what the accused partner has done to warrant these labels. The labels themselves are not only vague, but also provocative. If the purpose is to make the partner angry and alienate him/her from the task of problem-solving, there is no better way to do it than to substitute derogatory labels for behavioral descriptions. Since such name-calling leads to a feeling of being attacked, the response is usually a counter-attack (for example, "So I'm lazy, eh? Well at least I'm not insensitive and cold the way you are") or a self-defense (for example, "I'm not lazy!"). In either case, the problem-solving session has become, at best, a debate and, at worst, an argument. Time for the default option.

If, on the other hand, the complainant can remain focused on maintaining the other person's cooperation, he or she can simply describe the behavior that displeases him/her and forget the labels. Consider the advantages of redefining the four examples listed above in terms of behavior.

1. When you fix yourself something to eat at night, you often neglect to ask me if I want something." (vs. "You are inconsiderate.")

2. "Today you didn't make the bed, you left your dirty clothes on the floor, and you left used dishes in the living room." (vs. "You are lazy.")

3. "In past months, you have seldom touched me except during sex." (vs. "You are cold.")

4. "I've noticed that lately, when we discuss important decisions, you often interrupt me and insist upon your point of view." (vs. "You are dogmatic and intolerant.")

If couples find it difficult to give up these derogatory adjectives, they are probably not ready for PST. They are probably still feeling too much pain and vulnerability to focus on solving the problem.

One final word about the use of labels rather than behavioral descriptions and defining a problem. Our culture teaches us to try to view people as having personality traits that explain their behavior. Thus, when partners act in upsetting ways, they are called "repressed," "hysterical," "overprotective," "sadistic," "introverted," and so on. Often, there is a tendency to define relationship problems as either or both partners' possessing undesirable traits. These labels have all the drawbacks of derogatory adjectives and nouns. In addition, their use creates pessimism about being able to change, because personality traits are often thought of as permanent. The important question is not, "What personality trait does this person have?" but rather, "What is it about the partner's behavior that displeases the other?" Why stick to the behavior? Because some behavior can be changed!

Overgeneralizations. Couples often exaggerate the scope of their complaints. Words like "always" and "never" are typical ways that such exaggeration is accomplished, for example, "You *never* clean up the messes you make," or "you're *always* late." Not only are these overgeneralizations imprecise, but they are seldom accepted by the partner. In response to an overgeneralized complaint the receiver is likely to dispute the overgeneralization ("I am *not* always late!"), rather than discuss the problem per se. Whether the problem occurs "all" of the time or some of the time, it is a problem. Debates about frequency are usually not to the point. Partners should be encouraged to avoid over-generalizations.

Rule 3: Express Your Feelings.

- "I feel rejected and unloved when you don't include me in your Friday night plans."
- "It's very frustrating to me when I want sex but have to wait for you to initiate it."
- "I get angry when you leave your clothes on the floor."
- "I feel hurt when I think the time is right but you don't show me affection, like after we go to see a romantic movie."

Almost always, when behavior objectionable, it is because the be-havior (or lack of it) has an emotionally upsetting impact. If the be-havior doesn't have such an impact, it would not be the subject of a problem-solving session. It is important to make these feelings known, in addition to pinpointing the behavior that led to the feel-ings. When the discomfort is disclosed, the partner may be more sym-pathetic. Partners should not assume that their feelings are obvious. If feelings are stated directly, the other can avoid the hazardous, and often not very reliable, task of trying to guess what they are. Good problem-solving communication means sharing feelings as well as openly admitting to the behavior that is upsetting.

Rule 4: Be Brief When Defining Problems. In general, problem-solving is oriented towards the future. The question which pervades most problem-solving sessions is the following one: "Something is troub-ling one of us; what can we do in the future to prevent a recurrence of this discomfort?" The only exception to this focus on the future is when the problem is defined. Since problem definitions describe be-havior that upsets one or both partners, they must make reference to things that have occurred in the past. But the main objective in the problem-solving definition phase is for the one who is not defining the problem to understand exactly what it is that the partner is upset about and how he or she feels when the problem occurs. The defini-tion should be as brief as possible. Once both partners have a clear understanding of what the problem is, the focus should immediately turn to "What do we do about it?"

Couples often become bogged down in this definition phase. They spend an excessive amount of time engaged in an unproductive focus on the past. This makes the probability of an argument higher. It also lengthens problem-solving sessions unnecessarily, thereby making them less enjoyable and more tedious. Finally, these discussions often contribute nothing toward the ultimate solution. "Talking about" the problem may be interesting, but it is not problem-solving. Don't confuse the two. Here are common ways that couples devote excessive time to describing rather than solving a problem:

1.   Couples mention as many examples as they can remember of the problem's occurrence and then argue over the details of particular examples.

2.   Couples analyze their problem and try to come up with the cause of the problem.

3.   Couples ask "why" questions: "Why are you so stubborn?" "Why can't you just remember to be on time?" "Why do you hold your feelings in?" etc.

These are all appropriate topics for acceptance work, but they are not part of PST. There is no need to list example after example of the problem's occurrence in the past. Doing so is not conducive to solving the problem: the one about whom the complaints are being registered feels like defending his/her behavior every time it is mentioned, and the one who is defining the problem finds him/herself getting angrier and angrier just talking about all the awful things the partner has done in the past. Neither ends up in a frame of mind conducive to collaborative work on solving the problem.

It should be noted, however, that sometimes, in order for the partner to really understand what the spouse is upset about, he or she will ask for some specific examples of the behavior. This is certainly acceptable during the definition phase of problem-solving. The difference is that he/she is asking for examples in order to clarify what it is he/she is doing that is problematic vs. hearing an unsolicited diatribe on every past misdeed the partner can think of.

Nor is it useful to spend a lot of time trying to uncover the past cause of the problem. Often, such speculations about causality can be useful during acceptance work, but they are hindrances during PST. Even if the "cause" of the problem is discovered, that realization does not solve the problem per se. For example, "I get upset when you stay out until 1:00 a.m. because my parents used to leave me with baby-sitters a lot, and I felt insecure." This connection between a childhood event and current behavior may or may not be accurate; in either case, it makes little difference in terms of coming to agreement about what to do about the problem.

In addition, there is another type of "cause" that is relevant to the problem definition and should not be included in our general caution about irrelevant digressions. These are "immediate" causes, that is, events that occur along with the defined problem and seem to have some relationship to the defined problem. For example:

- "I don't intentionally hide my feelings from you; it's just that it seldom occurs to me to share them with you."
- "I have trouble thinking of things to do with the kids. That is one of the reasons I spend so little time with them."

In other words, mentioning the apparent reason for the occurrence or non-occurrence of some behavior often adds to the understanding of the problem. Although these factors should be mentioned, make sure that the discussion does not shift to them. The focus should remain on the defined problem, although the eventual solution may take these immediate causes into account. The danger is that one partner will blame his/her behavior on the immediate cause, and thereby deny responsibility for doing anything about it. Immediate causes are factors to be taken into account, not reasons for avoiding a direct focus on the problem.

"Why" questions are specific invitations to focus on the alleged cause of the problem rather than ways to solve it. In addition, "why" questions are usually experienced as critical. The recipient of a "why" question is likely to feel threatened and "set up." Couples should be discouraged from asking "why" questions during PST; instead they should be encouraged to expend their energy changing the situation so that the behavior ceases to be a problem.

Conclusions: A Well-Defined Problem

A well-defined problem includes a positive statement, a description of the undesirable behavior, a specification of the situations in which the problem occurs, and the consequences of the problem for the partner who was distressed by it. A list of well-defined problems follows:

1. I love to do things with you and when we have planned activities together I really feel close to you, but lately on Sundays when neither of us is working, you have seldom helped me plan things to do together. I end up feeling like the re-

sponsibility for our leisure time is all on my shoulders, and I resent it. At those times, I feel angry and unloved.

2. I have always enjoyed talking to you and finding out what you have been doing and thinking about, but now that our work schedules leave us so little time together, we've done very little talking. When you come home at night at 10:30 and watch television, I feel upset and hurt and left out.

3. I really appreciate the way you handle our finances and never go over our budget, but I get pissed off when I notice the checkbook is not balanced, particularly when you have let it go for more than two weeks.

4. Your opinion means a lot to me and I feel very good when you give me credit for doing something well, but I get a lot of criticism from you about how I do the housework, particularly the dishwashing. It really irks me when you do that since I do 90% of the housework, and I end up feeling angry and resentful.

5. I love it when you hug me when you come home from work and we talk about how our days went, but when you get up in the morning and are silent and don't say anything to me like "Good morning" or "Hello" or "Would you like some coffee?" I feel very distant from you.

6. I love to make love with you and I feel very special when you initiate sex, but when you let a week go by without initiating or telling me that you'd like to make love with me, I feel rejected.

7. I think you are a wonderful mother and really have good ideas about how to raise the children, but when you break in and discipline Annie while I'm in the middle of disciplining her myself, I get very angry at you.

8. You know, when you open up to me and tell me about your feelings, I really like it and I feel very close to you. The problem is that, although we've been talking more lately, we've not been communicating about things that are really important to me, like how you really feel about certain things. I tend to turn off to you when you don't talk more, and feel distant from you and rather lonely.

Rule 5: Both Partners Should Acknowledge Their Role in Creating and Maintaining the Problem. This is the first rule that applies to the receiver of the problem definition as well as the one who has stated

the problem. In the competitive disputes that all too commonly substitute for problem-solving, each partner tries to deny the validity of
the other's point of view or tries to blame the partner.

Example #1: The wife says: You spend very little time playing with
Linda.

Husband responds: I already play with Linda more than you do.
(*denial of responsibility*) Besides, whenever I try to play with Linda,
you interfere. (*blaming her for problem*)

Wife: That's not true. (*denying responsibility*)

In this example the husband first denies that there is any problem
with anything he's doing, and then goes on to blame his wife for there
being a problem at all. His wife feels attacked and also denies any
responsibility for the problem. Each partner competes to point the
finger at the other. They are blaming each other rather than accepting
responsibility and working together.

In a real problem-solving session, where couples are collaborating to
solve a common problem for the mutual gains that follow from an
improved relationship, both partners adopt the stance of admitting to
their role in the problem rather than casting blame.

Example #2: Wife: You spend very little time playing with Linda.

Husband: You're right, I don't spend a whole lot of time with her
these days. (*admitting to his role*)

Wife: I know that I can make it hard for you to play with Linda
because I sometimes step in and interfere. (*admits to her role in problem*)

Notice that in this example both are admitting that they have some
responsibility in creating the problem. Openly acknowledging their
role in contributing to the problem does wonders to change the spirit
of the problem-solving session from being very negative and blaming
to being an open, honest, collaborative experience.

The "listener" (the one not defining the problem) should go first in
accepting responsibility, as in example #2. There are various degrees
of accepting one's role and we are not suggesting that spouses admit
to more than they feel is justified. Their instructions are simply to
accept as much responsibility as they truthfully can. It could mean
simply saying, "I can see that you're upset and I'm willing to work on
it with you." Here they are at least acknowledging that the partner is
upset and expressing their willingness to work on the problem. To go
one step further and acknowledge more of a role, an example might
be, "Yes, I admit that I do that and I understand why you would be
upset by it. Let's work on it." The most collaborative stance to take

would be to admit to what the partner is complaining about, acknowledge some understanding of the partner's feelings, and add something like, "I'd be upset too if you were to do that to me, and I'd really like to work with you and try to resolve this." The main idea is to express willingness to work collaboratively on the issue.

Once the "listener" has accepted responsibility for his/her role in the problem, the one who defined the problem should also mention how he/she contributes to the creation of the problem. The idea is to acknowledge openly to the partner that he/she helped create or perpetuate the problem. Problems between two people usually involve both parties in some way.

General Rules

Before specifying the optimal strategies for generating good solutions to relationship problems, we will identify some general rules that should be observed during all phases of a problem-solving session, whether the immediate task is problem definition or problem solution.

Rule 6: Discuss Only One Problem at a Time. In a given problem-solving session, only one problem should be discussed. When an additional problem is brought in, it is referred to as side-tracking. Couples are frequently guilty of side-tracking, to the point where it often occurs without either party being aware of it. It takes many forms, as the following examples suggest:

1. W: The problem is that I would like you to be nicer to my mother.
   H: Since when are you nice to my mother? (*side-track*)

2. W: I wish we had more interesting conversations.
   H: What can we do about that?
   W: Maybe if you had more outside interests. That's another thing I've been meaning to talk to you about. (*side-track*)

3. H: We have to try to show each other more affection.
   W: I think you're right. It would be hard at first.
   H: It would be good for Michael as well as for ourselves to see us being more affectionate.
   W: That sort of disturbs me because I feel that Mike and I are very close, but that you and he have no relationship. I wish you could somehow get to know him a little bit. (*side-track*)

    H: I know you're right. It is difficult for me to get to know Mike.

4.   W: I think we should panel the walls, and then buy furniture.

    H:I think we should buy the furniture first, and then panel the walls to match.

    W:Don't forget this house was your idea in the first place. (side-track)

    H:Well, it was either moving or having to put up with your brother right across the street. (side-track)

    W:You have never really given him a chance.

In each of these examples, the couple has drifted from the original topic to a new one. In the first example a discussion of the relationship between husband and mother-in-law becomes refocused on the wife and her mother-in-law. In the second case, the couple is discussing how to have more interesting conversations and then changes the topic to whether or not the husband should expand his leisure time activities outside the home. In the third instance, the topic moves from affection to the husband's relationship with his son. Finally, in a "double side-track," the couple begins by discussing the interior design of their home, shifts to the question of whose decision it was to buy the house in the first place, and terminates on the topic of the wife's brother.

The reason for restricting discussion to one problem at a time is simple. Solving two problems simultaneously is twice as difficult as solving one problem in isolation. One of the reasons that spouses find problem-solving so difficult is that they cannot talk about a problem without bringing in every problem in their relationship. Such a task is overwhelming. It is amazing how straightforward problem-solving can be if discussion is limited to one problem at a time.

Bilateral Problem Definition

At times it is difficult to draw the line between a side-track and a statement that merely pinpoints a related problem. For example, consider a situation where the husband defines the problem as the wife nagging him about household tasks. The wife responds by pointing out that she only nags him after he has procrastinated for a day or more. Is this a side-track? Clearly, she is bringing in a new problem, which is our definition of a side-track. Yet, she is also doing something that we have previously labeled as good practice when defining a problem, namely, she is identifying the situations in which nagging occurs.

In such a case, there are two ways to handle the situation. The "listener" could simply continue through the regular steps of problem definition and see whether or not the partner mentions the other side of the problem in his acknowledgment of his own role. Often the partner will know exactly how he contributes to the problem and there is no need for the listener to tell him once again. In this example, the wife could just admit that she does nag (acknowledge role) instead of immediately pointing out to the husband that she only nags him when he procrastinates (the latter is likely to put him on the defensive and may be interpreted as blaming him). Hopefully, when her husband accepts responsibility for his role in the problem, he will recognize that he does delay in completing tasks and acknowledge that as a contribution to the problem.

Many times, however, the partner will not say exactly what the other had hoped when he acknowledges his role and original complainant will be left thinking that he contributes to the problem in some major or minor way that needs to be brought out. This is when a bilateral (or two-sided) problem definition is useful. Both people define different aspects of the same problem before moving into the solution phase. If, for example, the husband originally brings up an issue, the couple would first go through all the steps necessary for a good problem definition. If the wife thinks that there is another aspect to the problem that has not been mentioned and would serve to clarify their mutual roles in the issue, she would then state that she thinks the problem is bilateral and proceed to define the problem from her point of view. The couple would go through all the steps of a good problem definition once more. In the example of the nagging wife and procrastinating husband, the bilateral problem definition might look something like this:

H: You know, I appreciate the care you take to keep the house neat. I really like the fact that you care about how the house looks, but when you tell me more than once to do a particular task, I really get angry and I resent it. (*defining the problem*)

W: I realize I do keep reminding you, sometimes in a not so pleasant way, and I'd like to work on this with you. (*acknowledges own role*)

H: I realize that I am probably more sensitive to this than most people would be. (*acknowledges own role*)

W: I think there is another aspect to this that would help us understand the issue.

I really appreciate it that you do all the things that you do around the house—lots of men don't help at all—but what irritates me is when I ask you to do something and it takes you two or three days to start doing it. (*defines the problem, adding new information*)

H: I realize that I do procrastinate and I can see how that would irritate you. (*acknowledges own role*)

W: I realize that I don't always jump up and do things right away when you ask me to do something either. (*acknowledges own role*)

In this way, both are able to bring up their own sides of the problem in a way that is least likely to arouse anger or defensiveness in the partner. By having the additional information given in the second definition, the couple will be better able to propose solutions that include changes on the part of both individuals.

Rule 7: Paraphrase. When spouse A makes a remark, spouse B is encouraged to summarize it before responding. After the summary statement, B is advised to check its accuracy with A. If it was accurate, fine. Then B has the floor. However, if A does not think the summary statement was accurate, he or she should repeat the original remark, and B should try it again, until both feel that the summary and the original are one and the same. Below are examples:

1. W: I feel very close to you when you express interest and support in my activities outside. Lately I've been feeling rejected by you when I try to talk to you about work; you haven't been asking questions or making supportive remarks.

    H: You like it when I show interest and support for your job experiences, and lately you feel that I haven't shown much interest. Is that what you said?

    W: Yes.

    H: I wasn't aware of that. I can understand how that would be upsetting to you.

2. H: You're very physically responsive to me at times. That is very important to me. But I've been noticing lately that when I initiate affection you don't respond. That hurts me a lot, and I feel unloved.

    W: You are saying that you've had some doubts lately about whether or not I love you.

    H: No, I know that you love me. But you are not affectionate to me unless you are the one who initiates it.

W: Oh, so you're upset about my not returning affection
   when you initiate it.
H: That's it.

Summary statements can be powerful ways of clarifying and improving communication. First, knowing that they will have to summarize forces spouses to listen carefully. Second, the summary statement helps ensure that the speaker will understand what the other person has said. If the summary statement indicates misunderstanding, it will be immediately corrected. Third, summary statements minimize the likelihood of interrupting the other person's speech. Fourth, summary statements help each see things from the other person's perspective.

Rule 8: Don't Make Inferences. Talk Only About What You Can Observe.

- "I don't think you're mad at me because I criticize your driving. I think it had more to do with my refusing to have sex with you last night."
- "There's a lot of anger inside waiting to come out."
- "You're trying to get me to do things that you know I shouldn't have to do for you."
- "As soon as I become more independent, you're going to leave me. That's why you're coming to therapy."

All of the above examples constitute attempts on the part of one spouse to speculate about what the partner is thinking or feeling. We refer to this practice as mind-reading. Mind-reading is very useful in many modes of marital communication, including empathic joining and other types of acceptance work, but it is a hindrance to PST. The entire process is built on being specific and relying what can be observed. Also, people often don't like to have their minds read.

A particular form of mind-reading that is both common and dangerous to problem-solving is the attempt to infer the partner's intentions from his/her behavior. Consider the following example:

W: When you made fun of me in front of Rick and Barbara, it really pissed me off. I don't like it when you crack jokes at my expense in front of other people. You were trying to humiliate me.
H: I was not trying to humiliate you.

The wife is not only describing to her husband the behavior that was upsetting, but also accusing him of bad intentions. She has no way of knowing what his intentions were, and by insisting that he intended, with his remarks, to humiliate her she is focusing on the wrong issue. The husband is now obliged to defend his benevolent intentions, and the conversation has been diverted into an unproductive area. Disputes about what people are thinking or feeling cannot be resolved; only one partner has direct access to such an inner state. The real issue is his behavior, which was upsetting to her regardless of his intentions. Whenever one partner's behavior is upsetting to the other, it is legitimate to focus on it, but it is not legitimate in PST to leave the behavior aside and instead focus on the person's motivation. Stick to the behavior; this is the simplest and most effective way to problem-solve.

The confusion of intentions with behavior can interfere with problem-solving in still another way, as illustrated by the following example:

H: I don't like it when you criticize my housework.
W: But I'm just trying to be helpful.
H: But I don't like it.
W: But don't you see? I really don't mean any harm.

Here the wife is justifying her behavior on the basis of her good intentions. She is claiming that, given her good intentions, she does not have to change her behavior. But the husband is really asking her to stop criticizing his housework, regardless of whether or not her intentions are to be critical. Although her intentions are constructive, her behavior is destructive. If her behavior is upsetting to her husband, it is a legitimate problem, regardless of her intentions.

Rule 9: Be Neutral Rather Than Negative. When spouses are fighting rather than collaborating, their interaction is frequently punctuated by attempts to put down, humiliate, or intimidate each other. Such power struggles constitute the antithesis of problem-solving. As such, their presence serves as a clear indication that more acceptance work needs to be done.

Solving Problems and Forming Change Agreements

Rule 10: Focus on Solutions. Once a couple has agreed on a definition to a problem, the focus should henceforth be on solving it. The discussion should be future-oriented and should answer the question, "What can we do to eliminate this problem and keep it from coming back?"

Returns to problem definition should not occur; in fact, there should be no further discussion of the past.

The most effective way to maintain a focus on solutions and on the future is by brainstorming. This means the partners go back and forth, generating as many possible solutions to the problem as they can think of, without regard to the quality of the solutions. Solutions should include behavior changes on the part of both the husband and the wife. If the problem is a bilateral one, solutions should be generated to take into account both sides of the problem. Some of the proposed solutions should be completely absurd. The important point is that partners be encouraged to use their imaginations and say anything that comes into their minds, without censoring anything, no matter how silly and unworkable it may seem. Each proposed solution should be written down.

Brainstorming is so effective because it keeps couples focused on the task of arriving at a solution to the problem; also, if the rules are obeyed, couples are less inhibited in suggesting things. People often hold back from suggesting solutions because a given proposal may seem inadequate when it is considered privately; yet, when it is verbalized and later considered publicly, it often contains at least some merit.

As an example, consider a couple, Chester and April, who had difficulty in a social situation with another couple, Sam and Connie, because Chester did not like Connie. Even though the wives were close friends, almost every time the four of them got together Chester would either withdraw or make nasty remarks directed at Connie. After brainstorming, Chester and April came up with the following list of solutions:

1. We will not socialize with Sam and Connie anymore.
2. We will socialize with Sam and Connie only when other couples are present.
3. Chester will have an affair with Connie.
4. Chester will make a flattering remark to Connie at the beginning of an evening to set the mood.
5. The foursome will engage in activities that don't require entire evenings of conversation (e.g., movies, theater).
6. Sam and Connie will enter couple therapy.
7. The foursome will hold a joint problem-solving session.
8. Chester and April will relate positively to one another and not split up enough to allow opposite-sexed pairings between couples.

9. The couples will stay close to one another physically and sit so that Chester and Connie are not close together.

From this original list, proposals #3, 6, and 7 were eliminated as absurd, and #1 was eliminated since both Chester and April agreed that the foursome was worth preserving. This left them with #4, 5, 8 and 9. The eventual agreement was as follows:

> In future evenings with Sam and Connie, we will make sure that we function as a couple and not allow Sam and April or Chester and Connie to pair off. Physically, we will sit next to each other and put April in between Chester and Connie. We will suggest activities that provide us with breaks from an entire evening of conversation (e.g., movies). Chester will start the evening off by complimenting or flattering Connie.

Consider, as another example, Tim and Elaine, who had been plagued with a problem for years: Tim had a tendency to engage in extramarital affairs. A brainstorming session uncovered two factors which had never been brought out into the open before: first, the sexual aspects of Tim's affairs were really unimportant compared to Tim's wanting to maintain a diversified social life with people of both sexes; second, Elaine's concerns were not so much the relationships themselves, but the understandable feelings she had that she was being rejected for these other women. Here were the specific proposals generated during the brainstorming session:

1. Tim will sleep with any woman he is attracted to.
2. Elaine will start to sleep with men she is attracted to.
3. Tim will tell Elaine when he is attracted to another woman, and they will discuss it.
4. Tim will not form any kind of relationship with other women.
5. Tim will have platonic relationships with other women, but will not sleep with them.
6. Tim and Elaine will both have sex with the women whom Tim is attracted to.
7. Tim will discuss his daily social interactions with Elaine at night.
8. Tim will get together with other women only during the day.

9. Tim will see other women only in public places or at their home, with Elaine present.

From this list of solutions the following agreement was formed:

Tim agrees to forever stop sleeping with other women. He has the right to pursue friendships with women, under the following conditions: (1) he will get together with them only during the day; (2) He will get together with them only in public places or at his home, when Elaine is present; (3) he will discuss his activities upon coming home, on days when he gets together with a woman. In return Elaine will refrain from making suspicious or mistrustful remarks regarding Tim's activities.

Rule 11: Behavior Change Should Include Mutuality and Compromise. In the spirit of collaboration and cooperation, whenever possible, problem solutions should involve change on the part of both partners. This is true even in situations where the problem is clearly pointing to change on the part of one person. One reason for this is that both partners are more likely to be change if they are not doing it alone. Another reason is that a partner can often help the other person change by providing feedback or teaching the partner some skill. In this sense, providing feedback or teaching a skill is the change to which the second partner is agreeing. Finally, at times some behavior on the part of one partner may be serving as a reward for the negative behavior of the other partner, or the former may be able to do something following the change that will reinforce the latter for that change.

As an example of the first reason mentioned—being more willing to change if both people change—consider the husband who was upset because his wife left clothes on the floor. After battling over this problem for years, the husband finally asked, "How can I help you change?" They quickly reached an agreement that permanently settled the issue. Each night prior to bed the husband and wife walked through the house together, hand in hand, picking up clothes. It became a game they both enjoyed, and they went to bed every night feeling closer.

The second reason for offering to join in the change process is that the complainant can provide valuable feedback and instructions that may help the process of change along. Consider the husband who, as far as his wife was concerned, spent an insufficient amount of time playing with their three-year-old daughter. One factor that emerged from their problem-solving discussion was that the husband felt incompetent as a father and had difficulty thinking of things to do with the daughter. The wife offered to help her husband by planning activities for the husband and daughter to engage in. With her help he found it much easier to interact with his daughter and quickly became independent of his wife's instructions.

The third reason for changing at the same time as the partner changes, even when the problem is defined in terms of the other person's behavior, is that the behavior of spouse A may be related to spouse B's in such a way that a change in A would make it more likely that B would change. For example, a couple was in conflict over who should do what with the kids. The wife wanted her husband to put the kids to bed at night. In the service of her own request, she granted him complete control over this task; she would leave him alone while he put the kids to bed. This was a big help, since in the past she often interfered with his efforts out of fear that he would do something wrong. When she agreed to leave him alone, he unburdened her of this responsibility.

As a rule of thumb, it behooves complainants to begin the solution phase with an offer to change some aspect of their own behavior. As in the above examples, this offer can take one of two forms: either the complainant can offer to help the partner change or the complainant can change some aspect of his/her own behavior to make it more likely that the partner will change for the better. Thus, during brainstorming, we advise complainants to begin with an offer to change some aspect of their own behavior, prior to requesting a change from the partner.

Remind partners that they must be willing to compromise if they expect their partner to change. It is difficult to change. The more complete the change that people request, the harder it will be for the person who is supposedly changing. Yet spouses often act as if they have to have it all immediately; otherwise they don't want it. A wife who felt that she carried the full child-rearing load suggested, for example, that her husband take on 50% of the child-rearing beginning the next day, without considering the fact that he was working more than full-time outside the home and she was not working at all outside the home. May suggested that Benito change from a quiet partner to a man who talked about his feelings on a daily basis. Al expected Pam to change from being a procrastinator to someone who fulfilled all of her responsibilities on time without ever being reminded. Edgar asked Jackie to give up drinking beer completely, even though beer was her favorite drink. Distressed spouses frequently demand sweeping changes from their partners, changes that seem so overwhelming that partners simply refuse.

Couples should be encouraged to consider another strategy. What about starting with less than what they would ideally want, but something that seems more feasible? Complainees may be more willing to agree to such requests. Later one may want to ask for more, but by that time they will have already moved in the right direction and the request will not seem as overwhelming. Or, partners may even find that they are perfectly content with the amount of change that has already occurred. Not only can acceptance lead to change, but change can lead to acceptance.

Whenever change is desired, partners should be encouraged to formulate the problem in two ways:

1. What do I ideally want?
2. What am I willing to settle for?

The answer to question #2 should always be somewhat different from the answer to question #1. Otherwise, there is some collaboration missing, and PST may be premature.

Willard and Penny only had Sundays together. Penny virtually always planned their Sundays for the family and wanted Willard to play a role.

1. Ideally, she wanted to trade Sundays, so that every other Sunday it was Willard's responsibility to plan their time together.
2. As a compromise, she suggested that Willard plan one Sunday per month. He agreed, and she turned out to be satisfied with this solution.

Tom complained about Ann's high frequency of verbal criticism. He defined her nagging as, "reminding me to do things or commenting on the fact that I haven't done what I said I would do."

1. Ideally he wanted her to drop such verbal comments from her repertoire entirely. She found this extremely difficult.
2. He was willing to settle for a change in the "content" of her verbal comments. They agreed to set a deadline on particular tasks, and she agreed to comment only on the fact that the deadline had been reached if the task was not completed within the allotted period. The agreement worked, but it was never necessary to really test out the last part of it, since the setting of specific deadlines eliminated the problem of Tom not completing tasks.

Lenore had a tendency to drink a lot of beer on weekends. On a Friday night, she would typically consume a six-pack. This would result in her becoming tired early, which in turn would lead to an unwillingness on her part to engage in sexual activity. She would also become verbally abusive on occasion.

1. Ideally, Ralph wanted Lenore to stop drinking beer entirely. This wish was based on his belief that she could not control her beer drinking once it started. Since Lenore really liked the taste of beer, she refused to give it up.

2. He was willing to settle for her limiting her consumption to two beers during the course of an evening. Lenore agreed to do this and was able to stop with two.

In all of these examples, the complaining spouse was willing to settle for less than what he or she would have insisted on in the past. The partner was able to honor the new requests without cramping his/her style to any great degree, whereas the original, sweeping changes were more than he or she was willing to make. More often than not, the complaining spouse was so happy with the changes that the original request was no longer deemed necessary.

An exercise that is often valuable during a problem-solving session is to have spouse A explicitly tell spouse B what he or she would expect in the best of all possible worlds. Then the spouse B can respond by telling spouse A how close he or she is willing to come to granting that ideal wish.

Rule 12: Discuss Pros and Cons of Proposed Solutions. Many couples find that a structured approach to discussing the possible solutions works best. It keeps them from escalating into arguments and serves to accomplish the task (solving the problem) efficiently.

Consider the brainstormed list of solutions. Have one person lead the discussion by reading off the first proposed solution. The first question to ask is, "Is this absurd?" If both agree that the idea is completely ridiculous and was actually thrown in for some comic relief, it is crossed off and the next solution is read. If either thinks it is not absurd, the proposal is formally considered along with all of the others.

The format for discussing a proposal is to begin with the question, "If we were to adopt this solution, would it contribute to resolving the problem?" If the answer is "yes," they then discuss the benefits and costs of implementing that solution. Problem-solving is usually a more positive experience if all of the good or potentially good things about the solution are discussed before the costs are enumerated. For example, if spouse A had offered a particular solution and spouse B's first response was, "The thing I don't like about that is . . ." and then went on to list a whole host of reasons the solution wouldn't work, A would probably feel deflated or angry. The whole tone of the problem-solving session would quickly become very negative. If, however, B were to acknowledge that this solution did have some merit and say some good things about it, A would probably feel more positively about the level of collaboration and the prospect of discussing future problems.

After the "costs" of a proposal have been discussed, partners must decide whether to (a) eliminate it from the list, (b) include it as part of the solution or change agreement, or (c) defer a final decision until all proposals have been discussed. If (b), other proposals can be added; in other words, an affirmative response to one proposal does not preclude the adoption of others as well. If (c) is chosen, partners return to it later, after they have considered the rest of the proposals on the list. Whatever they decide to do with a given proposal, the process is repeated for each item on the list: (1) eliminate it if both agree that it is absurd; (2) decide whether it would contribute to solving the problem; (3) discuss the benefits of and costs to each spouse of adopting this proposal; (4) decide whether to eliminate, include, or defer.

Rule 13: Reach Agreement. Once brainstorming and related exercises have generated a series of possible solutions, the task becomes one of combining those solutions in such a way that change agreements are reached. Ultimately, the ability to agree on and implement behavior change is the acid test of effective problem-solving. After discussing the pros and cons of each proposed solution on the list, including the consequences of each proposal for each partner and for the relationship, the proposals should be combined into a final agreement. Keep in mind the following points:

- Final change agreements should be very specific. They should be spelled out in clear, descriptive, behavioral terms.
- The agreement should clearly state what each spouse is going to do differently. Too often couples agree to vague changes, and subsequently it is unclear exactly what the agreement was. When each person walks away with a different interpretation of the agreement, future clashes over what was

meant by the terms of the agreement frequently occur. Along the same lines, disagreements can arise in the future over whether the agreement was complied with.

- Change agreements should not be open to interpretation. From the terms of the agreement the behaviors that are required for compliance should be absolutely clear. The terms should include a description of the exact changes to be made, along with when these changes are expected to occur and, if possible, the frequency with which the new behaviors are to occur.

Here are some examples of bad agreements and the modifications that would be necessary to make them conform to this rule:

1. Bad: Adolfo agrees to come home on time from now on.
    Good: On Monday through Friday, Adolfo will be home by 6:30 p.m. If for some reason this is impossible on a particular night, he will let Marlene know by 4:30 p.m., and at that time will tell her when he will be home.

2. Bad: Mike will show more interest in Holly's day.
    Good: Each day when Holly and Mike get home, before dinner Holly will speak with Mike about the events of her day. Mike will ask at least five questions of Holly regarding her day. He will also avoid the use of put-downs and other derogatory remarks, which to Holly imply disinterest.

3. Bad: Dashel will make an effort to talk more about his feelings to Lillian.
    Good: On Tuesday and Thursday nights, Dashel and Lillian will engage in a discussion that covers events through the days since the last session. Lillian will describe feelings she had in the various situations she was in. Then Dashel will do the same thing with his past few days.

4. Bad: Dana will try to do more of her part around the house.
    Good: Dana will be responsible for washing the dishes (to be completed within an hour of dinner), walking the dog (twice per day, 7:30–8:00 a.m. and 9:30–10:00 p.m.), and sweeping the floor every other evening before bed.

5. Bad: Patty will not be as apprehensive about the future, and will have more confidence in Cosmo.
    Good: Patty will respond to Cosmo in conversation about his job when he initiates such conversation. During these

conversations she will not make pessimistic remarks about his future with the company.

6. Bad: Don will be more understanding when Laura is depressed.

Good: Don will actively listen and "reflect" Laura's verbalizations of her depression. He will not offer suggestions unless she asks for them. Nor will he express annoyance or frustration.

You will note that these agreements are quite structured in their content. They seem mechanical and artificial. It is true that to some extent these kinds of agreements are mechanical and artificial. However, don't forget that in many cases couples are trying to change very long-standing habits. Such habits are very difficult to change, and the changes do not come naturally. If the changes are to occur, a good deal of structure is necessary at first. Later, after the changes have been in place for a while, they will become more natural and the need for such explicit structure will be reduced. Chances are that clarity and structure were missing from their previous attempts to deal with these problems.

- Final change agreements should include cues reminding both partner of the changes that they have agreed to make.

In many instances, the problem is not that an individual is unwilling to comply with the partner's request, but that when the time comes he/she simply forgets. This is particularly likely with long-standing habits. In such cases, the agreement should include some way of reminding the other person of the change to which he/she has agreed. Sometimes the agreement itself, written down and posted where it is likely to be seen, is sufficient. At other times the agreement can include reminders from the spouse. One of the more inventive uses of an external cue involved a husband's placing a sign on the dashboard of his car that read "EXTJ"; this meant, "express feelings to Judy."

- Final change agreements should be recorded in writing.

This has been mentioned before, and it is very important. First, writing down agreements means less reliance on memories. Memories tend to distort in directions most beneficial to our interests. Second, when agreements are put in writing, partners will be more precise; ambiguities in communication will become obvious and be ironed out in the writing process. Third, the written agreement, conveniently posted somewhere in the house, will remind partners of what they have agreed to.

Closing Comments

Once couples have formally written up an agreement, they should take a few minutes to read over the problem definition and the final agreement and check to make sure that the agreed-upon solutions really address the problem. Each partner should be satisfied with the changes specified in the agreement. If the problem was a unilateral one, it demonstrates collaboration if the spouse asks the one who defined the problem how satisfied he or she is with the solution. That is, if the husband was the one who raised a particular problem, the wife might ask at the end of the problem-solving session how happy he is with the proposed solution and if he thinks this will be a significant step in resolving the issue for him. If he is not satisfied, it is best to do some more work (either then or at a later time), rather than accepting a poor agreement that is not likely to help rectify the problem.

In any case, every agreement that is made should be reviewed at some specified future date to evaluate how well it is working and to determine whether it has successfully solved the problem. When an agreement is signed, partners should set a date for this evaluation. Every agreement should have a "trial run" for a specified period of time.

Reviewing every agreement and renegotiating those that are not working constitute important steps in the process of conflict resolution. Sometimes the first agreement will work, and the review will serve to reinforce the changes that have been made. However, often the first agreement will not be the perfect solution and may even create new problems. It is crucial that partners renegotiate the agreement by brainstorming some new ideas or reevaluating the original solutions. No one wants to be locked into an agreement forever, particularly if it is not working.

In an ideal world, PST becomes a natural part of the couple's relationship. Even after spouses have solved their major problems in therapy, they should have time put aside for occasional problem-solving sessions. These "state of the relationship" sessions provide opportunities to deal with any conflict that has arisen since the last problem-solving session and to go over prior agreements and discuss how they are working. If an agreement is not working well or if circumstances have changed such that the agreement is impractical, it should be renegotiated.

Conclusion

In this chapter, we have reviewed strategies for teaching communication skills, the role of such strategies in ICT, some of the subtleties in communication training—which can be used either in the service of acceptance or change—and PST. While it is not for all couples, PST remains an important component of the ICT repertoire.

— 10 —

DIVERSITY IN GENDER, CULTURE, ETHNICITY, CLASS, AND SEXUAL ORIENTATION: CLINICAL IMPLICATIONS

We use the word "couple" rather than "marital" in the title of this book because the approach is intended to be applicable to unmarried as well as married couples, same-sex as well as heterosexual couples. In our clinical practices, we have found that ICT is applicable to all of the above groups, with few fundamental alterations in the basic strategy. Moreover, we have had occasion to work with African American, Asian, and Latino couples, and have applied ICT successfully.

ICT has as its cornerstone a recognition of diversity. In fact, any functional analytic approach is idiographic by definition and is thus adaptive to wide variations in behavior-environmental relationships. Thus far, we have discussed diversity in terms of individual differences in couples on various dimensions: severity of distress, level of commitment, age, degree of incompatibility, and theme, just to name a few. Yet, there are also group differences between couples as a function of their gender, race, culture, or sexual orientation that have treatment implications. There has been no research done on the ways in which ICT will need to be altered as a function of these macro-contextual variables. However, based on some information and our own clinical experience, we will offer some opinions on these matters in this chapter. Some of our observations may be applicable to any type of couple therapy, not just ICT. Others may be particular to our approach.

The Politics of Intimacy: Gender Issues

As Jacobson has argued elsewhere (Jacobson, 1983, 1989), a growing body of literature suggests that the traditional marriage contributes to life satisfaction more for men than it does for women. In fact, the protection that marriage offers from physical and mental health problems may be true only for men. Some epidemiological studies (Radloff & Rae, 1979) have actually found that women are at increased risk for depression if they are married, while married men are afforded protection from depression. Thus, it is fair to say that marriage has generally been beneficial to both men and women, but that many of its benefits have been greater for men. Moreover, in some respects women may be better off single, especially when it comes to mental health problems. For example, married mothers with young children are at higher risk for major depression than single women or married women without children.

Certainly, the clinical literature suggests that men are more satisfied with their marriages than women are. Margolin and colleagues (1983), for example, found that wives wanted more change in every aspect of their marriages, except for sex, than did their husbands. We know from our own research that wives are the ones who seek therapy 70–80% of the time: often, the wives come into therapy eager for change, while husbands come grudgingly, if at all, and either enter therapy satisfied with the relationship as it is or desiring changes that are in the opposite direction to those desired by the wife.

And what are the typical changes that wives want? They want greater intimacy with their husbands, more involvement from their husbands in housework and childcare, and more companionship (Christensen & Heavey, 1993). Husbands typically want to maintain the current level of intimacy, stay as uninvolved as they currently are, and keep the amount of time spent in companionship constant. If they want change, it is often in the direction of greater distance, less involvement, and more time to themselves.

This is the essence of the "closeness/distance" theme described in Chapter 3, the most common theme among couples we have studied and treated. In this theme, as well as others (e.g., control/responsibility), women tend to be in the role of "demanding" change, while men tend to be in the role of "withdrawing" from change (Christensen & Heavey, 1993). This demand-withdraw pattern is the most common way that couples polarize. Thus, both the most common theme and the most common polarizing phenomenon in couples seeking therapy are gender-linked.

Wives, in other words, have historically been the "barometers" of marital satisfaction (Floyd & Markman, 1983). The structure of the marriage often suggests unequal power. Not only is the inequality implied by the fact that women want to change the structure, but it is also implicit in the roles played by men and women in traditional marriages. Using one or more of many existing yardsticks, wives and mothers have less status in the culture than those who achieve through work outside the home: the self-esteem implications follow directly from these cultural contingencies. However, when married women work, the situation may actually get worse, since in dual-career households married women maintain their housework and parenting responsibilities, whereas married men continue to play subordinate roles in these areas; in fact, there is some evidence that working women actually do more housework relative to their husbands than nonworking women (Brines, 1994). Thus, although there may be additional self-esteem derived from the work outside the home, this is counteracted by the burden of having essentially two full-time jobs. It is pretty clear why women are dissatisfied with the structure of marriage: it is a better deal for men than it is for them!

In addition to the factors mentioned above, there are others that make marriages more distressing for women and marital distress more damaging to women. The power differential is exacerbated by the resources held by men that are desired by women: the husband's sharing of himself and his internal life, his time, his attention, and his involvement in instrumental activities are all relatively scarce resources. Since the wife wants these resources that the husband is withholding, he has power over her, as anyone does when he has something that the other wants, but won't give it. When marriages become dissatisfying or unstable, the consequences are often greater for women because more of their personal happiness is bound up in the success of their intimate relationships (Koerner et al., 1994). This issue will be delineated further in the next chapter.

For all of these reasons, marriage as an institution is more oppressive to women than it is to men. Because of these built-in cultural influences, each couple seeking therapy presents in part a microcosm of these factors. These cultural practices have to be taken into account when conducting ICT. The pronouncements of a therapist both reflect the culture and influence the culture; thus, therapist remarks can either reinforce or undermine the oppressive nature of marriage for women. Couple therapy, like any other form of psychotherapy (Halleck, 1970), is inherently political in this sense (Jacobson, 1989).

The way we attempted to cope with this issue in traditional behavioral couple therapy (TBCT), based on this analysis, was to share our pro-egalitarian values with our clients and to directly advocate for peer as opposed to traditional marriages. This seemed to us the only honorable, ethical, and morally defensible position to take. Since our own views and values were likely to influence the process of therapy in more insidious ways if we kept them to ourselves, it also seemed to make good therapeutic sense to be explicit about our values.

Now, several years later, and after the development of integrative couple therapy (ICT), we see things somewhat differently. First of all, neither of us has ever seen a traditional marriage become egalitarian as a result of the couple's knowing that we favor egalitarianism. Nor have we found covert attempts to promote egalitarianism successful. For example, we have tried suggesting behavior exchange (BE) tasks and promoting change agreements in problem-solving training (PST) that move the couple in the direction of greater intimacy, a more equitable sharing of housework, and equal control over finances. It was almost as if couples had a structural "set point." They would inevitably revert and gravitate toward interactional patterns that maintained whatever level of traditionality they started with.

On the face of it, ICT would seem to compound the problem. Since we promote "acceptance" at least as much as "change," our approach could be viewed as contributing to the status quo, thus consolidating the oppression of women in their marital relationships. However, as we explained in Chapter 1, our definition of acceptance and our continued incorporation of change techniques act collectively to preclude this danger. Nevertheless, the stance of the therapist in ICT does preclude the didactic, psychoeducational approach inherent in providing the client with our opinions about what kinds of relationships work best. Furthermore, our functional analytic perspective leads us to the recognition that couples vary in how they maximize their marital satisfaction: as much as we would like the general cultural factors to make life simple for us, the fact is that not all wives suffer in traditional marriages and not all women are liberated from oppression in peer marriages. The world is more complicated than any ideology based on group norms. ICT has that complexity built into its structure. ICT therapists are permissive: they create conditions in therapy which foster the kind of relationship that works best for a particular couple. We have compassion for distancers as well as closeness seekers, whether they be men or women. We believe that there are multiple paths to a close relationship and even allow for the possibility that a "close" relationship is not always a good one or one that the partners want. Just as we are opposed to pathologizing closeness seeking by calling it "dependency," so are we opposed to pathologizing distancing by attributing it to a "fear of intimacy." We are pluralistic in our outlook of what constitutes a good marriage. This follows directly from our analysis of differences between partners: differences do not reflect the rights and wrongs of married life. In fact, it is the fundamental mistake that couples make to assume that differences imply a right and a wrong. Differences are just that, nothing more: not good, not bad, just different. Gottman's (1993) research confirms this pluralistic view: there are multiple paths to marital satisfaction, and each couple must find its own. If we adopt a non-evaluative stance toward differences, and help couples do the same, we almost invariably succeed in enhancing the quality of their marriage.

Nevertheless, we have noticed something interesting. When we avoid pathologizing differences and help spouses let go of their condemnation of the other for those differences, the trajectory they follow tends to be in the direction of egalitarianism. In other words, the more successful we are at avoiding advocacy of a particular kind of marriage, the more likely couples are to "choose" an egalitarian path. In a recent case, when Carla stopped blaming Jack for his distancing, and Jack stopped making false promises to be more intimate than felt comfortable to him, their relationship evolved into a more intimate one. We think that, as Carla stopped demanding that Jack be more intimate, he began to take risks that made him more vulnerable. Without another person telling him that he had to disclose personal feelings, he began to confide in Carla, gradually but steadily. Then the natural contingencies took over. Carla reinforced him for these intimate behaviors, not because the therapist told her to, but because these behaviors were naturally reinforcing for her, and she displayed their reinforcing value by softening toward him and showing him more love and appreciation. Jack responded to this love and appreciation by displaying more of himself to Carla, and they gradually moved toward a relationship that was satisfying for both of them and more egalitarian. But now it was what they both wanted.

This example is not atypical. It does not always turn out this way, but it happens more often than it did when we tried to force-feed the process through direct advocacy. Thus, the less you need it, the more likely you are to get it. There may be something inherently more rewarding about peer marriages for both partners. But they have to discover this for themselves. All the therapist can do is create a window of opportunity.

Same-sex Couples

Our limited experience suggests that ICT can be applied to same-sex couples without substantial modification of clinical procedures. Yet, unlike heterosexual couples, same-sex couples have to deal with a culture that is hostile to their very existence (Brown, 1995). This and other factors contribute to certain issues arising in such relationships that are unique to them and thus require some special consideration. We will mention some of them in this section. For more information, see Brown (1995).

One factor to consider is that, since men and women are socialized differently, with same-sex couples we have two individuals who share similar gender-based socialization backgrounds, whereas the opposite is true with heterosexual couples (Rutter & Schwartz, in press). The second factor is the hostility and prejudice that the culture has toward same-sex couples, which affect the experience of virtually every partner in a same-sex relationship in ways that have no counterpart in heterosexual couples. Often, the sources of relationship distress in these couples are directly related to these two unique factors. Since therapists who are heterosexual may be insensitive to these factors, they may not adequately consider them in their evaluation and formulation.

One consequence of hostility in the culture toward same-sex couples is that they must commonly deal with insults, violence, and prejudice perpetrated by the majority culture. Another is that they are not legally allowed to partake in the rituals that solidify heterosexual relationships, such as marriage. Support from families is often absent, and same-sex couples often fail to reap one of the primary benefits of marriage: acceptance as a couple within one's social and familial community. Role models of happy and/or realistic gay and lesbian relationships are seldom available within popular culture to guide young gay and lesbian people in developing their values about intimate relationships. Partners in same-sex relationships may feel ambivalent and hostile toward themselves and their partner because of these cultural biases, a phenomenon commonly referred to as internalized oppression. We prefer to characterize internalized oppression in terms of repertoires that have been shaped by cultural contingencies involving prejudice and oppression toward gay men, lesbian women, and same-sex couples. Gay men and lesbian women often dislike themselves for their sexual orientation, and the experience of self-hate or ambivalence is a product of their learning histories that continues to be reinforced by the culture, not a structure in the brain that has its own separate existence. However, we will keep to the vernacular of internalized oppression because it is a widely recognized term in the literature.

Jon and Adam entered therapy because they were in conflict about money: how much of it to keep separate, who was going to control decision-making, and how they would decide whose "stuff" was whose in the event of a breakup. This issue arose because they viewed an eventual breakup as an inevitability—not because of anything that was happening in the relationship, but rather because they had bought into the cultural stereotype that gay relationships are transient. This connection between their financial problems and internalized oppression had to be inferred by the therapist: the couple did not articulate the connection, although when the therapist did they immediately resonated to it. From this connection, other consequences of cultural oppression emerged; for example, the culture does not recognize community property in same-sex relationships. Division of resources is much more closely tied to relationship satisfaction in same-sex couples than it is in heterosexual ones (Berzon, 1988): same-sex couples who overcome internalized oppression and divide their resources just like a heterosexual couple would are more likely to be happy. In other words, in this one area, conducting oneself as a heterosexual couple would is a barometer of relationship satisfaction.

Often, problems that appear to be confusing to the therapist and difficult to understand (e.g., Why are they so compulsive about money? Does this indicate a lack of commitment? But they "seem" committed) are the result of this history of oppression, which has become part of their context. Without recognition of this context of oppression, the relationship may seem fragile, the sources of the problems may seem obscure, and it may be hard to determine what the theme is. Therapists who are homophobic or uncomfortable with same-sex relationships should not be working with such couples; this may disqualify most heterosexual therapists from treating gay and lesbian couples, although we would not carry the logic of this argument that far. But, as Brown (1995) notes, it is important to know oneself with respect to attitudes and values about same-sex relationships, and to understand the subtle ways that prejudice can manifest itself, before taking on such cases.

To the extent that gay men are socialized the way men typically are, their problems in relationships with one another are likely to reflect the themes that one would expect when men try to be intimate. Since men are more likely to be distancers, the theme of "distance/competition" is probably much more common among gay men than it is among heterosexual and lesbian couples. William and Harrison were competitive and territorial about issues both within and outside of the relationship. Within the relationship, they each tried to remain one-up in terms of their lack of commitment and quarreled frequently about who was going to have decision-making power in particular domains. They also found themselves experiencing jealousy when the other's career seemed to be advancing and found it difficult to be supportive when the other needed a confidant regarding work-related matters. They polarized by withdrawing rather than becoming combative: to do otherwise would be tantamount to experiencing oneself as vulnerable and committed, feelings that were anathema to both of them.

The behavior of gay men in relationships has also been extraordinarily influenced by the AIDS epidemic. For one thing, it has impinged upon their tradition of having an open sexual relationship despite an understanding that they would remain a couple with a primary commitment to one another. The fear of AIDS, along with the socialization of gay men as men, has helped to create a common problem: there is a need in many gay relationships for both partners to pay attention to the emotional integrity of their bond, a job that is often left to women in heterosexual relationships. Men may seek therapy because neither is equipped for that role: "This relationship needs work: why don't you do something?" is one way of characterizing the theme. Whereas in the past such problems may have precipitated a breakup, concern about STDs may now propel gay couples into therapy to learn the skills that they didn't need when terminating the relationship seemed easier and more practical.

ICT can be a very effective way of fostering the support and compassion that gay men need to navigate these troubled waters, provided that the therapist has the knowledge and awareness to separate core from derivative issues. One of the primary needs of gay couples in therapy is to learn that it is safe to be vulnerable and supportive in a relationship. The acceptance work in ICT merges nicely with this need. Therapists must not impose heterosexual norms onto gay relationships. For example, if a couple is making a transition from an open relationship to a monogamous one, we should not assume that this is a sign of greater emotional closeness: it may be driven by fear, and the transition may actually create distance—which neither is willing to express. Armed with the knowledge that the norms for gay relationships are changing, and that it was once the norm for sexual openness to coexist with a committed relationship, a therapist is much more likely to pinpoint the ambivalence, reformulate in a way that normalizes it, and create conditions where the fear and ambivalence can be openly discussed.

Another common problem in gay relationships is competition over status. If they present, for example, with conflict over housework, it may turn out that the one earning more expects the other to be doing the lion's share of the housework, whereas in heterosexual relationships there are cultural norms that the woman is the homemaker, even when she is employed outside the home. Differences in occupational status may affect the perceptions of both partners, even though they seldom emerge as themes unless the therapist is sensitive to these issues.

In the same way, many of the sources of conflict in lesbian relationships can be better understood by considering the fact that the relationship consists of two women. Since the skills that women bring to relationships are often devalued or even pathologized in our culture, a therapist working with lesbian couples needs to understand female socialization and how it affects women's functioning in close relationships (Koerner et al., 1994).

There is a high risk of internalized oppression in lesbian partners. Women are not raised in the culture to value women simply because they are women, and the internalized oppression may have as its counterpart resentment of the other. Sometimes this leads to very high expectations in lesbian relationships: the theme is, "Because you aren't a man, you must be perfect in all ways." Such expectations may lead to polarization because the partner, sharing the same values, may be particularly insulted that she is being criticized by a woman. The same criticism coming from a man in a heterosexual relationship would be less likely to polarize the partner, because women in heterosexual relationships may put up with more than do women in lesbian relationships (Brown, 1995).

The "closeness/closeness" theme is more common in lesbian than in other couples. This is a theme where both become upset when the other shows signs of distancing. This is a popular and much debated topic within the literature, and many explanations for the apparent "fusion of boundaries" have been put forth (Chodorow, 1979; Luepnitz, 1988). We see it simply as a logical theme when two women are involved: women are more likely than men to be closeness seekers and to be dissatisfied with distance. Thus, it follows that this theme would be more likely to appear in lesbian than in heterosexual or gay relationships.

Finally, there are unique issues faced by both gay and lesbian couples when it comes to having children. Problems are likely because of what the couple has had to go through in order to have children and the complicated multifamily structure of many gay and lesbian families, where the children become part of a stepfamily, an adoptive family, and a biological family (where one of the women was impregnated by artificial insemination). Many lesbians bring children, usually from a previous heterosexual relationship, into the current lesbian relationship. Since the law does not recognize or protect gay and lesbian families, they are fragile. The insensitive therapist can make the problem worse by treating the family as somehow less important and by minimizing the impact of changes and transitions on children.

We think that ICT can deal with any of these themes, as long as the therapist is knowledgeable and sensitive enough to develop an accurate formulation. But without an adequate awareness of the oppressive cultural prejudices that affect every gay and lesbian American, and without some information about the norms for relationships in the gay and lesbian community, the therapist is likely to be ineffectual at best and harmful at worst. When in doubt, refer to a gay or lesbian couple therapist. But don't assume that expertise in heterosexual relationships generalizes to expertise in gay and lesbian relationships. It doesn't.

Ethnic Diversity, Working with Multiple Cultures, and Class

An understanding of cultures other than European ones will often illuminate themes that would otherwise remain a mystery. Moreover, ICT seems particularly indicated for certain ethnic and cultural groups, but with others there is no basis—empirical or otherwise—for making recommendations at this point.

As an example where some prediction may be possible, consider African American couples. They have a divorce rate over twice as high as Caucasians (Tucker & Mitchell-Kerman, 1995). An important longitudinal study of the early marriages of African American and Caucasian samples indicates differential predictors of marital stability in these groups. A major risk factor in African American but not in Caucasian couples was the husband's anxiety about being able to provide adequately for his family. This finding undoubtedly reflects the economic stresses on African American males, as so many continue to be marginalized in the work force. The appropriate intervention for these risk factors is more likely to be societal than psychological. Nevertheless, individual African American couples must struggle with their economic situation and the feelings it arouses in each. ICT, with its emphasis on expressing vulnerability in the relationship, may enable partners to support one another more effectively in dealing with their stresses than the rational, change-oriented TBCT.

A more problematic and complicated example involves Asian couples, Japanese couples in particular. A number of writers have suggested that Asian Americans are more likely to have a collectivist value system, in contrast to the individualistic value system dominant in European American culture (Dion & Dion, 1993; Ho, 1990). Collectivism is characterized by the subordination of personal, individual goals to group goals. Ho describes a number of values, attitudes, and behaviors that differentiate each of these value systems. He suggests that people in an individualistic culture are "well prepared for negotiation," while those in a collectivist culture are "unprepared in negotiation." With its emphasis on problem-solving, negotiation, and compromise, TBCT would seem to more easily fit Caucasian than Asian cultural backgrounds. Ho also suggests that collectivist cultures are more likely than individualistic ones to accept differences between people in relationships, particularly differences in power. Because ICT tries to promote the acceptance of differences, although not necessarily differences in power, it may fit more easily with Asian than with Caucasian couples.

The complication is that Asian cultures are often extremely patriarchal, and collectivist values can mean, at the relationship levels, collectivist values as defined by the husband. Thus, ICT could play into the hands of these cultural norms by reinforcing acceptance of differences that perpetuate the subordination of women. This is why the "integrative" component of ICT is so important. Despite the antagonism between Asian culture and concepts such as negotiation and compromise in close relationships, these skills may be particularly important to include in the treatment of Asian couples in order to help balance power in the relationship. Thus, what fits compatibly within the culture does not always determine where therapy is targeted. The path of least resistance is not always the optimal path.

There has been more attention paid to cross-cultural marriages in the marital and family therapy literature than there has been to cultural differences between the couple and the therapist. The issue of cultural differences between the partners is an interesting one for ICT, because the differences are often such an obvious source of conflict. Since ICT is based on the inevitability of differences and "acceptance work" essentially means "learning to deal with differences," ICT is a natural for problems created by marriages reflecting two different cultures or ethnic groups. In fact, Falicov (1995), in her chapter on treating cross-cultural marriages, describes "polarization" as the outcome of an unbalanced view on the part of spouses regarding cultural differences. An unbalanced way of handling cultural differences may result from either maximizing or minimizing them. Whereas marriage is a major life transition for any couple, when the spouses come from different cultures or ethnic backgrounds there is a second major transition, a cultural transition. During this phase, couples try to find a balance between their similarities and differences, so that they can best utilize their similarities and accommodate their differences.

Falicov (1995) has identified three main patterns where cultural differences appear to be unbalanced. First, there can be conflicts in the cultural code. Second, there can be conflicts with extended family members, when at least someone from one family disapproves of the family member's choice of partner. Third, couples somehow allow their cultural differences to serve as a barrier during times of stress, creating distance between them and interfering with their effective coping as a team.

Conflicts due to discrepant cultural norms are tricky to deal with in therapy, because it is not always easy to distinguish them from other types of marital problems. There is at least as much variability within as between cultures in marital dynamics. Cultural differences about how marriage should work are of particular interest to ICT. When couples are in conflict, they are not always aware that the conflict stems from different cultural norms. Reformulations noting how the positions the partners are taking are consistent with their cultures can be quite therapeutic in these instances. But the therapist has to be aware of the cultural norms in order to lend credibility to these reformulations. Furthermore, such familiarity is important because some couples pretend that there are no cultural differences in order to make things go smoothly and are not likely to attribute the problems they are having to those differences. One sign of minimizing cultural differences is when one or both know little about the other's culture. In these instances, a characteristic that is culturally normative can be perceived initially as negative behavior but later accepted when the connection is made to the cultural norm. However, if there is no opportunity for accommodation and compromise, the interpretation of such differences may generate a sense of fatalism or hopelessness. Therefore, the need for change should not be ignored when working with such couples. Moreover, if the cultural "gap" appears too wide, the result might be greater distance rather than acceptance. While this can be true with any acceptance-based intervention, the wording of reformulations is especially important in the case of cultural characteristics.

Parental attitudes toward partners still carries a great deal of weight in most subcultures. In some families, extended families also want to have a voice. Cultural, racial, or ethnic differences can increase the likelihood of disapproval, especially in families that have been insular in the past. Although some of this disapproval may be exactly what it seems to be, i.e., based on dedication to culture, race, or preservation of ethnic identity, at times this disapproval can be a disguised way of keeping a child from creating desired (for the child) emotional distance. Similarly, the parents can avoid dealing with their reactions to the child's leaving home by focusing on the other's cultural difference

(Friedman, 1982). We believe that parental disapproval, and to some extent disapproval from extended family, can be a major source of stress for couples, even for those in which the progeny claim to be emancipated from their families of origin. Sometimes the outcome is that one person breaks ties with the family of origin; but that broken tie then becomes a source of marital stress in the future. At other times, the family of origin wins, and the marriage doesn't last. This, however, is a pyrrhic victory, since the issues of divided loyalties are still present, marriage or no marriage.

Falicov's (1995) distinction between maximizing and minimizing differences, as a reaction to not getting permission to marry, is useful from an ICT perspective. When couples maximize their differences, they resemble their family members and either polarize with one another or lead parallel lives, both of which are highly predictive of marital instability (Gottman, 1994). With couples who are already using their cultural differences as a weapon and siding with their families of origin, acceptance work is less likely to be successful. This is one place where we would begin by exploring avenues for accommodation. If we knew that permission to marry had been denied, we might do acceptance work, but the reformulation would not focus on the cultural differences. Rather, we would focus on the pain inherent in having to choose between family of origin and lover.

When couples minimize cultural differences to deal with the lack of permission, they might severe all ties with the family of origin, deny that there are cultural differences, or adopt a third culture. For these kinds of couples, reformulations that emphasize the lack of permission seem clearly indicated.

When under stress, cultural differences can be used as weapons, and long-festering irritants can emerge as full-blown insults and epithets directed at the partner's culture. Usually, when cultural differences erupt in such an acute manner, there are other precipitating issues; however, it is possible that neither partner is aware of them. Reformulations that reflect the stress can save the marriage, or at least get the partners through the crisis. But it would be a mistake to take the cultural stereotypes as literal interpretations of the speaker's belief system. Through communication training (CT), prompting of softer emotions, or reformulating by the therapist, the epithets should be neutralized by getting some discussion going regarding the stress.

We consider class conflict between partners to be a very important and not very well understood phenomenon. Often, race and class get confused: therapists tend to assume that conflicts between African American and Caucasian partners are about race, for example, when they could be about class. Class conflicts could be between partners who come from different strata of society, or they could be conflicts about class, where spouses clash about issues that are literally forced upon them by their class.

As the middle class shrinks and our society becomes increasingly divided into haves and have-nots, the pressures on American couples are unlike those experienced by previous generations. We alluded earlier in the chapter to problems where the solutions lie more in societal change than in psychological interventions. In our final chapter, we will be talking about some problems that are not best solved by couple therapy, even though marital problems clearly exist. One of the primary responsibilities of a therapist is to decide not just *how* to treat, but *when* to treat. There are couples in life circumstances so stressful that no sane human being would be expected to carry on an intimate relationship that would not be seriously compromised. The circumstances are made even more stressful by the vague nature of the stress: at times, people feel the stress, but have difficulty characterizing it concretely, let alone verbalizing it to their partner. Conflicts emerge, without either understanding exactly what it is that they are fighting about.

For example, couples in their twenties are facing tremendous uncertainty about their economic future, and the majority of them are convinced that they will be worse off than their parents were. At the same time, they are not certain about much of anything. For forty years, middle-class men and women came of age optimistic about the future, believing that their future was secure and predicting that they would be as happy and secure as their parents were. Most of us who came of age during that period now know the difference between the post-World War II optimism and the uncertainty about the future that keeps people from feeling secure in the 1990s. How do we know? Because we middle-class professionals don't feel as secure as we once did. We feel ourselves slipping in terms of financial security and status. Perhaps we won't be able to make a living as practitioners or find university positions as academics. We have an inkling of what it is like to be in one's twenties in the 1990s. Ultimately, what people fear is slipping from the realm of material security and social status into the realm of personal failure and material worry. This is indeed a scary prospect.

But there are some, an increasingly growing number, who have been not only insecure but hopeless for so many generations that it feels like home to them. Not that it is enjoyable. It's not. But it is familiar. There is a sense among adolescents from poor families that the only way to improve one's life situation is by ignoring the law and becoming an entrepreneur in illegal activities. Indeed, being an entrepreneurial outlaw is not only where the money is but where the status is as well: in communities where status is hard to come by people will take it where they can get it. So would many who are currently members of the shrinking middle class, if they were in a similar situation.

The stresses and strains of material insecurity, not to mention poverty, on couples are staggering. When couples whose mortgage has just been foreclosed seek therapy, it seems ridiculous on the face of it to talk about acceptance or change within the dyad. Very likely their marital problems are largely a function of the poverty, material needs, and sense of personal failure. Of course, the marital problems are significant and an important source of variability in day-to-day life satisfaction. But at times a therapist fails to see the forest from the trees when a couple facing tremendous economic stress is treated for their failure to communicate.

Sometimes issues get attributed to race when in fact they are largely a function of class. Racial stereotypes and prejudice are perpetuated by these failures to distinguish between race and class. The high divorce rate among African Americans is most likely a function of poverty and racial prejudice, not anything inherent in African American culture about the importance of monogamy or commitment. Domestic violence rates are higher among Blacks than they are among Whites also, but only until one controls for class. Middle-class Black Americans are no more likely to batter their partners than are middle-class White Americans.

Therapists in private practice probably don't need to think much about the material in this section. Invisible couples, couples in poverty, usually do not seek the help of mental health professionals unless they get into trouble with the law. But on those occasions when therapists are confronted with couples facing poverty and/or members of minorities, especially those who are victims of racism, it is important that economic and societal stresses not be interpreted as communication problems. There are environments so stressful that they would affect any relationship; in such situations the ability of a therapist to become involved in helping couples in concrete, practical ways cannot be overestimated.

Andy and Myrna were an African American couple from an inner-city ghetto that had come under the control of crack dealers and criminals. They were in conflict over whether or not their son Matthew should go to the police: a local gang had taken a contract out on his life. Myrna was terrified that her son would end up dead if the family didn't handle this without involving the police, while Andy felt equally strongly that Matthew's only chance, "slim instead of none," as he put it, was to involve the police. Although there were themes with this couple as there are with all couples, and it would have been possible to do ICT as it is typically done, under the circumstances it seemed inappropriate for the therapist to conduct psychotherapy as usual.

As enthusiastic as we are about ICT, we recognize that not all problems are best solved by psychotherapy. The therapist has several options in a situation like this. One of them is to conduct couple therapy, as if the primary problem were between the partners. He could focus on the theme of conventionality/nonconformity that characterized all of the conflicts faced by the couple. Myrna tended to be mistrustful of the dominant power structure and felt that they were better off expecting nothing from it and operating according to the rules of the streets. Andy recognized that neither state nor federal institutions were likely to be helpful; nevertheless, he had licked a heroin habit that he had picked up as a teenager, he had a job, and he still believed that social conformity with the dominant culture was the better alternative. One could identify polarization processes and mutual traps. But to work with them in this way would be insensitive to say the least. Their son was about to be murdered. Under such circumstances, the normal response for a parent is to be terrified and marital conflict is natural.

A second option is for the therapist to help the couple in a directive, supportive way deal with the immediate crisis, by brainstorming with them and suggesting possible solutions. Although couple therapy may be indicated at some point in the future, concrete help in getting through the crisis is what is often indicated when victims of poverty and racism desperately seek help from a therapist. But if the therapist is going to take this tack, he better know what he is doing. This leads to the third option: recognize when you are in over your head, and seek consultation when necessary.

Myrna's position about the police is not based on psychopathology around authority issues. She has good, reality-based reasons to be skeptical about the police being willing and able to save their son's life. Knowing when to seek consultation is a clinical skill in and of itself. In this case, the consultation has to come from someone who knows the culture of the inner-city and understands the interrelationships among community institutions, and between those institutions and the larger culture. The most common mistake made by therapists in these situations is to make assumptions based on their own experience as privileged professionals and to give advice based on what they would do if the lives of their own children were in danger. If therapists are not knowledgeable about the socioeconomic class with which they are dealing, the best action they can take is to not act and seek consultation. This requires, of course, that the therapist know where to go in order to get such consultation. All couple therapists need contingency plans for situations like this.

In the case of Myrna and Andy, the therapist brought in a community leader (a paraprofessional with no advanced degree) who took over, with the therapist continuing to follow up and provide continuity of care. The African American community activist negotiated the interested parties through the crisis, and the police were never involved. Once the parents and the son felt safe, other factors in the environment required attention. There was a teenage pregnancy to deal with: their daughter needed to decide whether to have an abortion, but she would not talk to the parents about it. If she was going to carry the child, she needed housing, welfare, and prenatal care. The therapist was able to bring the teenager into the office, help her with decision-making, and mobilize the family to deal with the practical issues at hand. When these crises were dealt with, communication between partners improved and the couple, grateful to the therapist for her help, decided to discontinue therapy.

One additional class-related issue worthy of mention is the stress of economic insecurity as middle-class people discover that they may not be able to do what they were trained to do. Therapists should have great empathy for this fear of slipping from middle- to lower-middle-class status, since it is a fear voiced by many professionals within the psychotherapeutic community. ICT can be helpful in such situations, but only if therapists realize that the stresses are normal and natural, especially in an era of "downsizing" when there is a realistic chance that middle-class privileges will be revoked. There are all sorts of unspoken antecedents of couple conflict in such situations. First, there are the reality-based stresses of reestablishing some plan for economic survival—not necessarily at the level expected prior to the crisis, but at least at a level that eliminates the immediate concern. Second, there is a sense of personal failure that often goes unacknowledged but makes irrational anger directed at the other more understandable and eventually more acceptable. Third, there is the often unspoken blaming of the spouse expected to provide material security by the partner: when these issues remain implicit, the spouse whose earning power is threatened may report not being adequately supported, which the disappointed partner angrily denies. A formulation can be built around this dynamic, and the polarization process can be deciphered. ICT can be very helpful with such couples. However, as in the case of the couple plagued by survival issues, there has to be some recognition of and dealing with the real problems that need to be solved; again, if the therapist is ill-equipped to solve the problems related to class realignment or the prevention thereof, perhaps consultation might be helpful. Whatever the solution, the willingness on the part of the therapist to deal directively with real-world stress is vitally important: change may even take precedence over acceptance.

In short, the therapist who knows when to switch from an ICT "clinical" mode to a "socioeconomic problem-solving" mode is going to have a much greater impact on conflicts related to class than one who treats every problem as if it were business as usual for psychotherapy. Today therapists need to be able to play multiple roles. As the societal safety net shrinks further and further, and as polarization of haves and have nots continues, more and more therapists will be faced with situations such as these. If we want to make ourselves useful, we better be prepared to deal with them.

Diversity as a Relative Term

Earlier we alluded to the fact that there is at least as much diversity within cultures, ethnic groups, classes, gender, and sexual orientation as there is between these groups. If the term "diversity" is extended to its logical extreme, we need to consider when we decide to label a phenomenon and give it special status. "Diversity" has been used in recent decades to distinguish between ethnic groups, gender, and, to a lesser extent, sexual orientation. Rarely is the term used to make class distinctions, as important as such distinctions are. "Cross-cultural" and "cross-ethnic" issues in marriage and family therapy are also starting to emerge as buzzwords. The attention paid to them is often more style than substance, as evidenced by the paucity of research on relevant topics in the couple area. However, our addition of "class" to this mix shows how relative the whole question of diversity can be. There are literally an infinite number of factors along which people, and couples, can be diverse. Where one chooses to define the relevant variables must be understood like everything else, from an examination of existing contingencies in the environment.

For example, the reaction to the O.J. Simpson verdict drew much attention to racial divisions in this country. To paraphrase James Carville with a slightly different slant, "It's race, stupid!" became the buzzword among pundits, since most African Americans thought that Simpson was innocent and most Caucasians thought that he was guilty. However, to us the most interesting division was between Caucasian and African American feminists, because within the feminist community there is an intersection of race and gender that results in shifting alliances and competing loyalties. African American feminists, who tended to emphasize "race" and the widespread racism among dominant American institutions such as the police, celebrated the verdict, while Caucasian feminists, who viewed "violence against women" as the primary issue, thought the verdict to be a travesty.

This example shows how, depending on one's focus, one's view of the dimensions along which diversity should be considered changes. Within the Black community, race is considered primary, gender secondary, even among African American women. Within the Caucasian community, gender is where the focus is among women. Often, both race and gender can be subsumed under a more generic "diversity dimension" called "class." Others may come up with yet another source of variation.

Where diversity should be located is a decision that occurs within a specific context. In ICT, we see a great deal of "diversity" in our couples, and when doing couple therapy we believe that these forms of diversity are often more important than the ones discussed in this chapter. To us, recognition of diversity implies not just being sensitive to culture, race, gender, sexual orientation, and class, but also adopting a functional analytic perspective. This means starting from ground zero with each couple: a functional analysis makes no assumptions about why couples seek therapy. Rather, its implicit premise is naive: the "why" will be determined by the functional analysis, and we are prepared to modify any rules that are being formulated about what constitutes marital distress based on the results of a particular functional analysis. A functional analytic perspective assumes infinite diversity: if one takes the perspective seriously, he or she lets the contingencies do the talking. One is informed by facts about group differences but decides based on the histories of particular couples.

~ 11 ~

SPECIAL PROBLEMS AND CONSIDERATIONS IN INTEGRATIVE COUPLE THERAPY

In this final chapter, we address a variety of important special issues not covered in other chapters. Now that we have described the basic integrative couple therapy (ICT) approach, we can turn to a number of clinical, practical, and contextual issues that come up for couple therapists, regardless of theoretical orientation.

Assessment and Treatment of Domestic Violence

Couple and family therapists often see "domestic violence" as a specialty area in which they do not need to have expertise (e.g., Bograd, 1992). For example, since Jacobson began engaging in collaborative research on domestic violence with John Gottman, he has given numerous workshops on "treatment of domestic violence." The audiences are entirely different from those attending Jacobson's or Christensen's couple therapy workshops: the latter consist largely of couple and family therapists; the former are mostly "specialists"— advocates, shelter workers, people who run treatment programs for batterers, police, lawyers, and feminist therapists. One of the couple therapists who works for us recently stated, "It would never occur to me to attend a workshop on domestic violence. The material just doesn't seem relevant to my couple therapy practice."

Often, training in domestic violence assessment and treatment is not offered by marriage and family therapy studies programs. Thus, a substantial proportion of couple therapists is lacking in skills regarding the detection, assessing the dangerousness of, safety planning in, and crisis intervention for couples where the husband is a batterer. Yet, such skills are essential for all couple therapists, because close to 50% of all couples seeking therapy have engaged in physical aggression within the year prior to therapy (O'Leary, Vivian, & Malone, 1992). Moreover, a majority of couples seeking therapy have engaged in physical aggression at some point in the marriage, even if it hasn't been in the past year (O'Leary et al., 1992). If these rates seem high, it is because couple therapists frequently treat couples who engage in domestic violence without knowing that the violence is occurring. The failure to detect domestic violence has multiple causes. First, if questionnaires are not used to ask about violence, it often goes unreported by couples, especially if spouses are always seen together: the wife may be too frightened to disclose the violence, for fear of reprisal by the husband. Second, some couples, despite the occurrence of physical aggression, do not view it as part of the problem and therefore do not disclose it (O'Leary et al., 1992). This is especially true when the physical aggression is relatively low-level and non-injurious. In this section, we discuss methods for detecting domestic violence, assessing dangerousness, and safety planning. We also discuss the role of couple therapy in treating domestic violence.

Detecting Domestic Violence

Even when battered women are seen individually and can report on domestic violence without fear of the husband finding out immediately, they are often reluctant to disclose such information. For one thing, they may be concerned that someday the husband *will* find out about the disclosure, even if the therapist does not tell the husband immediately. Furthermore, they may have had bad experiences in the past when they have tried to get help from professionals. Historically, therapists, police, lawyers, and judges have been insensitive to complaints brought by battered women; although all of these groups have become more aware of the problem in recent years, many clients may be operating based on those previously unsatisfying experiences (Dutton, 1995; Holtzworth-Munroe et al., 1995). Victims of domestic violence are more likely to check domestic violence on a questionnaire than they are to acknowledge its occurrence during a clinical interview (O'Leary et al., 1992). Therefore, we routinely include the Conflict Tactics Scale (CTS; Straus, 1979) in the assessment battery that partners complete prior to the initial interview.

Although the CTS does not do a very good job of assessing either the function or the impact of domestic violence (Jacobson, 1994), it is an excellent screening instrument, since it does provide a reliable and valid method of determining whether or not physical aggression is occurring at all. If there is any physical aggression reported on a screening instrument, it is essential that the therapist interview the wife separately.

Given the deterrents to wife disclosure during an interview, it is important that the therapist move slowly and gradually toward a verbal acknowledgment. Therapists should begin their inquiry in the same way that inquiries are conducted with any other individual, by trying to assess the severity of marital distress, the commitment to the current relationship, the current areas of conflict, and how conflict is dealt with. Once the therapist is at the point of assessing what happens to the couple when faced with conflict, he or she will ask about typical sequences of arguments, perhaps by asking for a description of the most recent one. Then the therapist can move to an inquiry about the most severe argument the wife can remember the couple ever having. If the description of this argument does not spontaneously elicit descriptions of battering or emotional abuse, then and only then should the therapist directly ask about them. Here are a series of questions recently asked by Jacobson of a suspected battered woman, designed to detect whether or not physical and emotional abuse were occurring:

Therapist: When Tom gets angry, how does he act?
Client: He yells, and cusses, and calls me names.
Therapist: Do you ever get scared during these arguments?
Client: Yeah, I'm afraid a lot of the time.
Therapist: Sometimes, when people get mad and they start yelling, they get physical, pushing, shoving, things like that. Has any of that ever happened to you?
Client: Yeah, I guess. I push him too. But I can't hurt him like he hurts me.
Therapist: Does it ever get worse than pushing and shoving?
Client: Yeah, he's beat me up a couple of times.

Determining the Level of Dangerousness

Once violence has been established, as in the above dialogue, the therapist must evaluate exactly how dangerous the situation is for both husband and wife. The inquiry should proceed in such a way as to ascertain the impact that the husband's violence has on the wife, how long it has been going on, how frequently it occurs, the typical level of severity, and how the level of violence has been changing over time.

There are certain "red flags" that might indicate a high probability of serious injury: when severe violence has occurred in the past, when injuries have occurred in the past to either party, when the violence includes sexual assault, when either drugs or alcohol are involved in the violent episodes, when homicidal threats have occurred in the past, and when either spouse has attempted suicide in the past. Batterers are particularly dangerous if certain types of emotional abuse are prevalent along with physical abuse: when the pattern of abuse indicates that the husband considers the wife to be his property, or when his entire life revolves around her to the point where he keeps track of her comings and goings, tries to isolate her from others, and seems willing to risk jail if necessary in order to maintain his sense of ownership. Batterers who break into their partners' houses or apartments during separations, who badger members of her family, who minimize, deny, or distort their level of violence, or who violate restraining orders in order to maintain their power and control over their wives are potentially quite dangerous. If any red flags show up during the evaluation, the couple assessment must be dropped and the task shifted to ensuring the wife's safety.

But before safety planning can begin, therapists must express their grave concern for the safety of both partners. Given their reluctance to disclose such information, therapists have to respond with obvious concern, compassion, and sensitivity if they want to be effective at the safety planning stage. Battered women need to be believed, not treated with skepticism. They need to be told that the violence is not their fault and that it is the husband's responsibility, and his alone, to stop the violence. It is also important to debunk for them the family systems theoretical notion that the violence is caused by some marital dynamic implicating her. Any marital problems other than the violence have to be put on hold until the therapist is certain that the woman is safe.

Safety Planning

Safety planning requires finesse on the part of the therapist, because he/she is trying to attain two goals at once: ensuring the wife's safety, and improving her self-care skills so that she can protect herself. In order to be effective, therapists have to know what resources in the community are available for battered women: what agencies, shelters, and legal options will aid the therapist in supporting her safety needs? What are the wife's sources of support other than the therapist? Can she name and call on supportive family members, friends, professionals? She needs the phone numbers of local shelters, along with encouragement to use them if necessary. It is also important to discuss with her the legal options at her disposal, including the meaning of legal terms such as "mandatory arrest," "orders of protection," and the like. All of this assumes, of course, that the therapist is familiar with community resources, the advocacy community, and has some understanding of the law and the extent to which it protects battered women in a particular community. It would be ideal if all marriage and family therapists went through advocacy training themselves, since once violence against a wife is detected, the therapist essentially operates as an advocate.

But the heart of safety planning is the plan itself. A safety plan must be appropriate to the wife's particular situation. Battered women need to be trained to recognize high-risk situations, if they are not already aware of them. More commonly, battered women are acutely aware of what the high-risk situations are, and the therapist needs to be educated about these situations so that he or she can help the wife figure out ways of protecting herself, given the occurrence of each particular risk cue. Once an escape plan has been established, the therapist and client must verbally rehearse how the plan would function from various locales both inside and outside the couple's residence. The battered woman should be encouraged to prepare a "safety package" and store it in a safe place in case she has to escape quickly. The safety package might include clothing, cash, important documents, and a "hard copy" of the escape plan. It is usually a good idea for this safety package to be kept outside the residence, perhaps with a relative or trusted friend.

Whatever the specifics of the safety plan, the process by which the plan is arrived at should be a dialogue where brainstorming occurs, rather than a lecture, with the therapist simply telling the client how to stay safe. This process pertains to the goal of helping the wife develop the ability to take care of herself.

If the outcome of safety planning is that other resources replace the therapist as primary contact, it is still important for the therapist to maintain contact with the wife to ensure some continuity of care. Having a plan and implementing it are two distinct processes. There may be a number of unsuccessful attempts before a safety plan is adequately implemented. The plan may need to be changed and reviewed; approximations to implementation must be reinforced. If the wife does succeed in getting out of the relationship, there must be follow-up, since women are often at greatest risk *after* they physically separate from their husbands. When the wife perceives various deterrents to escape, the therapist must be prepared to provide a reality check regarding the validity of these deterrents. Although some deterrents are quite real, others may be based on distortions which are inevitable when one is experiencing the trauma of being in an abusive relationship. When considering whether or not to leave an abusive relationship, battered women may conclude that, as bad as the abuse is, it is preferable to being alone: the fear of being stalked and physically harmed, the fear that reprisals may be made against children, the financial costs of getting out of the relationship are all realistic blocks to getting out of the relationship that must be taken seriously by the therapist. On the other hand, at times women stay because they blame themselves for the violence or mistakenly believe that they cannot survive without the partner. All deterrents, whether or not they are realistic, need to be carefully explored in a dialogue between therapist and client; when they are not realistic, they need to be gently challenged and debunked. We are still talking about a dialogue rather than a prescription handed to the client by a therapist. At all stages of the process, the helplessness and hopelessness expressed by the client should not transfer to the therapist. At the same time, the battered woman should not be patronized during the process of safety planning, since a patronizing stance replicates her experience with her husband.

The Importance of Written Documentation

All episodes of violence must be documented in writing by the therapist. Since couples in relationships where the husband is a batterer are at high risk for injury, murder, and suicide, it is important for therapists to demonstrate that they have attained state-of-the-art standards of care. The documentation is also important because the therapist may be the only person with whom the wife has shared her secret regarding domestic violence. Since battered women are often isolated and have few sources of contact and support, the therapist's notes may constitute the only official record of the violence. This information may be quite useful in subsequent criminal and civil proceedings.

The Role of Couple Therapy in Domestic Violence

The question of whether or not couple therapy is indicated when domestic violence has entered the relationship is fraught with controversy. Representatives of the advocacy community and specialists in the treatment of battering tend to see couple therapy as contraindicated (e.g., Kaufman, 1992; Meyers-Avis, 1992; Pence & Paymar, 1993; Walker, 1995). In contrast, systemic thinkers, even those with a feminist perspective, tend to advocate couple therapy, at least for a sub-group of batterers and battered women (e.g., Goldner et al., 1990).

In identifying an appropriate role for couple therapy in the treatment of domestic violence, it is first important to distinguish between "battering" and "physical aggression without battering." "Battering" can be defined in one of two ways: in terms either of form or of function. The formal or structural definition of battering is vague; it usually is identified somewhere along a dimension of severity of aggression. It is clear that we are talking about battering when women are being injured as a consequence of the violence. It is also clear that when men slap women or hit them with closed fists, the women are being battered. However, when verbal arguments escalate to pushing and shoving, without any physical pain or harm, it is less clear. The problem with defining battering solely in terms of severity is that it doesn't take into account what we consider to be the central feature of battering: that it is an act of aggression where the function is to control another human being through violence, the threat of violence, or a previous history of violence. Battering, in other words, is not just physical aggression: it is physical aggression with a purpose. The purpose of battering is to control, intimidate, and subjugate another human being. When the violence results in injury, or when the wife reports fear as a result of the abuse, one can safely infer that we are talking about battering.

In contrast, there are a great number of distressed couples who engage in low-level violence where typically no one gets hurt and the wife is not afraid of the husband. Even though the physical aggression in these situations is potentially dangerous (people can get hurt, even accidentally), the absence of fear, control, or injury distinguishes it from battering. When there is physical aggression without battering, the violence serves other functions: it may be a classically conditioned frustration response, it may be a voluntary response where the function is to reduce frustration, or it may be an ineffectual attempt to fight back in response to emotional or physical abuse from the partner.

In cases where there is low-level violence, what we call physical aggression without battering, couple therapy is indicated, just as it would be for any other couple problem. However, we recommend "no-violence" contracts as a precondition to doing ICT. Even low-level violence can lead to injury, and thus is something that cannot be tolerated during the course of ICT. This issue can be directly addressed during the feedback session by pointing out the necessity of adhering to such a contract in order for the treatment to proceed. The advantage of a contract is that it defines the nature of the rule, thus relieving the therapist of a policing function that would be inconsistent with ICT. The contingencies should be very clear in the contract: in most instances, violation of the no-violence contract, for any reason, would mean: (a) that couple therapy would be immediately terminated, and (b) that the perpetrator, as identified by the *therapist*, must agree to individual therapy in advance, so that if termination is necessary some acceptance of responsibility and follow-up is already established. The contract must be explicit about what constitutes grounds for negative consequences, and the therapist must check on adherence to the contract at every session.

Successful contracts typically include not only the behavior that constitutes grounds for termination, but also steps that couples can take in high-risk situations to avoid physical aggression. For example, "time-out" is usually listed as one of the actions to be taken when either partner recognizes that a situation is high-risk (Holtzworth-Munroe et al., 1995). Also, common cues for high-risk situations should be identified.

Once the contract is in place, ICT can proceed as usual. In fact, couple therapy is the ideal treatment for physical aggression without battering. Moreover, if couples with a history of low-level violence were excluded from couple therapy, couple therapy would rarely be used: most couples seeking therapy have at least some history of low-level physical aggression (O'Leary et al., 1992). As we stated earlier, if this claim seems exaggerated, it is because physical aggression is inadequately assessed by many marriage and family therapists; as a result, they are treating physically aggressive couples without realizing it.

For couples where there is battering, couple therapy is contraindicated. Typically, in heterosexual relationships, batterers are men. Those who claim otherwise distort the findings from the national survey conducted by Straus and Gelles (1990), which show approximately equal frequencies of physical aggression in men and women. However, as Vivian and her colleagues (O'Leary et al., 1992) and Stets and Straus (1990) have shown, women are far more likely than men to be injured as a result of physical aggression. Equally important is the finding that only in men does violence function as an effective method of control (Jacobson et al., 1994). Despite occasional exceptions, battering is something that men predominantly do to women in marriage, during courtship, and after the breakup. Even when women are arrested for domestic violence, they are not batterers: two-thirds of them are battered women themselves, and the rest are not using violence as a method of power and control (Hamberger, 1995).

One reason not to do couple therapy with batterers is that it may increase the risk of violence. Some couples regulate violence by avoid-ing conflict whenever possible. Couple therapy, including ICT, forces couples to confront conflict areas on a regular basis, thus making vio-lence more likely for many couples. Furthermore, couple therapy im-plies joint responsibility for the battering. No matter how the treat-ment is presented, and no matter how many times the therapist says that battering is unacceptable, the structure of therapy belies those presentations and statements. The conjoint structure suggests that the battered wife is somehow part of the problem, when the violence should be viewed as the husband's responsibility and his alone. In fact, the conjoint format, in addition to blaming the victim for her own abuse, colludes with the husband's explanation for the violence. Typically, batterers claim that the wife is to blame for the violence because her criticism and contempt drove him to beating her. A sys-temic view inevitably creates the impression that the husband is at least partly right. The fact is that battering has very little to do with actions on the part of the wife; therefore, not only is couple therapy victim-blaming but it is unlikely to stop the violence (Jacobson et al., 1994).

Thus, couple therapy is contraindicated, dangerous, and may even be unethical as a treatment for batterers and battered women. When batterers and battered women present themselves to us for therapy, we refuse to treat them and explain why in the feedback session. We refer the husbands for individual therapy, specifically designed to stop the violence. If the wives also want therapy, we make that available to them, while also providing advocacy information and support. If the husband admits that he has a problem and is willing to enter individ-ual therapy to work on it, a possible step toward stopping the violence has been taken. If the husband refuses the individual referral and im-plicitly or explicitly denies responsibility for, minimizes the signifi-cance of, or in other ways distorts the impact of his violence, then the violence is unlikely to stop and may get worse (Jacobson, Gottman, et al., 1996). Thus, the therapist should be prepared for playing the role of advocate in a therapeutic relationship with the battered wife.

Referring the batterer to individual or group therapy should not be viewed as a panacea, since it is unclear at present whether or not currently existing treatment programs for batterers are effective (e.g., Holtzworth-Munroe et al., 1995). Recent reviews suggest that bat-terers who complete group treatments have similar recidivism rates to those who drop out prematurely, even though the batterers who drop out should be at greater risk, not only because they dropped out but because of the kinds of batterers who drop out (e.g., unemployed, alcohol problems, etc.). Moreover, there is little evidence that psychotherapy of any kind reduces the risk for recidivism, compared to simply arresting the batterer. Thus, there is certainly no guarantee that even a referral for individual therapy will solve the problem. In fact, the husband's entry into treatment may put the battered wife at increased risk, since she is lulled into a false sense of security and may, for example, move back home from a shelter because the husband has sought treatment.

We have to remember that not all problems are best solved by psychotherapy. Battering is best thought of as a problem for the criminal justice system and a public health problem of enormous proportions. Batterers are primarily criminals, not clients. Arrest, prosecution, and punishment should be routine and not mitigated by whether or not the batterer is willing to enter into psychotherapy. If batterers want to seek treatment voluntarily, rather than as a strategy for avoiding imprisonment, fine; however, psychotherapy should not be used as an alternative to legal sanctions, if a crime has been committed. If a husband is willing to enter into treatment even though he will still face legal sanctions, then at least he is taking responsibility for the violence. If the violence does stop, couple therapy may very well be appropriate at some point in the future. And sometimes, the violence does stop!

Extramarital Affairs

One of the most common questions we hear at workshops is: how does ICT handle extramarital affairs? We always hope that we will get away from a workshop without having to respond to this question, because it is so hard to answer. There is no easy, let alone perfect, method for handling couples where one spouse is engaging in an affair. Yet, some estimates are that extramarital affairs are the norm rather than the exception when couples divorce (Pittman & Wagers, 1995). While there are no reliable statistics on the proportion of therapy-seeking couples with coexisting affairs, in our opinion there is often some third party or force to reckon with when couples with chronic marital discord suddenly consider separation, especially when one person has unilaterally suggested it.

The therapist faces numerous dilemmas in dealing with this problem. First, people engaging in affairs often fail to disclose them to either the partner or the therapist; thus, the therapist is often treating couples where an affair is going on without even knowing it. Second, couple therapy is very unlikely to succeed when an affair is going on, especially if it is kept secret, because the "perpetrator" is putting his or her energy into a new relationship and the commitment to therapy is disingenuous. The deception simply compounds the problem. Third, the alternative of admitting to an affair will almost invariably create an even more severe crisis in the marriage, perhaps leading to separation or divorce.

In ICT, we take a position on affairs that departs from the recommendations by Jacobson and Margolin (1979). The traditional behavior therapy stance on affairs is that, unless the affair stops, therapy cannot commence. We no longer consider this position justifiable. For one thing, such a stance has the effect of simply increasing the likelihood that ongoing affairs will not be disclosed, thus maintaining the marital discord and making it impossible for the therapist to help the couple improve their marriage. Furthermore, if an affair is going on, the crisis engendered by disclosure can actually be the first step in improving the relationship, despite the severe discord that almost invariably precedes the improvement. ICT offers a way out of the crisis, but only if the affair is disclosed.

Thus, if an affair is going on, and we find out about it during the individual session, we strongly encourage disclosure during the feedback session, usually in the presence of a therapist. This gives the therapist an opportunity to intervene, using the strategies described in previous chapters, and to attempt to move the couple in a direction involving both acceptance and change. Although it would be inconsistent with ICT to take a position one way or the other regarding the continuance of an affair, "acceptance work" can often produce spontaneous cessation of the affair. In contrast, failure on the part of the offending spouse to disclose the affair or the therapist's insistence on terminating therapy with a couple when an affair is ongoing is practically guaranteed to result in no change or deterioration in the marriage.

This policy is consistent with our general stance toward information revealed to us by clients during the individual assessment sessions. We explain that, even though we are meeting individually, we are doing so in preparation for couple therapy. Therefore, our obligations are to both individuals. Although we will not betray a confidence, if a secret is revealed that is relevant to treatment, we strongly encourage disclosure and reserve the right to refuse to treat if we cannot persuade the client to disclose the relevant information.

If a partner discloses an affair to us during an individual session, he or she is strongly encouraged to disclose the affair during the feedback session. If the partner refuses, we will not force the disclosure, but we will not be a party to the deception either. Thus, we refuse to treat couples where there is an undisclosed affair. Furthermore, we require that the perpetrator explain to the partner during the feedback session that he/she is insufficiently committed to engage in couple therapy. We leave it in the perpetrator's hands to decide how much elaboration to provide. The therapist should be ready to provide support during this session, but should not continue with therapy unless the secret is revealed.

The perpetrator also has the option of breaking off the affair. Unless the two people having the affair are working in the same office, breaking it off means no further contact. If the perpetrator chooses this option, it has to be shared with the partner, and the partner is allowed to have whatever proof he or she requires that all contact has been broken off, including access to the third party to confirm that the affair is over. We usually recommend a joint letter, written by both perpetrator and victim to the third party, explaining that couple therapy has been chosen as the number one priority, and that this requires no further contact with the third party. Typically, the therapist helps the couple in the construction of this letter, which can be the first step toward repairing the wounds that the affair has caused to all involved. Often, it is a good idea for the couple to even mail the letter together.

If the perpetrator is willing to share the illicit relationship, either in its current or discontinued form, with the victim, the therapist should offer the perpetrator all of the support that ICT provides for any partner. Remember that in ICT, through attempts to create an atmosphere of empathy and compassion, we try to encourage open discussions about all areas of conflict, no matter how severe the feelings of betrayal and mistrust. Through our own efforts to validate and reformulate negative behavior, we communicate and model nonblaming and nonaccusatory stances toward both parties, whatever their past and present actions. This is true even when we are forced to take a stand on the unacceptability of certain behaviors.

Thus, we offer the perpetrator our protection from blame when the victim, quite understandably, condemns the partner for both the affair itself and the deception. This protection comes in the form of attempting to bring out the affective experiences that occur in the wake of the disclosure and to show how this affair is simply another consequence of polarization and an ineffectual attempt to escape from a mutual trap. Similarly, we try to help the victim express the pain and suffering that he or she experiences now, regarding the affair, and has experienced in the past.

For example, Scott revealed to Emily during a therapy session that he was having an affair. Although he entered therapy with every intention of continuing both relationships, since he regarded them as independent, he decided to end the affair and disclose it to Emily after the therapist encouraged him to do so during their individual session. The disclosure occurred during the feedback session. Following the disclosure, the couple entered a period of acute crisis during which they were seen twice a week. During the sessions, the therapist attempted to draw out Emily's sense of vulnerability and Scott's guilt and shame. At the same time he helped them work together on the "Dear Jane" letter to the third party. Such a letter is a form of "unified detachment," as the couple works together against a third force, which in this case was the distance that had been created between them as a result of the affair.

Once the affair had ended and the letter had been written, Scott and Emily began to quarrel over "moving on with their lives," as Scott put it. He wanted to be forgiven, because he had given up the affair, and started to become angry at Emily for not letting go of her mistrust. Emily, on the other hand, seemed to want more contrition from Scott; in addition, she resented his efforts to get her to give up her sense of betrayal. Through a combination of intimacy-enhancing and tolerance-building acceptance exercises, the therapist helped Emily develop sympathy for Scott's desire to put the past behind him: it was understandably hard for him to be reminded of her suspiciousness and mistrust on a daily basis. At the same time, Emily's experience of betrayal was not something over which she had voluntary control: she could not give Scott a timeline for a resumption of trust. Thus, the therapist had to reformulate Emily's suspiciousness and foster her expressing her mistrust in nonblaming terms, in order for Scott to soften toward it. In this case, softening meant being able to tolerate, and even develop compassion for, Emily's inability to "turn off" her experience. Indeed, Emily would have preferred to not feel betrayed. The struggle this couple had, in the wake of the affair, was to decide whether they could live together and perhaps even appreciate each other's natural, understandable, and inevitable human reactions to what had happened. Gradually, Emily grew more comfortable with Scott's impatience, and Scott grew more comfortable with Emily's involuntary mistrust. As she let go of the struggle to get him to be more patient, and as he let go of the struggle to get her to feel more trusting, he became more patient and she became more trusting.

This case exemplifies a strategy for dealing with extramarital affairs that is in some ways antithetical to traditional behavioral couple therapy (TBCT). TBCT really had no way of dealing with mistrust, since it is an experience that cannot be problem-solved or contracted away. Nor can it be targeted for a behavior exchange (BE) exercise. Through acceptance work, we can foster intimacy and at the very least build tolerance, where behavior therapists from the 1970s and 1980s would have simply thrown up their hands in defeat.

Finally, it is important to note that our strategy is very different when it comes to affairs from the past. If an affair came and went, and the third party is no longer part of the ex-perpetrator's life, we don't advocate disclosure. In these instances, disclosure causes unnecessary pain in the victim and typically provides little benefit to the relationship. We do not advocate that partners share every negative behavior in their repertoire with one another at every moment, or in retrospect. All couples keep secrets from one another: no two people have access to everything that the other experiences. This is good. Relationships would be both less interesting and more painful if each was an open book to the other. Past affairs that are of little consequence for the current relationship are best left as one of those many experiences that the individual holds onto alone. Marriage creates enough mischief on its own, without total and absolute honesty.

Special Considerations in the Treatment of Alcohol and Substance Abuse

Most married people who are dependent on drugs and alcohol have couple problems. These problems are sometimes antecedents, and sometimes consequences of, the drug and alcohol problems. Indeed, couple therapy does have an important role to play in the overall treatment plan for drug and alcohol abusers (e.g, McCrady & Epstein, 1995). While we do not believe that couple therapy, in and of itself, is a solution to alcohol or drug problems, it can be a valuable ancillary treatment, when combined with individual therapy.

Our approach is usually to let some other professional treat the individual with the drug and alcohol problem, and keep our focus on the couple issues. As long as the alcohol or drug problem is being targeted in individual or group therapy, the ICT therapist can focus attention on the relationship issues. This way, the therapist avoids two major pitfalls: the temptation to have an identified patient, and the need to "police" the substance abuse.

The propensity for using addiction as a scapegoat is almost unavoidable if the couple therapist is trying to deal simultaneously with the substance abuse problem and the marital issues. From an ICT perspective, there is never an identified patient in couple therapy, except in cases of battering. However, the substance abuse problem must be addressed in some way. By structuring treatment such that a different therapist is treating the substance abuser, the couple therapist is free to focus on the formulation, as in all other ICT cases. The substance-abusing episodes will undoubtedly be discussed, but only as exemplars of a theme and as part of a polarization process or a mutual trap.

Although we are not experts on the treatment of substance abuse, it seems to us that most currently existing treatments include some sort of policing function: this is certainly true of A.A. Moreover, there is a directive, confrontational approach to many treatments for addictive behaviors that cannot be easily integrated into ICT. To the extent that treatments for substance abuse result in the therapist deviating from a validating, nonblaming stance, they are incompatible with ICT. Unlike TBCT, ICT requires interventions that differ so markedly from most currently existing treatments for substance abuse that the problems should be dealt with by different therapists. Then ICT can proceed as usual, with an occasional consultation between the couple and the individual therapists.

Couple Therapy as a Treatment for Depression

In the past six years, couple therapy has emerged as a viable treatment for some forms of major depression, either as an adjunct to individual therapy or as a primary intervention strategy (Prince & Jacobson, 1995). The rationale for treating depression with couple therapy stems from different bodies of research (see Prince and Jacobson, 1995, for a review): the moderate correlation between depression and marital discord, the ability of marital discord to predict relapse, the continuance of marital discord even following recovery from depression, and the protective value of a supportive partner in preventing depression following stressful life events.

The evidence thus far regarding the efficacy of couple therapy as a treatment for depression is mixed. Weissman and colleagues (Klerman, Weissman et al., 1988) compared Interpersonal Psychotherapy (IPT) with the partner involved to IPT without partner involvement and found trends favoring the spouse-involved treatment, although the differences were not statistically significant. To further complicate interpretation of these findings, even spouse-involved IPT is not really couple therapy; rather, it is an individual therapy with a spouse present, playing a role somewhere between co-therapist and a co-client.

Two studies have evaluated TBCT as a treatment of major depression. The first (O'Leary & Beach, 1990) found that both cognitive behavior therapy (CBT) with the depressed spouse and TBCT were more effective than a control group in alleviating major depression in women, but not differentially effective from one another. However, only TBCT was effective in alleviating marital discord, which was important, since all couples in the sample came to therapy for marital discord as well as major depression. Unfortunately, TBCT was no more effective than CBT at preventing relapse in depression at a one-year follow-up. Since the primary rationale for treating the marital discord is that an improved marriage should lead to less relapse, these outcomes at the one-year follow-up are disappointing. Moreover, there are some additional problems that make the results of this study hard to interpret: questions as to the representativeness as well as the competence with which CBT was performed; the possibility that the allegiance of the investigators, which was decidedly an interpersonal/pro-TBCT stance, inflated the differences between CBT and TBCT; the relatively mild nature of the sample in terms of depression severity; and the fact that, despite the statistically significant differences between groups, only a minority of TBCT-treated couples actually ended up in the normal range on measures of marital satisfaction after therapy.

The second study was conducted by Jacobson and colleagues (Jacobson et al., 1991; Jacobson et al., 1993). This study attempted to include a broader sample of depressed women, and thus did not require that the couple report coexisting marital discord in order to be accepted into the study. Unfortunately, although this tactic was laudable from the standpoint of ensuring better comparability to previous clinical trials, it resulted in only a minority of couples who were maritally distressed. Not surprisingly, nondistressed couples failed to benefit from TBCT: the depressives stayed depressed, and the marriages did not improve. However, for the maritally distressed subsample, Jacobson and colleagues found that TBCT was as effective as CBT in treating major depression, and was the only treatment that significantly increased marital satisfaction. Unfortunately, the latter study replicated O'Leary and Beach in documenting no relapse prevention effect for couple therapy.

In short, based on the two studies from TBCT, it appears that the type of therapy advocated by Jacobson and Margolin (1979) works as well as CBT in alleviating depression in that subgroup of depressed women who are both married and report marital distress. However, depressed women are no less likely to relapse after being treated with TBCT than they are when treated with CBT.

To date, no studies have been done evaluating ICT as a treatment for major depression. However, we have reason to believe that ICT may be well suited for couples where one spouse has a major depression, especially if the depressed spouse is a woman (Koerner, Prince,

& Jacobson, 1994). As Koerner and colleagues note, girls, and later women, are socialized in our culture to be more "relational," that is, to value and base their self-worth on the success of their intimate relationships. Therefore, they are more vulnerable to depression when their marital relationships are discordant. They are also likely to blame themselves for the marital problems and see it as their job to fix them. ICT, with its nonblaming, validating stance toward marital problems, directly counters this tendency on the part of women to blame themselves, as well as their partner's tendency to blame the marital problems on the depression. Moreover, the intimacy-enhancing acceptance techniques, to the extent that they are successful, produce the kind of relationship that women tend to value: these techniques foster a sense of connectedness, even in the face of differences between the husband and the wife. Even if the husband does not become as relationship-focused as the wife, the increased closeness makes the relationship considerably more satisfying for the wife.

At the same time, as we mentioned in Chapter 1, an acceptance-based model has the potential to accentuate what is already an oppressive relationship for the wife. The wife, for example, might become more accepting of her lower status and getting less than she wants and needs in the relationship. That is why it is important to remember that: (1) we focus our efforts on using the problems as vehicles for intimacy rather than simply resigning ourselves to the status quo, and (2) we emphasize change as well as acceptance. The fact that our approach is integrative protects men from hiding behind the acceptance focus and using it as an excuse not to change.

When couples enter therapy and one is depressed, an important assessment question pertains to the temporal relationship between the depression and the marital discord (Jacobson, 1992; Prince & Jacobson, 1995). Although we can never be completely sure of the causal relationship between the two, couples often agree on which came first, and these views tend to coincide with their perceptions of the causal relationship. Thus, if the marital problems preceded the first episode of depression, ICT might very well be a necessary and sufficient treatment. In Jacobson's clinical trial, 42% of the couples with a depressed wife were maritally distressed, and about half of those viewed the marital distress as primary. Thus, we estimate that, of those couples who enter therapy with coexisting marital discord and depression, about half might be adequately treated with couple therapy. However, for the other half, some form of individual therapy will probably be necessary: either psychotherapy, antidepressant medication, or both.

The individual therapy should be conducted by a different therapist;

otherwise, the couple therapist can't help but have competing loyalties. In ICT, the client is clearly the couple, and even though our definition of good couple therapy emphasizes the well-being of both individuals, there are times when the interests of an individual compete with the best interests of the relationship. When therapists attempt to treat the depression individually and concurrently perform couple therapy, they may find themselves facing some difficult dilemmas, with the two therapies working at cross-purposes. In short, the entire therapeutic structure is likely to be "cleaner" and less complicated if there is bifurcation between the couple work and the individual work.

Couple Therapy in an Era of Managed Care

As this book is being written, more and more therapists are faced with time limits and finite numbers of sessions imposed upon them by third-party payers. As a result, we have been forced to experiment with briefer versions of ICT and ways of streamlining the process to accommodate the managed care conglomerates who will only pay for a few sessions. Of course, there is wide variability in the limitations set by insurance companies, and many do not reimburse therapists for couple therapy at all. Although we are aware of no formal statistics in this area, our impression is that, even though the insurance coverage is less than optimal for many couples, it is more likely now than it was prior to the age of managed care that third-party payers will cover at least some couple therapy. Given the uncertainty of how mental health care will be covered in the future, it is hazardous to make recommendations. Nevertheless, based on the current climate, and some possible scenarios for health care coverage in the future, we can make some general statements that may be helpful to couple therapists wanting to use ICT.

First, remember that many of your clients who are limited to between five and eight sessions of coverage now were not covered by insurance at all ten years ago and were paying out of pocket for couple therapy. For couples who think they can afford to pay out of pocket if necessary, we would present them with a choice. We could contract for only those sessions they are covered for, and then evaluate their progress during the last session. If they want to recontract for further therapy, they are entitled to do so, but they would be paying for the remaining sessions themselves. We would try to give them an estimate of how many more sessions we think would be necessary. Therapists who offer couples this option should make it clear that the truncated version is only an approximation of ICT as it is described in this book.

A related option for couples who can afford to pay if necessary is simply to begin ICT as we have described it and have as many sessions as the insurance company allows. Then, they can decide whether to continue or discontinue treatment. The difference between this option and the first one is that here ICT is not truncated in any way, and we simply stop and evaluate whether to continue when the insurance coverage runs out.

In deciding between these two options, one relevant question is: how long does ICT take in its ideal form? Unfortunately, we do not have the data to answer this question as yet. In our pilot study, described in the first chapter (Jacobson et al., 1996), our protocol allowed couples up to 25 sessions if necessary, counting the two evaluation sessions and the feedback session. However, it should be noted that this choice was arbitrary. We wanted to make sure that we allowed sufficient numbers of sessions for all couples, and so we erred on the side of offering too many rather than two few sessions. Even knowing that they could have up to 25 sessions, not all couples availed themselves of this option. Session numbers varied from 13 to 25. It is entirely possible that we would have achieved the same results if we had limited our protocol to fewer sessions.

Jacobson's TBCT research is potentially instructive in this regard. His first two studies tested an eight-session protocol (Jacobson, 1977, 1978a). The next trial tested a 12-session protocol (Jacobson, 1979). In the study where TBCT was compared to each of its components, the protocol allowed for a variation of 12 to 16 sessions. Finally, in the two most recent TBCT outcome studies (Jacobson et al., 1989; Jacobson et al., 1991), he tested a 20-session protocol. Outcome did not improve as the number of allowed sessions increased. In fact, the two largest effect sizes were achieved in the first two studies, where couples only had eight sessions! Given these data, why did Jacobson and colleagues keep increasing the length of the protocol? Because with each phase of treatment development, more was added to the manual. But, as we can see in retrospect, more was not necessarily better.

Therapists and therapy researchers tend to adjust their intervention strategies to the time allotted to them. Clients may do the same. Brief therapists have long argued that both clients and therapists work harder, and accomplish more, when there are external constraints imposed upon them either in terms of time or number of sessions. In our clinical practices, even though we average 20 sessions per ICT case, some couples have been successfully treated in as few as five sessions. When we have had to work within time or session constraints im-

posed by managed care, we offer truncated versions of ICT, and sometimes they work beautifully. In fact, we have no empirical basis for
asserting that a truncated version would not work equally well. However, based on our clinical experience, we believe that more extensive
work is needed with severely distressed couples.

Clinical research generally proceeds in a programmatic fashion.
First, it is necessary to establish an effect, using a strong manipula-
tion. Thus, in order to establish a treatment effect, one errs on the
side of maximizing the potency of the treatment, in order to make
sure that if there is an effect we will be able to detect it. In the case of
ICT, we want first to establish that ICT has some unique benefits, and
therefore we are maximizing its "dose" in order to make sure we will
find any effect that is there. However, once an effect has been established, questions regarding its generalizability take precedence: Can it
be done with less experienced therapists? Can it be done in fewer sessions? Can it be done with less training and supervision? It takes
years to answer these questions. However, we must remember that, up
until now, therapists have been reinforced in a variety of ways for
constructing treatments that require a large number of sessions. It
may turn out, in the end, that a truncated version, yet to be defined,
works as well as or better than the version described in this book,
applied in its totality.

When we are restricted in terms of time or number of sessions, here
are some of the considerations:

1. *Don't be tempted to drop the acceptance work.* At first glance, it
might appear that if you only have six to eight contacts with the couple, the only alternative is to attempt change in the most expeditious
way possible. This would imply starting with BE, since it does produce change quickly and, at times, quite dramatically. However, as we
reported in Chapter 1, the long-term outcomes following an exclusively BE approach are quite dismal. We are concerned that the same
thing may be true of solution-focused therapy, when applied to couples (Weiner-Davis, 1992). Since there has been no outcome research
done on the solution-focused approach to couples, there is no way of
knowing. But BE resembles solution-focused therapy in a number of
ways. We learned from one study (Jacobson, 1984) that it is easy to
generate short-term change, but considerably more difficult to make
it last. By not force-feeding change, the acceptance work renders the
changes that do occur more durable.

2. *Streamline the assessment process.* If therapists make adequate
use of questionnaires, they can have a working formulation prior to
any contact with the couple. Then, during the first session, the focus
can be on the six assessment questions discussed in Chapter 4, with

the goal being a mini-feedback session at the end of the session. In short, there would be no individual sessions except in cases of domestic violence (where items indicative of physical aggression are endorsed on the CTS), and the first session would combine the first conjoint interview, the two individual sessions, and the feedback session. The courtship history, focus on strengths, and any information about family of origin would probably be minimized, and the emphasis would have to be on delineating a formulation. There would also not be time for a formal presentation of a treatment plan. However, we have conducted assessments such as these, and if enough information is obtained from questionnaires and good assessment instruments (see Chapter 4), and the therapist is willing to scrutinize them carefully to develop hypotheses, it is possible to come up with a formulation and present it to a couple at the end of the first session.

3. *Schedule more time than usual between sessions.* There is nothing magical about the 50-minute hour or the weekly session. If we are limited to a few sessions and the couple cannot afford to pay for the additional sessions without the aid of insurance, we may meet every other week, every three weeks, or even once per month. This way, the typical duration of therapy is four to six months, even though the number of sessions remains within the limits of third-party coverage. If the couple is working on either BE or communication/problem-solving training (CPT), the tasks to be completed between sessions can be more ambitious, with brief, weekly phone calls just to check in and make sure the tasks are being implemented as they are supposed to be. If the focus is on acceptance work, at times long intervals between sessions actually facilitate progress, giving couples a greater opportunity to incorporate the therapist's reformulations into their relationship.

When couples do not have frequent conflicts, but do have destructive arguments at less frequent intervals, longer periods of time between sessions make it more likely that incidents will occur that provide the therapist with opportunities for acceptance work during therapy sessions. For example, Christensen is currently working with a couple who have sufficient money to pay for therapy and were anticipating weekly contact. However, based on his formulation and his observation that the couple had infrequent conflict he recommended only biweekly contact. They agreed that biweekly meetings would provide more incidents to discuss.

Finally, certain tolerance-building strategies, such as role-playing negative behavior, have more of an opportunity to take hold with longer intervals between sessions. Recall that these exercises are designed to prepare people for inevitable slip-ups. Since slip-ups are more likely to occur with longer intervals between sessions, the therapist has more of an opportunity to check up on whether the preparation led to increased tolerance, as it was supposed to.

4. *Schedule sessions at the time incidents occur, rather than according to specified time intervals.* Jacobson is now seeing a couple, Marie and Mario, who have insurance that covers eight sessions and would prefer a truncated version of ICT to paying out of pocket. Their typical conflicts occur when Marie and Mario clash over how to spend their weekends. Mario is task-oriented, and Marie wants to engage in recreational activities. The polarization process involves Mario getting angry and losing his temper when tasks are not accomplished. Marie responds to his anger by reacting to the anger rather than the content of the issue: she may say something like, "I will not be spoken to like that!" This makes Mario even angrier, and his escalation of anger makes Marie even less willing to participate in the discussion.

The formulation was presented to Mario and Marie at the end of the first session, and even though a month passed before having another session, they did not report a single incident during the second session. Neither Jacobson nor the couple knew what to make of this. Mario was saying that, somehow, hearing the formulation was helpful. Marie was saying that they always have these honeymoon effects when they start therapy, and it doesn't really mean anything. That session was spent role-playing a typical conflict, and they were given the task of faking the polarization process. The faked behavior was rehearsed during the session.

Then, a month later, they met for a third session. Still, not a single incident. She complied with her part of the faking task, whereas he did not. She tried to provoke him into yelling at her by ordering him around and making unilateral decisions about recreational activities, but he would not be provoked into yelling at her. He thought about yelling at her at other times, as a fake, but for some reason could not get himself to do it. A decision was made to have our remaining sessions organized according to their incidents. Both of them seemed certain that there would be incidents in the future. But since this had now been the longest stretch without an incident in the history of their 20-year relationship, a regular time was left open for them each week, but they were expected to keep the appointment only when an incident occurred, and cancel within 24 hours if there had been no incident. They left messages confirming the cancellation on Jacobson's voice mail. Thus far, they have gone four additional months without an incident and canceled every session (Jacobson has made contingency plans for filling the hour when they cancel.) They still have six more sessions to be covered by their insurance company. In the meantime, they have been in contact with their therapist for six months and have had the best six months in their 20-year history has a couple.

More progress tends to be made in acceptance work when there are incidents to discuss. When spouses enter a session upset with one another over an incident related to their theme, and find themselves polarizing as they typically do, the therapist has an opportunity to provide them with the experience of softening and being softened during the session. These experiences can be quite powerful. If the number of sessions is limited, whenever possible we would want to make maximum use of each one and "strike while the iron is hot."

5. *Request extensions when necessary.* We have been surprised to discover the flexibility that managed care representatives have shown when we have been able to justify extensions in the number of sessions covered. It usually requires a persuasive argument and documented need for more sessions, but with some organizations it is possible to obtain extended coverage when clinically indicated. We have even obtained extensions where the written policy is not to grant them. But we have found that, in order to win these arguments, we have to have at least three factors going for us: (1) there must be some evidence that therapy has begun to reap some benefits (2) there must be some reason to believe that further therapy would reap further benefits, and (3) we must be providing a treatment with at least some empirical validation. If therapy has not yielded any progress after eight sessions, the agents are not likely to grant an extension. Moreover, if we cannot persuade them that there is more room for improvement, and that we have some specific plans for how to generate improvement in those particular areas, the extension is not granted.

It seems reasonable to place the burden of proof in our hands. Given the lack of evidence supporting long-term psychotherapy, including long-term couple therapy, and given the existence of very brief therapies, there is some logic to the limitations imposed by insurance companies. Some of them are more flexible than others. And, if all else fails, you can bring out the heavy artillery: the prevention argument.

6. *Use the prevention argument!* In the long run, costs are minimized by keeping people from reentering the system following a relatively permanent improvement in their condition. We have reason to believe (cf. Jacobson & Addis, 1993) that it is easier to prevent marital problems than to deal with them after they have had time to fester. In the same way, while one can change couples quickly for brief periods of time, long-term change appears to require more complicated interventions, which by their very nature take longer (Jacobson, 1984).

When couples relapse continuously, or divorce, become depressed, and develop health problems, health care actually becomes more expensive to provide. We already have some evidence from TBCT that a more complex intervention, which tackles more components of a couple problem, yields fewer relapses as well as fewer divorces (Jacobson et al., 1987). In the long run, couples are better off getting as much of their problem taken care of "now" as possible, rather than tackling a piece of it now and then waiting for the problem to return. And with very brief approaches, most couples will either return or deteriorate, which will increase the demand for mental health services, and probably for other medical services as well. The prevention argument is persuasive; more importantly, it is valid!

Acceptance in a Broader Context:
Psychotherapy and Spirituality

ICT is part of a broader movement, within and outside of behavior therapy, to integrate acceptance-based and change-based treatment strategies in psychotherapy. Since the field of psychotherapy has become so fragmented and so disorder-based (e.g., depression, alcoholism, marital problems), there have been many missed opportunities for cross-fertilization and collaboration. However, both of us participated in a conference specifically devoted to the integration of acceptance and change, organized in January 1993; the proceedings of that conference were recently published (Hayes, Jacobson, Follette, & Dougher, 1994). A simple perusal of the table of contents reveals that this integration has become central to work in many areas, particularly within the field of behavior therapy: there is the pioneering work of Linehan (1993) with parasuicide and borderline personality disorder; the creative contributions of Hayes (e.g., Hayes, 1987) in the application of "Acceptance Commitment Therapy" (ACT) to a variety of difficult types of clients, especially anxiety disordered people and drug abusers; and rational-emotive therapy (Ellis, 1962) has always been oriented toward integrating acceptance and change. More recently, the role of acceptance has even been explored in such intractable populations as sex offenders (LoPiccolo, 1994). Finally, acceptance approaches have been integrated with traditional behavior therapy in the "harm reduction" approach to treating addictive behaviors (Marlatt, 1994) and in defining the stance of the therapist in the radical behavioral approach to psychotherapy called "Functional Analytic Psychotherapy" developed by Kohlenberg and Tsai (1991).

This movement, both within and outside of behavior therapy, has potentially far-reaching consequences for psychotherapy. Prior to it, most theoretical models of therapy focused primarily either on acceptance (e.g., Greenberg & Safran, 1987; Kohut & Wolf, 1978; Rogers, 1951), or on change (e.g., traditional behavior therapy, strategic therapy [Haley, 1987; Watzlawick, Weakland, & Fisch, 1974], and solution-focused therapy [de Shazer, 1985; Weiner-Davis, 1992]). Moreover, in the acceptance based approaches of the past, strategies and clinical techniques were seldom described in sufficient detail to clearly delineate how specific therapist tactics were supposed to generate particular types of acceptance. Finally, in the past, "acceptance" was often implicitly rather than explicitly discussed; in many cases it was never actually defined.

Now, with the development of these new descriptions, integrative models are becoming more accessible to therapists in training, as well as to trained therapists. Many experienced therapists who practice integrative techniques have welcomed a unified theoretical framework to describe their eclectic ways of doing therapy.

Despite the convening of the Reno conference on acceptance in 1993 and the subsequent publication based on that conference (Hayes et al., 1994), there have been no systematic efforts to examine the similarities and differences between integrative models. Certainly, such an exploration is far beyond the scope of this volume. But it is our guess that such an examination would be fruitful both in terms of developing more comprehensive theories of change and in broadening the clinical repertoires of integrative therapists. For example, we have described a model of couple therapy that distinguishes between two types of acceptance work: intimacy-enhancing and tolerance-promoting strategies. In ICT, we have also delineated how traditional change techniques fit into the model both theoretically and clinically. We have argued that "change" looks different when it emerges from the contextual shift promoted by acceptance work than it does when it follows the rule-governed behavior generated by traditional behavior therapy.

In Linehan's dialectical behavior therapy (DBT) for borderline personality disorder (BPD), one acceptance strategy is "mindfulness," which involves the incorporation of concepts from Eastern meditation (Kabat-Zinn, 1990). In DBT, these concepts are taught as skills: observing, describing, participating spontaneously, being nonjudgmental, focusing attention on only one thing at a time, and being effective in particular situations. When these skills are learned effectively, people learn to observe their own and others' behavior without needing to either get away from them when they are unpleasant or prolong them when they are pleasant. They also learn to discriminate between events in the environment and one's thinking and feeling about these events.

Linehan describes a process that is quite similar to what Hayes used to refer to as "comprehensive distancing." The mindfulness component of her DBT has some parallels to the goals of tolerance in ICT, except that, rather than getting individuals to stay "in the present," as Linehan's approach teaches, we try to get couples to stop trying to avoid or escape from their partners' negative behavior. In fact, Hayes advocates the cessation of "emotional avoidance" with anxious and depressed clients, the ability to *feel* good as opposed to simply feeling *good*.

In other words, both Linehan and Hayes promote acceptance of self in part by teaching individuals to experience whatever they experience without needing to do something about it, whether that "something" is escaping from it or trying to change it. Our tolerance-promoting techniques are designed to accomplish the same end, except the context is the partner's negative behavior. Furthermore, the distancing of events from one's thinking and feeling bears some similarity to unified detachment in ICT. The difference is that our goal is to get couples to look at a problem in their relationship as outsiders, to observe the problem together from a distance, whereas Hayes and Linehan are focusing on individuals' detaching themselves from events in their environment that might otherwise be too painful to endure.

An additional mindfulness skill taught in Linehan's approach is "participating," which means experiencing events in the moment without evaluating them. Although she is referring to the adoption of a nonblaming and non-accusatory stance toward oneself, the parallel to ICT is clear: our entire approach, from the stance of the therapist to the reformulating that goes on in empathic joining, is to help partners experience one another without blame or accusation.

"Distress tolerance" is Linehan's summary term for techniques designed to follow directly from mindfulness: the ability to accept one's experience without needing to change it. The skills include distraction, self-soothing, improving the moment through imagery and self-talk, and a sort of problem-solving, where the advantages and disadvantage of distress tolerance are contrasted. Some of the tolerance techniques in ICT are quite similar, especially self-care. On the other hand, some of the distress tolerance techniques seem more like our TBCT techniques: distraction is something we would classify as a BE technique, Linehan's problem-solving is more like problem-solving training (PST) than any of our acceptance techniques, and imagery and self-talk resemble some cognitive techniques that are not really part of ICT but do comprise an important part of the TBCT cognitive repertoire, as practiced by the approaches of Baucom and Epstein (1990; Baucom, Epstein, & Rankin, 1995) and Halford, Sanders, and Behrens (1993).

The relapse prevention model of treating addictive behaviors developed by Marlatt and Gordon (1985) emphasizes treatment strategies designed to counteract the "abstinence violation effect." This effect leads the recovered alcoholic to say, when he or she has a drink, "Oh well, I have had a drink; I might as well get drunk." To counteract this effect, the relapse prevention model of treatment accepts "lapses" as understandable, natural, and inevitable, and tries to prevent them from turning into full-blown relapses. The strategies used to prevent relapse in the 1980s were largely cognitive behavioral, resembling TBCT more than ICT. However, the philosophy of Marlatt and Gordon is remarkably similar to the rationale for tolerance that we present to couples, especially when having them role-play negative behavior or fake negative behavior at home.

The relapse prevention model of the 1980s has become the "harm reduction" model of the 1990s (Marlatt, 1994). Harm reduction procedures are designed to help substance abusers cut their losses, even if they cannot achieve abstinence. People who reject relapse prevention treatments or who cannot or will not abstain might be persuaded to reduce the harm that their addictive behaviors cause. For example, if a heroin addict persists in heroin use, a harm reduction approach would consider it a victory if the addict uses a clean, sterilized needle. Moving to smoking marijuana would be even better. Getting alcoholics to avoid driving when drunk would represent another treatment goal for a harm reduction approach. What is interesting about this model, and parallel to ICT, is that the harm reduction approach implicitly acknowledges the difficulties in changing addictive behavior and attempts to develop strategies that follow from this more realistic, albeit pessimistic, view of change. In ICT, the entire approach follows from the recognition that we will have more success in helping couples if we acknowledge their inability to change and develop treatment approaches that follow from that reality. According to Marlatt (1994), some officials involved in the "war on drugs" are beginning to advocate a harm reduction approach as social policy.

Thus, there is much obvious convergence when one examines other approaches to acceptance in even a cursory manner. However, one of the striking aspects of many self-acceptance protocols is that they have been heavily influenced by Eastern religion, especially Buddhism. Recently, a colleague approached us at a meeting and said, "I finally understand what you guys are getting at with this acceptance stuff. It is about spirituality." We were initially befuddled by these remarks, since we developed ICT from an entirely secular theoretical model, and were, to the best of our awareness, influenced by aspects of our learning history that would be hard to label spiritual. We asked him to explain what he meant by spirituality. He said, "You are trying to get couples to a place where they are feeling peaceful and comfortable with themselves and with each other. You are trying to help them appreciate the moment, love even things that they now don't like about life, and essentially create this sense of contentment with who the other person is. It is very Eastern."

Is it possible that we have inadvertently begun to view relationships in a spiritual way? We don't know. But it is striking that other acceptance-based innovators in behavior therapy have drawn inspiration from spiritual and philosophical ideas that are decidedly Eastern. We will have to check them out. Meanwhile, we will enjoy the moment.

BIBLIOGRAPHY

Bateson, G. (1958). *Naven* (2nd ed.). Stanford, CA: Stanford University Press.

Bateson, G., Jackson, D. D., Haley, J., & Weakland, J. (1956). Toward a theory of schizophrenia. *Behavioral Sciences, 1,* 251–264.

Baucom, D. H. (1982). A comparison of behavioral contracting and problem-solving/communications training in behavioral marital therapy. *Behavior Therapy 13,* 162–174.

Baucom, D. H., & Epstein, N. (1990). *Cognitive behavioral marital therapy.* New York: Brunner/Mazel.

Baucom, D. H., Epstein, N., & Rankin, L. A. (1995). Cognitive aspects of cognitive-behavioral marital therapy. In N. S. Jacobson & A. S. Gurman (Eds.), *Clinical handbook of couple therapy* (pp. 65–90). New York: Guilford.

Baucom, D. H., & Hoffman, J. A. (1986). The effectiveness of marital therapy: Current status and applications to the clinical setting. In N. S. Jacobson & A. S. Gurman (Eds.), *Clinical handbook of marital therapy* (pp. 597–620). New York: Guilford.

Baucom, D. H., Notarius, C. I., Burnett, C. K., & Haefner, P. (1990). Gender differences and sex-role identity in marriage. In F. D. Fincham, & T. N. Bradbury, (Eds.), *The psychology of marriage: Basic issues and applications.* New York: Guilford.

Beach, S. R. H., & O'Leary, K. D. (1992). Treating depression in the context of marital discord: Outcome predictors of response of marital therapy vs. cognitive therapy. *Behavior Therapy, 23,* 505–528

Berzon, B. (1988). *Permanent partners.* New York: Dutton.

Belsky, J. (1990). Children and marriage. In F. D. Fincham & T. N. Bradbury (Eds.), *The psychology of marriage: Basic issues and applications* (pp. 172–200). New York: Guilford.

Belsky, J., & Pensky, E. (1988). Marital change across the transition to parenthood. *Marital and Family Review, 12,* 133–156.

Bograd, M. (1992). Values in conflict: Challenges to family therapists' thinking. *Journal of Marital and Family Therapy, 18,* 245–256.

Bradbury, T. N., & Fincham, F. D. (1990). Attributions in marriage: Review and critique. *Psychological Bulletin, 107,* 3–33.

Brines, J. (1994). Economic dependency, gender, and the division of labor at home. *American Journal of Sociology, 100,* 652.

Brown, L. S. (1995). Therapy with same-sex couples: An introduction. In N. S. Jacobson & A. S. Gurman (Eds.), *Clinical handbook of couple therapy* (pp. 274–291). New York: Guilford.

Chodorow, N. (1979). *The reproduction of mothering*. Berkeley: University of California Press.

Christensen, A. (1983). Intervention. In H. H. Kelley, E. Berscheid, A. Christensen et al. (Eds.), *Close relationships* (pp. 397–448). New York: Freeman.

Christensen, A. (1987). Detection of conflict patterns in couples. In K. Hahlweg & M. J. Goldstein (Eds.), *Understanding major mental disorders: The contribution of family interaction research* (pp. 250–265). New York: Family Process Press.

Christensen, A., & Heavey, C. L. (1993). Gender differences in marital conflict: The demand-withdraw interaction pattern. In S. Oskamp & M. Costanzo (Eds.), *Gender issues in contemporary society*. Newbury Park, CA: Sage.

Christensen, A., & Jacobson, N. S. (1991). *Integrative behavioral couple therapy*. Unpublished treatment manual.

Christensen, A., & Jacobson, N. S. (in press). *When lovers make war*. New York: Guilford.

Christensen, A., Jacobson, N. S., & Babcock, J. C. (1995). Integrative behavioral couple therapy. In N. S. Jacobson, & A. S. Gurman (Eds.), *Clinical handbook of couples therapy* (pp. 31–64). New York: Guilford.

Christensen, A., & Nies, D. C. (1980). The spouse observation checklist: Empirical analysis and critique. *American Journal of Family Therapy, 8*, 69–79.

Christensen, A., & Pasch, L. (1993). The sequence of marital conflict: An analysis of seven phases of marital conflict in distressed and non-distressed couples. *Clinical Psychology Review, 13*, 3–14.

Christensen, A., & Shenk, J. L. (1991). Communication, conflict and psychological distance in non-distressed, clinic, and divorcing couples. *Journal of Consulting and Clinical Psychology, 59*, 458–463.

Christensen, A., & Walczynski, P. T. (in press). Conflict and satisfaction in couples. To appear in R. J. Sternberg & M. Hojjat (Eds.), *Satisfaction in close relationships*. New York: Guilford.

The college dictionary (1972). New York: Random House, 1984.

Cordova, J. V., Jacobson, N. S., & Christensen, A. (in preparation). *Acceptance versus change interventions in behavioral couples therapy: Impact on client communication process in therapy sessions*.

Craske, M. G., & Zoellner, L. A. (1995). Anxiety disorders: The role of marital therapy. In N. S. Jacobson & A. Christensen (Eds.). *Clinical handbook of couple therapy* (pp. 394–410). New York: Guilford.

deShazer, S. (1985). *Keys to solution in brief therapy*. New York: Norton.

Dion, K. K., & Dion, K. L. (1993). Individualistic and collectivistic perspectives on gender and the cultural context of love intimacy. *Journal of Social Issues, 49*, 53–69.

Dutton, D. G. (1995). *The domestic assault of women: Psychological and criminal justice perspectives*. Vancouver BC: UBC Press.

Ellis, A. (1962) *Reason and emotion in psychotherapy*. New York: Lyle-Stuart.

Emery, R. E., & Forehand, R. (1995). Parental divorce and children's well being: A focus on resilience. In R. J. Haggerty, N. Garmezy, M. Rutter, & L. Sherrod (Eds.), *Risk and resilience in children*. London: Cambridge University Press.

Emmelkamp, P., van der Helm, M., MacGillawry, D., & van Zanten, B. (1984). Marital therapy with clinically distressed couples: A comparative evaluation of system-theoretic, contingency contracting, and communication skills approaches. In K. Hahlweg & N. S. Jacobson (Eds.), *Marital interaction: Analysis and modification*. New York: Guilford.

Falicov, C. J. (1995). Cross-cultural marriages. In N. S. Jacobson & A. S. Gurman (Eds.), *Clinical handbook of couple therapy* (pp. 231–246). New York: Guilford.

Floyd, J. F., & Markman, H. J. (1983). Observational biases in spouse observation: Toward a cognitive/behavioral model of marriage. *Journal of Consulting and Clinical Psychology, 51,* 450–457.

Floyd, F. J., Markman, H. J., Kelly, S., Blumberg, S. L., & Stanley, S. M. (1995). Preventive intervention and relationship enhancement. In N. S. Jacobson & A. S. Gurman (Eds.). *Clinical handbook of couple therapy* (pp. 212–230). New York: Guilford.

Friedman, E. (1982). The myth of the shiksa. In M. McGoldrick, J. K. Pearce, & J. Giordano (Eds.), *Ethnicity and family therapy* (pp. 499–526). New York: Guilford.

Goldner, V., Penn, P., Sheinberg, M., & Walker, G. (1990). Love and violence: Gender paradoxes in volatile attachments. *Family Process, 29,* 343–364.

Gottman, J. M. (1979). *Marital interaction: Experimental investigations*. New York: Academic Press.

Gottman, J. M. (1993). The roles of conflict engagement, escalation, and avoidance in marital interaction: A longitudinal view of five types of couples. *Journal of Consulting and Clinical Psychology, 61,* 6–15.

Gottman, J. M. (1994). *What predicts divorce?* Hillsdale, NJ: Erlbaum.

Gottman, J., Notarius, C., Gonso, J., & Markman, H. (1976). *A couple's guide to communication*. Champaign, IL: Research Press.

Greenberg, L. S., & Safran, J. D. (1987). *Emotion in psychotherapy*. New York: Guilford.

Guerney, B. (1977). *Relationship enhancement*. San Francisco: Jossey-Bass.

Guerney, B., Brock, G., & Coufal, J. (1986). Integrating marital therapy and enrichment: The relationship enhancement approach. In N. S. Jacobson & A. S. Gurman (Eds.), *Clinical handbook of marital therapy* (pp. 151–172). New York Guilford.

Hahlweg, K., Schindler, L., Revenstorf, D., & Brangelmann, J. C. (1984). The Munich marital therapy study. In K. Hahlweg & N. S. Jacobson (Eds.), *Marital interaction: Analysis and modification* (pp. 3–26). New York: Guilford.

Haley, H. (1987). *Problem-solving therapy: New strategies for effective family therapy* (2nd ed.). San Francisco: Jossey-Bass.

Halford, W. K., Sanders, M. R., & Behrens, B. C. (1993). A comparison of the generalization of behavioral marital therapy and enhanced behavioral marital therapy. *Journal of Consulting and Clinical Psychology, 61,* 51–60.

Halleck, S. (1970). *Politics of therapy*. New York: Jason Aronson.

Hamberger, L. K. (in press). Female offenders in domestic violence: A look at actions in context. *Aggression, Assault and Abuse.*

Hayes, S. C. (1987). A contextual approach to therapeutic change. In N. S. Jacobson (Ed.), *Psychotherapists in clinical practice: Cognitive and behavioral perspectives* (pp. 327–387). New York: Guilford.

Hayes, S. C., Jacobson, N. S., Follette, V., & Dougher, M. (1994). *Acceptance and change in psychotherapy*. Reno: Context Press.

Heatherington, M. E. (1989). Coping with family transitions: Winners, losers, and survivors. *Child Development, 60,* 1–14.

Heavey, C. L. Christensen, A., & Malamuth, N. M. (1995). The longitudinal impact of demand and withdrawal during marital conflict. *Journal of Consulting and Clinical Psychology, 63,* 797–801.

Ho, M. K. (1990). *Intermarried couples in therapy.* Springfield, IL: Charles Thomas.

Holtzworth-Munroe, A., Beatty, S. B., & Anglin, K. (1995). The assessment and treatment of marital violence: An introduction for the marital therapist. In N. S. Jacobson & A. S. Gurman (Eds.), *Clinical handbook of couple therapy* (pp. 317–339). New York: Guilford.

Hooley, J. M., Richters, J. E., Weintraub, S., & Neale, J. M. (1987). Psychopathology and marital distress: The positive side of positive symptoms. *Journal of Abnormal Psychology, 96,* 27–33.

Huston, T. L., & Houts, R. M. (in press). The psychological infrastructure of courtship and marriage: The role of personality and compatibility in romantic relationships. In T. Bradbury (Ed.), *The developmental course of marital dysfunction.* New York: Cambridge University Press.

Jacobson, N. S. (1977). Problem solving and contingency contracting in the treatment of marital discord. *Journal of Consulting and Clinical Psychology, 45,* 92–100.

Jacobson, N. S. (1978a). Specific and nonspecific factors in the effectiveness of a behavioral approach to the treatment of marital discord. *Journal of Consulting and Clinical Psychology, 46,* 442–452.

Jacobson, N. S. (1978b). Contingency contracting with couples: Redundancy and caution. *Behavior Therapy, 9,* 426–427.

Jacobson, N. S. (1979). Increasing positive behavior in severely distressed adult relationships. *Behavior Therapy, 10,* 311–326.

Jacobson, N. S. (1983). Beyond empiricism: The politics of marital therapy. *American Journal of Family Therapy, 11,* 11–24.

Jacobson, N. S. (1984). A component analysis of behavioral marital therapy: The relative effectiveness of behavior exchange and problem solving training. *Journal of Consulting and Clinical Psychology, 52,* 295–305.

Jacobson, N. S. (1989). The politics of intimacy. *The Behavior Therapist, 12,* 29–32.

Jacobson, N. S. (1991). To be or not to be behavioral when working with couples: What does it mean? *Journal of Family Psychology, 4,* 373–393.

Jacobson, N. S. (1992). Behavioral couple therapy: A new beginning. *Behavior Therapy, 23,* 493–506.

Jacobson, N. S. (1994). Rewards and dangers in researching domestic violence. *Family Process, 33,* 81–85.

Jacobson, N. S., & Addis, M. E. (1993). Research on couples and couple therapy: What do we know? Where are we going? *Journal of Consulting and Clinical Psychology, 61,* 85–93.

Jacobson, N. S., & Anderson, E. A. (1980). The effects of behavior rehearsal and feedback on the acquisition of problem solving skills in distressed and nondistressed couples. *Behavior Research and Therapy, 18,* 25–36.

Jacobson, N. S., Christensen, A., Prince, S. E., & Cordova, J. (in preparation). *Efficacy of integrative behavioral couple therapy.*

Jacobson, N. S., Dobson, K., Fruzzetti, A. E., Schmaling, K. B., & Salusky, S. (1991). Marital therapy as a treatment for depression. *Journal of Consulting and Clinical Psychology, 59,* 547–557.

Jacobson, N. S., Dobson, K., Truax, P., Addis, M. E., Koerner, K., Gollan, J. K., Gortner, E., & Prince, S. E. (1996). A component analysis of cognitive behavioral treatment for depression. *Journal of Consulting and Clinical Psychology, 64*, 295–304.

Jacobson, N. S., & Follette, W. C. (1985). Clinical significance of improvement resulting from two behavioral marital therapy components. *Behavior Therapy, 16*, 249–262.

Jacobson, N. S., Follette, W. C., & McDonald, D. W. (1982). Reactivity to positive and negative behavior in distressed and nondistressed married couples. *Journal of Consulting and Clinical Psychology, 50*, 706–714.

Jacobson, N. S., Follette, W. C., & Pagel, M. (1986). Predicting who will benefit from behavioral marital therapy. *Journal of Consulting and Clinical Psychology, 54*, 518–522.

Jacobson, N. S., Follette, W. C., & Revenstorf, D. (1984). Psychotherapy outcome research: Methods for reporting variability and evaluating clinical significance. *Behavior Therapy, 15*, 336–352.

Jacobson, N. S., Follette, W. C., & Revenstorf, D. (1986). Toward a standard definition of clinically significant change. *Behavior Therapy, 17*, 308–311.

Jacobson, N. S., Follette, W. C., Revenstorf, D., Baucom, D. H., Hahlweg, K., & Margolin, G. (1984). Variability in outcome and clinical significance of behavioral marital therapy: A reanalysis of outcome data. *Journal of Consulting and Clinical Psychology, 52*, 497–504.

Jacobson, N. S., Fruzzetti, A. E., Dobson, K., Whisman, M., & Hops, H. (1993). Couple therapy as a treatment for depression: II. The effects of relationship quality and therapy on depressive relapse. *Journal of Consulting and Clinical Psychology, 61*, 516–519.

Jacobson, N. S., & Gortner, E. (in press). Biosocial aspects of domestic violence. In D. P. Farrington & S. A. Mednick (Eds.), *Biosocial bases of violence*. New York: Plenum.

Jacobson, N. S., Gottman, J. M., LaTaillade, J., Babcock, J., Gortner, E., Shortt, J., & Burns, S. (1996). *The course of battering over time*. Submitted for publication.

Jacobson, N. S., Gottman, J. M., Waltz, J., Rushe, R., Babcock, J., & Holtzworth-Munroe, A. (1994). Affect, verbal content, and psychophysiology in the arguments of couples with a violent husband. *Journal of Consulting and Clinical Psychology, 62*, 982–988.

Jacobson, N. S., & Holtzworth-Munroe, A. (1986). Marital therapy: A social learning/cognitive perspective. In N. S. Jacobson & A. S. Gurman (Eds.), *Clinical handbook of marital therapy* (pp. 29–70). New York: Guilford.

Jacobson, N. S., & Margolin, G. (1979). *Marital therapy: Strategies based on social learning and behavior exchange principles*. New York: Brunner/Mazel.

Jacobson, N. S., & Moore, D. (1981). Spouses as observers of the events in their relationship. *Journal of Consulting and Clinical Psychology, 49*, 269–277.

Jacobson, N. S., & Revenstorf, D. (1988). Statistics for assessing the clinical significance of psychotherapy techniques: Issues, problems, and new developments. *Behavioral Assessment, 10*, 133–145.

Jacobson, N. S., Schmaling, K. B., & Holtzworth-Munroe, A. (1987). Component analysis of behavioral marital therapy: Two-year follow-up and prediction of relapse. *Journal of Marital and Family Therapy, 13*, 187–195.

Jacobson, N. S., Schmaling, K. B., Holtzworth-Munroe, A., Katt, J. L., Wood, L. F., & Follette, V. M. (1989). Research-structured versus clinically flexible versions of social learning-based marital therapy. *Behaviour Research and Therapy, 27,* 173–180.

Jacobson, N. S., & Truax, P. (1991). Clinical significance: A statistical approach to defining meaningful change in psychotherapy research. *Journal of Consulting and Clinical Psychology, 39,* 12–19.

Jacobson, N. S., Waldron, H., & Moore, D. (1980). Toward a behavioral profile of marital distress. *Journal of Consulting and Clinical Psychology, 48,* 696–703.

Jarvis, I. L. (1982). Decision-making under stress. In L. Goldberger & S. Brezmitz (Eds.), *Handbook of stress: Theoretical and clinical aspects* (pp. 69–87). New York: Free Press.

Johnson, S. M., & Greenberg, L. S. (1995). The emotionally focused approach to problems in adult attachment. In N. S. Jacobson & A. S. Gurman (Eds.), *Clinical handbook of couple therapy* (pp. 121–141). New York: Guilford.

Kabat-Zinn, J. (1990). *Full catastrophe living.* New York: Delacorte.

Karney, B. R., & Bradbury, T. N. (1995). The longitudinal course of marital quality and stability: A review of theory, method, and research. *Psychological Bulletin, 118,* 3–34.

Kaufman, G. (1992). The mysterious disappearance of battered women in family therapists' offices: Male privilege colluding with male violence. *Journal of Marital and Family Therapy, 18,* 233–243.

Kelley, H. H. (1979). *Personal relationships: Their structures and processes.* Hillsdale, NJ: Erlbaum.

Kelley, H. H., Berscheid, E., Christensen, A., Harvey, J. H., Huston, T. L., Levinger, G., McClintock, E., Peplau, L. A., & Peterson, D. R. (1983). *Close relationships.* New York: Freeman.

Kelly, E. L., & Conley, J. J. (1987). Personality and compatibility: A prospective analysis of marital stability and marital satisfaction. *Journal of Personality and Social Psychology, 52,* 27–40.

Klerman, G., Weissman, M. M., Rounsaville, B. J., & Chevron, E. S. (1984). *Interpersonal psychotherapy of depression.* New York: Basic Books.

Knox, D. (1971). *Marriage happiness: A behavioral approach to counseling.* Champaign: Research Press.

Koerner, K., Prince, S., & Jacobson, N. S. (1994). Enhancing the treatment and prevention of depression in women: The role of integrative behavioral couple therapy. *Behavior Therapy, 25,* 373–390.

Kohlenberg, R. J., & Tsai, M. (1991). *Functional analytic psychotherapy: Creating intense and curative therapeutic relationships.* New York: Plenum.

Kohut, H., & Wolf, E. S. (1978). The disorders of the self and their treatment: An outline. *International Journal of Psycho-Analysis, 59,* 413–425.

Leonard, K. E., & Roberts, L. J. (in press). Marital aggression, quality, and stability in the first year of marriage: Findings from the Buffalo newlywed study. In T. Bradbury (Ed.), *The developmental course of marital dysfunction.* New York: Cambridge University Press.

Liberman, R. P. (1970). Behavioral approaches to family and couple therapy. *American Journal of Orthopsychiatry, 40,* 106–118.

Liberman, R. P., Wheeler, E. G., deVisser, L. A., Kuehnel, J., & Kuehnel, T. (1981). *Handbook of marital therapy: A positive approach to helping troubled relationships.* New York: Plenum.

Lindahl, K., Clements, M., & Markman, H. (in press). The development of marriage: A nine-year perspective. In T. Bradbury (Ed.). *The developmen-*

tal course of marital dysfunction. New York: Cambridge University Press.

Linehan, M. (1993). *Cognitive behavioral treatment of borderline personality disorders.* New York: Guilford.

LoPiccolo, J. (1994). Acceptance and broad spectrum treatment of paraphilias. In S. C. Hayes, N. S. Jacobson, V. M. Follette, & M. J. Dougher (Eds.), *Acceptance and change: Content and context in psychotherapy.* Reno, NV: Context Press.

Luepnitz, D. (1988). *The family interpreted.* New York: Basic.

Maccoby, E. E., & Mnookin, R. H. (1992). *Dividing the child: social and legal dilemmas of custody.* Cambridge, MA: Harvard University Press.

Margolin, G (1983). Behavioral marital therapy: Is there a place for passion, play, and other non-negotiable dimensions? *The Behavior Therapist, 6,* 65–68.

Margolin, G., Christensen, A., & Weiss, R. L. (1975). Contracts, cognition, and change: A behavioral approach to marriage therapy. *The Counseling Psychologist, 5,* 15–26.

Margolin, G., Talovic, S., & Weinstein, C. D. (1983). Areas of change questionnaire: A practical approach to marital assessment. *Journal of Consulting and Clinical Psychology, 51,* 920–931.

Marlatt, A. (1994). Addiction and acceptance. In S. C. Hayes, N. S. Jacobson, V. M. Follette, & M. J. Dougher (Eds.), *Acceptance and change: Content and context in psychotherapy* (pp. 175–197). Reno, NV: Context Press.

Marlatt, G. A., & Gordon, J. R. (Eds.), (1985). *Relapse prevention: Maintenance strategies in the treatment of addictive behaviors.* New York: Guilford.

McCrady, B. S., & Epstein, E. E. (1995). Marital therapy in the treatment of alcohol problems. In N. S. Jacobson & A. S. Gurman (Eds.), *Clinical handbook of couple therapy* (pp. 369–393). New York: Guilford.

Meyers-Avis, J. (1992, July). Where are all the family therapists? Abuse and violence within families and family therapy's response. *Journal of Marital and Family Therapy, 18,* 225–232.

O'Farrell, T. J. (1986). Marital therapy in the treatment of alcoholism. In N. S. Jacobson & A. S. Gurman (Eds.), *Clinical handbook of marital therapy* (pp. 513–536). New York: Guilford.

O'Leary, K. D., & Beach, R. H. (1990). Marital therapy: A viable treatment for depression and marital discord. *American Journal of Psychiatry, 147,* 183–186.

O'Leary, K. D., Vivian, D., & Malone, J. (1992). Assessment of physical aggression in marriages: The need for multimodal assessment. *Behavioral Assessment, 14,* 5–14.

Patterson, G. R. (1975). *Families.* Champaign, IL: Research Press.

Patterson, G. R., & Hops, H. (1972). Coercion, a game for two: Intervention techniques for marital conflict. In R. E. Ulrich & P. Mounjoy (Eds.), *The experimental analysis of social behavior* (pp. 424–440). New York: Appleton.

Pence, E., & Paymar, M. (1993). *Education groups for men who batter: The Duluth model.* New York: Springer.

Pepper, S. C. (1942). *World hypotheses: A study in evidence.* Berkeley, CA: University of California Press.

Pittman, F. S., & Wagers, T. P. (1995). Crisis of infidelity. In N. S. Jacobson, & A. S. Gurman (Eds.) *Clinical handbook of couple therapy* (pp. 295–316). New York: Guilford.

Prince, S. E., & Jacobson, N. S. (1995). A review and evaluation of marital family therapies for affective disorders. *Journal of Marital and Family Therapy, 21,* 377–401.

Radloff, L. S., & Rae, D. S. (1979). Susceptibility and precipitating factors in depression: Sex differences and similarities. *Journal of Abnormal Psychology, 88,* 174–181.

Repetti, R. L. (1989). Effects of daily work load on subsequent behavior during marital interaction: The roles of social withdrawal and spouse support. *Journal of Personality and Social Psychology, 57,* 651–659.

Rogers, C. R. (1951). *Client-centered therapy.* Boston: Houghton/Mifflin.

Rutter, V., & Schwartz, P. (in press). Same-sex couples: Courtship, commitment, context. In A. Auhagen & M. v. Salisch (Eds.) *The diversity of social relationships.* London: Cambridge University Press, and Germany: Hogrefe.

Schwartz, P. (1994). *Peer marriages.* New York: Free Press.

Shoham, V., Rohrbaugh, M., & Patterson, J. (1995). Problem- and solution-focused couple therapies: The MRI and Milwaukee models. In N. S. Jacobson & A. S. Gurman (Eds.), *Clinical handbook of couple therapy* (pp. 142–163). New York: Guilford.

Skinner, B. F. (1966). *The behavior of organisms: An experimental analysis.* Englewood Cliffs, NJ: Prentice Hall.

Snyder, D. K. (1979). Multidimensional assessment of marital satisfaction. *Journal of Marriage and the Family, 41,* 813–823.

Spanier, G. B. (1976). Measuring dyadic adjustment: New scales for assessing the quality of marriage and similar dyads. *Journal of Marriage and the Family, 38,* 15–28.

Stets, J. E., & Straus, M. A. (1990). Gender differences in reporting marital violence and its medical and psychological consequences. In M. A. Straus & R. J. Gelles (Eds.), *Physical violence in American families: Risk factors and adaptations to violence in 8,145 families* (pp. 151–166). New Brunswick, NJ: Transaction.

Straus, M. A. (1979). Measuring intrafamily conflict and violence: The conflict tactics (CT) scales. *Journal of Marriage and the Family, 41,* 75–88.

Straus, M. A., & Gelles, R. J. (1990). How violent are American families? Estimates from the national family violence resurvey and other studies. In M. A. Straus & R. J. Gelles (Eds.), *Physical violence in American families: Risk factors and adaptations to violence in 8,145 families* (pp. 95–112). New Brunswick, NJ: Transaction.

Stuart, R. B. (1969). Operant-interpersonal treatment for marital discord. *Journal of Consulting and Clinical Psychology, 33,* 675–682.

Stuart, R. B. (1980). *Helping couples change: A social learning approach to marital therapy.* New York: Guilford.

Surra, C. A. (1990). Research and theory on mate selection and premarital relationships in the 1980s. *Journal of Marriage and the Family, 52,* 844–865.

Thibaut, J. W., & Kelley, H. H. (1959). *The social psychology of groups.* New York: Wiley.

Tucker, M. B., & Mitchell-Kerman, C. (1995). Trends in African American family formation: A theoretical and statistical overview. In M. B. Tucker & C. Mitchell-Kerman (Eds.), *The decline in marriage among African Americans.* New York: Russell Sage Foundation.

Walker, L. E.(1995). Current perspectives on men who batter women—Implications for intervention and treatment to stop violence: Comment on Gottman et al. *Journal of Family Psychology, 9*, 264–271.

Watzlawick, P., Beavin, J., & Jackson, D. D. (1967). *Pragmatics of human communication.* New York: Norton.

Watzlawick, P., Weakland, J., & Fisch, R. (1974). *Change: Principles of problem formation and problem resolution.* New York: Norton.

Weiner-Davis, M. (1992). *Divorce busting.* New York: Summit.

Weiss, R. L. (1984). Cognitive and strategic interventions in behavioral marital therapy. In K. Hahlweg & N. S. Jacobson (Eds.), *Marital interaction: Analysis and modification* (pp. 337–355). New York: Guilford.

Weiss, R. L., Birchler, G. R., & Vincent, J. P. (1974). Contractual models for negotiation training in marital dyads. *Journal of Marriage and the Family, 36*, 321–331.

Weiss, R. L., & Cerreto, M. C. (1980). The marital status inventory: Development of a measure of dissolution potential. *American Journal of Family Therapy, 8*, 80–85.

Weiss, R. L., Hops, H., & Patterson, G. R. (1973). A framework for conceptualizing marital conflict, technology for altering it, some data for evaluating it. In L. A. Hamerlynck, L. C. Handy, & E. J. Mash (Eds.), *Behavior change: Methodology, concepts, and practices* (pp. 309–342). Champaign, IL: Research Press.

Wile, D. B. (1981). *Couples therapy: A nontraditional approach.* New York: Wiley.

Wile, D. B. (1995). The ego-analytic approach to couple therapy. In N. S. Jacobson & A. S. Gurman (Eds.), *Clinical handbook of couple therapy* (pp. 991–120). New York: Guilford.

Wills, T. A., Weiss, R. L., & Patterson, G. R. (1974). A behavioral analysis of the determinants of marital satisfaction. *Journal of Consulting and Clinical Psychology, 42*, 802–811.

Wood, J. V., Saltzberg, J. A., & Goldsamt, L. A. (1990). Does affect induce self-focused attention? *Journal of Personality and Social Psychology, 58*, 899–908.

Index

abuse
  emotional, association with physical
      abuse, 234
  physical or emotional, contraindication
      to couple therapy, 18
acceptance, viii–ix, 99–100
  affair abandoned following, 241
  versus attack on problems, xiii
  capacity for, clients', 77
  and change
    integrating, 15–19, 254–55
    reducing the costs of, 183
  of clients, noncompliant, 19, 96–97,
      155
  versus communication, 178
  context for
    intimate relationships, 12–14, 95
    psychotherapy and spirituality, 254–
        58
  of differences, 137–38
  as a goal
    in integrative couple therapy, 76–77
    of therapy, 83–84
  interventions for achieving, 92–93
  and intimacy enhancement, 103–29
    effect on depression, 247
  limitations on, 17–18
  Patrick and Michelle, 144–45
  reaching, from change, 1–21, 205
  therapist's role in discussing, 78
  in time-limited therapy, 250–51
  through tolerance, 130–50
  and traditional behavior therapy, 10–12
  through validation, 172
  work on
    if problem-solving is abandoned, 185
    relating to specific incidents, 253
    with same-sex couples, 219
accommodation
  capacity for, and success of therapy,
      10–11
  as a goal in therapy, 83–84

acknowledging a role, in problem defini-
    tion, 197
active listening, 170
  agreement during, 177
  in anger, 108
  empathy through, 108
  paraphrasing during, 176
  reflection during, 176
  types of, 176–78
addiction
  as a scapegoat in couple therapy, 244–
      45
  work with
    acceptance and change in, 254
    relapse prevention model, 257
Addis, M. E., x, 6, 21, 249, 253
advocacy
  community of, around domestic vio-
      lence, 236–37
  of a position, by the therapist, 16–
      17
affairs, extramarital, 240–44
affect, as a clue, 98–99
  in finding controlling variables, 89–
      90
affective experience, inaccessibility to
    problem-solving techniques, 180
African American couples, 226–28
  economic stress of, 221
age, and success of marital therapy, 7
agenda, for problem-solving, 182–83
aggression, physical, contraindication to
    couple therapy, 18
agreement
  during active listening, 177
  on solutions after brainstorming, 207–
      10
agreements, for change, clarity of, 208–
    10
AIDS, effect of, on gay men, 219
alcohol abuse/alcoholism
  difference in views of, 111